8/
/08   2.50

D0379727

I HAVE KNOWN Dr. Henrietta C. Mears for approximately fifteen years. She has had a remarkable influence, both directly and indirectly, on my life. In fact, I doubt if any other woman outside of my wife and mother has had such a marked influence. Her gracious spirit, her devotional life, her steadfastness for the simple gospel, and her knowledge of the Bible have been a continual inspiration and amazement to me. She is certainly one of the greatest Christians I have ever known!

—BILLY GRAHAM

HENRIETTA MEARS
and how she did it!

HENRIETTA MEARS
and how she did it!

By ETHEL MAY BALDWIN
and DAVID V. BENSON

G/L
REGAL
BOOKS
TM

A DIVISION OF G/L PUBLICATIONS
GLENDALE, CALIFORNIA 91205 USA

Second Printing, 1967
Third Printing, 1970
Fourth Printing, 1972
Fifth Printing, 1974

Published by Regal Books Division,
G/L Publications, Glendale,
California 91209 U.S.A.

ISBN 0-8307-0018-8

"WE ARE TOO PRONE to forget how many-sided were her strenuous labors during the more than thirty years she spent in California: (1) She was the inspiration and genius of the great Sunday School of the First Presbyterian Church of Hollywood, with its some 6000 members! (2) In that Sunday School she herself for many years taught its now famous college class—and administration and teaching gifts do not very often go together. (3) She was the founder of the Gospel Light Publications, whose literature has done so much to save many Sunday Schools from compromising or destructively liberal Sunday School study books. (4) She saw come into reality her vision of a Bible conference center at Forest Home, where, I think it can be said, a greater work has been done each year in the College Briefing Conference than in any similar gathering since those conferences held at Northfield by Dwight L. Moody. (5) Dr. Mears' own messages at conventions across our entire land brought inspiration and a deeper understanding of the essential task of a Sunday School teacher to unnumbered multitudes."

—DR. WILBUR M. SMITH
Author, preacher and formerly professor of
English Bible at Fuller Theological Seminary

CONTENTS

Four Talks by
Henrietta C. Mears

Foreword

While Henrietta Mears was visiting the Taj Mahal in India, her guide, in order to prove the unusual acoustics of the high-domed structure, stood on the platform in the center of the main hall and shouted: "There is no God but Allah, and Mohammed is his prophet!" His cry rang sonorously through all the chambers of the monument. Then Dr. Mears asked if she too might say something, and when permission was granted, she ascended the steps and exclaimed in her low, powerful voice: "Jesus Christ, Son of God, is Lord over all!" Like peals of thunder rolling through the canyons and across the valleys of an alpine mountain range, her words raced from wall to wall and down the corridors of the minareted shrine: "Lord over all, over all, over all!"

The Lordship of Jesus Christ was the message of Henrietta Mears, and she proclaimed it from platforms and pulpits across the English-speaking world — in churches, on campuses, at conventions, through writings, and by the lives of hundreds of young men and women she trained in the gospel ministry. She was the builder of the largest Presbyterian Sunday School in the world, the founder of a Sunday School publishing house that has placed the gospel in millions of hearts, the pioneer of one of the nation's most popular Christian conference centers—where thousands upon thousands have been won to the Saviour—and the divinely chosen instrument for one of the most significant revivals of modern times.

Henrietta Mears hiked in rhino-infested jungles in Africa, climbed mountains on Formosa, and walked amid the dying in India—all in order to obtain a better view of world missions. But she encountered her greatest adventure in Hollywood, where, in the midst of klieg lights and cameras, she raised an altar to the Lord Jesus Christ, which Dr. Wilbur Smith said was "the most significant work among our nation's youth done by a woman in the twentieth century."

This book is the story of an adventurous, daring, dedicated, zestful and talented woman who believed in a great God. Those who want to know her secrets of spiritual success will find them on these pages.

1

Adventurer

Adventurer

There is no magic in small plans. When I consider my ministry, I think of the world. Anything less than that would not be worthy of Christ nor of his will for my life.

—HENRIETTA MEARS

Silhouetted against the azure sky loomed the white-marbled Parthenon, the home of the gods. A little beyond it stood the Wingless Victory Temple. And to the south was the Hill of the Muses, with its graceful memorial. The blue waters of the Aegean Sea stretched out to the horizon. Below lay the Agora, or Market Place, with the Temple of Vulcan. And nearby stood the Temple of Jupiter. The modern city, with its Olympic Stadium, sprawled for miles to the west and north, its narrow streets and gray buildings bathed in the brilliance of a Mediterranean morning.

The sun was hot, and there was no shade, but the visitor in the white summer dress and her traveling companion found a stone smooth enough to sit on and rest.

All the history of ancient Greece seemed to pass by in a breathless moment: Here Zeno taught his pupils on the famous Stoa, or Porch. Socrates posed his perplexing questions to the youth of Athens, and was condemned to drink the hemlock. Plato and Aristotle gave free vent to their theories about God and society. And new ideas on democracy were put to the test.

The traveler's mind raced with thoughts excited by the ruins all around. But her most thrilling memory was of one who two thousand years before had come to this city "so full of idols," had argued with the passers-by in the Agora below, and then had been led to this same spot to defend his teaching about Jesus and the Resurrection. Perhaps he had sat on this very stone while talking to some of those who expressed interest in his ideas.

As she recalled the story, the traveler opened the book she had been carrying. It was bound in hand-tooled light-brown leather and was well-worn. She turned to the seventeenth chapter of the Book of Acts and began to read to her companion:

Now while Paul waited for them at Athens, his spirit was stirred in him, when he saw the city wholly given to idolatry . . . and they took him, and brought him unto Areopagus, saying, May we know what this new doctrine, whereof thou speakest, is? (Acts 17:16,19).

Reading had always been hard for her. (While she was in college, the doctors told her she was going blind and would have to give up her studies.) Holding the brown Bible close to her face she made out the words:

Then Paul stood in the midst of Mars' Hill, and said, Ye men of Athens, I perceive that in all things ye are too superstitious. For as I passed by, and beheld your devotions, I found an altar with this inscription, TO THE UNKNOWN GOD. Whom therefore ye ignorantly worship, him declare I unto you (Acts 17:22,23).

As the women continued to read aloud, they were interrupted by a young Greek who was offering his service as a guide. But they did not want a guide. They had come up Mars' Hill to think about the glories of Greece and to read the account of Paul in Athens, and they had no wish to be disturbed. Continuing to read, they ignored the young man; but after a minute they realized that he was sitting nearby listening to them with genuine interest.

"Do you understand what we are reading?" the woman with the Bible asked.

"If you read slowly enough," responded the Athenian.

When they came to the end of the story, she said to him, "Do you know this Christ that Paul was teaching your people about?"

"No," the Greek replied. They began to talk about Jesus, and before long they were praying together. As the three of them descended the hill, the youth held the Americans' coats and talked incessantly. Near sundown the two women said farewell to him in front of the British and Foreign Bible Society, where they had bought him a Bible.

The next day the visitors again met the young Greek.

"I could not sleep last night," he told them.

"Were you ill?" concernedly questioned the Americans.

"No, I was up all night reading that Book."

That evening, Henrietta Mears wrote in her travel journal:

On Mars' Hill we had the glorious privilege of introducing a twenty-three-year-old Greek youth to Jesus Christ as Saviour and Lord. What a thrill! On the very spot where Paul had presented this same Jesus nearly twenty centuries ago, we found that preaching Christ's claims brought the same results today. This wonderful experience was one of the highlights of the trip.

As she wrote, she could not have realized that less

than ten years later nearly one hundred thousand Greek youths would in their own language be reading her lessons on the Bible, and that they, too, would be finding THE UNKNOWN GOD and knowing him as their personal Saviour.

Henrietta Mears chose travel as a means of extending her education, for she had a broad appreciation of the beauties of God's creation and man's cultural attainments. Visiting foreign lands gave expression for her enormous energies as she thrived on the adventures she found among other peoples. But travel served, first of all, as inspiration for her driving compulsion to life—to see Christ proclaimed to all nations.

India is a far cry from modern Greece: If Greece awes the traveler with past glories, India oppresses him with present agonies. Miss Mears and her faithful co-worker, Esther Ellinghusen, had just arrived in Calcutta. There was a great religious festival going on, and the streets were jammed with processions carrying fantastic figures of their gods. Beggars of every description were taking advantage of the crowds. Coming to the railway station, the visitors were horrified: Thousands of displaced persons were gathered inside, huddled in groups, cooking their food and sleeping. Many of them were coughing and spitting in the last stages of T.B. Miss Mears could not sleep that night.

The next day the two women visited temples and shrines. At the notorious Kali Ghat a frenzied mob carried them along. The hot blood of a freshly killed goat was running over the pavement, and the pilgrims were darting forward to dip their fingers in it and make marks on their foreheads. A huge Hindu priest, stripped to the waist because of the intense heat, led the two Americans about. The odor from the mob was overwhelming, and everywhere the worshipers were giving themselves over to moral license.

Miss Mears wrote that night:

No wonder the pioneer missionaries to India had their very hearts eaten out by the condition of the heathen—without God and without hope in this world! Oh that many of us now would match their devotion! We must if we are to do anything about the lostness of this world. India seems so ripe for communism. "Anything is better than nothing," the people say. But if they knew Christ, they would soon do away with the sacred bulls ambling over the streets, eating everything and leaving their dung on the sidewalks, where thousands of the poor sleep with only their cloth wrapped around them. Over a hundred thousand human bundles on the streets! This is their only resting place. In the winter they lie down to shiver and die.

And a few days later, in Benares, India's holiest city, she observed:

It is good for one to visit this city with its innumerable shrines and temples to understand the degradation of idol worship. Thousands of pilgrims visit this place every day. If they can only bathe in the holy water of the Ganges and die in this place, they think they will be blessed. They will not come back to this earth again. About sundown we pushed through the crowds and went down the hundreds of steps through the processions to the water and got into a little boat. We were rowed out onto the Ganges. The water was teeming with boats carrying

21

the images of the gods ready for the water ceremony. Natives dipped gods into the water and left them there. The sun was setting a brilliant red. Hot steam from the water rose around us. Odors and weird sounds of the worshipers filled one with horror. Ugly buildings—pseudo palaces of the maharajahs—lined the banks. Burning ghats were being lighted to cremate the dead. The bathers were dipping their bodies into the filthy holy water, putting it to their lips, then lifting their faces in prayer with locked hands raised in reverence. One can hardly take it all in. I feel satanic spirits in this place.

Snake charmers in hotels, thousands of monkeys scampering between temple idols, camel caravans passing by miles of beggars, and starving, naked children lying in ditches—all of these scenes left horrid impressions on Miss Mears. Her resolve to bring these people the gospel took firmer root in her mind. Many people travel to the sordid spots of this earth never really understanding the hopelessness of those suffering about them. Their attitude is one of either complete disassociation from the dying, as though they were not of the same human race, or of a passing pity that never excites the heart to action. Few stand on the hilltop and weep over Jerusalem. But wherever Henrietta Mears went she was crushed by the black despair of people on whom the privileges of the gospel had never dawned. Every country she visited ignited determination to do something, although at the time she did not know what it would be. But God was to channel this concern, and frequently the results were unexpected.

Once, while visiting Beirut, Lebanon, Miss Mears was surprised to find herself the guest of honor at a reception given by several missionary families. They were on the foreign field, as four of them pointed out, because of a challenge they had heard from Miss Mears years before in Berkeley, California. And they recalled fifty more who were either out on the mission field or preparing to go as a result of her challenge.

On another occasion, Miss Mears and her traveling companions were in Jerusalem attending a service at the site of the Garden Tomb. A minister from Cincinnati, recognizing Dr. Mears, asked her to tell of her Sunday School work in Hollywood. Two missionaries from Bangkok interrupted, saying that they had been using her Sunday School materials for years. After her talk, a minister from Greece volunteered that her translated lessons were being used extensively in his country, even in the royal house, and that in his Sunday School alone there were 650 students studying them.

While in Israel, Dr. Mears met a guide who had been reading the Bible for twenty-six years and was well steeped in its history. As the two of them sat in front of their hotel on the shores of Lake Galilee, they talked about Christ, the Messiah. The stars studded the deep blue satin sky, and one cast a path of light right up to their feet. Tears rolled down the cheeks of the Jew as he said, "Yes, Miss Mears, I would like to let Christ into my heart, but do you know why it is so hard? I would be a second Stephen—stoned to death!" They talked on into the night, and afterwards Mr. Samuels expressed his appreciation for this fellowship, as he said, "like Jesus had with his disciples." A year after Miss Mears had returned to California, Mr. Samuels sent a message by one of her friends, for whom he had acted as a guide: "Tell Miss Mears I did what she asked me to do."

Africa was one of her favorite countries. Her adventures ran the gamut from spending a few days on King

Farouk's yacht and riding camels across the desert, to hiking in a rhino-infested reserve and retracing Livingstone's steps to the mightiest river wonder in the world, the thundering Victoria Falls. Once when her party was braving jungle roads, their car broke down not far from the white rhino territory. It was nearing the end of the day before the engine finally responded. They inched their way along in the semi-darkness, not daring to put on the headlights lest a rhino charge.

The safari continued, and their next stop was Kruger National Park, the world's greatest wild life sanctuary. Here they could see wild game in their natural habitat.

Dr. Mears' diary abounds with excitement:

The next morning we started out for game. There before our very eyes near the road was a giraffe raising its head eighteen feet above the ground. It posed for us like a Hollywood star. We drove along slowly looking through the woody bush which conceals the animals. Stop! A herd of zebras crossed over the road! Impala leaped in front of us, the most beautiful fauna in the world. One of these graceful creatures had been dragged up into a tree by a leopard and left in the branches. Think of a leopard carrying this large beast up into a tree! The Bristol gnu, an ugly black creature, the blue wildebeest, the huge baboon with its young, the sable antelope, the warthog that turns his tail straight up when running, and the duiker were other animals we encountered. . . . But I suppose the most exciting event was the 200 mile plane trip over the game reserve at Victoria Falls. At dawn we flew into the air to begin our search for wild animals. All went smoothly for a time, then our plane banked to almost a 90 degree angle, and we were looking at a herd of giraffe on the ground not more than 75 feet below us. The pilot skimmed along less than 50 feet above the ground. When he saw the animals, he turned quickly, dipping and banking until we could shoot a picture straight below. We saw zebras by the hundreds and all the other animals we had seen in Kruger, but we were searching for elephants. Back and forth across the waste and jungle we flew. Everyone was straining for a glimpse of the great beast. At last we sighted one, then another and another. We had found our game for the day!

On Sunday morning at 6:30 the wings of our plane carried us to Rhodesia, to Livingstone, the city that bears the name of the renowned missionary explorer. A few miles away are the Victoria Falls, "the Smoke that Thunders," viewed by Livingstone first on November 16, 1855. My thoughts were much with this missionary hero when I considered his utter loneliness in these jungles with only the roar of wild animals and a black man for company. Now everythings bears his name, but I fear many have forgotten his work.

Later, the travelers visited a missionary station in the Congo set high in the mountains, overlooking a chain of volcanoes. Miss Mears thrilled as Mel Lyons, with his arm around her shoulder, pointed out the villages which faded into the foliage, and it warmed her heart to hear him tell of the evangelistic work he was doing there. During the week he was training Bible teachers who would go to villages just like these to expound the Word of God. How little had she ever thought that this big football player, who jerked sodas at Forest Home, would one day be preaching the gospel in far off Africa! And Mary, whom he had met at Forest Home and later married, helped in the hospital of this teeming compound. They now had four lovely children.

As she did everywhere, Teacher ministered to the missionaries of this station. She always felt that the missionary must be inspired and fed from the Word, as he was constantly giving out. Over fifty of the young people gathered one evening to meet Teacher and hear her. God had been speaking to her from Philippians 2:13, and she gave them what he had laid upon her heart. *For it is God which worked in you both to will and to do of his good pleasure.* When she had finished, a young woman came up and said, "You won't remember me, but I was in your college class. I married a doctor and came to the Congo to serve." The surprise came when Teacher remembered her well, and her two sisters. In that group of missionaries was also one Marjory Shelley, who was destined to join in the effort to translate and publish for those living in the Gold Coast Miss Mears' Gospel Light Sunday School lessons. She heard Miss Mears only once, but well recalls her message on the will of God. The world drew closer for those missionaries that night.

Miss Mears bore adventure in her soul. She overflowed with the thrill of life. When she was a college student, she dedicated her life to God wondering if missions in the Far East was his call, but God closed this door. His plan was that through her influence many would go as missionaries sent to the Orient and around the world. But her vision encompassed the world. Wherever she labored—before audiences of thousands throughout the English-speaking nations, in the Sunday School which she built to be one of the largest in the world, at the Forest Home Christian Conference Center, among the stars of Hollywood, or through her numerous writings—she was an open lifeline of power; and her contribution to the international cause of the gospel ranks as one of the most important in the twentieth century.

The narrative of her life is a story of adventure and accomplishment, of faith in Jesus Christ, and of proving his power and love.

2

Beginnings

Beginnings

*Will is the whole man active. I cannot give up my
will; I must exercise it. I must will to obey. When
God gives a command or a vision of truth, it is never
a question of what he will do, but what we will do.
To be successful in God's work is to fall in line with
his will and to do it his way. All that is pleasing to
him is a success.*

          —HENRIETTA MEARS

"I was born with a silver spoon in my mouth," Miss
Mears would laughingly tell her friends, "but it was
yanked out before I got a chance to taste it."

Henrietta Cornelia Mears was born in Fargo, North Dakota, on October 23, in the year of the Great Panic of
1890, when many of the twenty banks her father owned
were closed. "Praise God, it's a girl! I couldn't face rearing another son!" exclaimed her father. But Henrietta managed to keep the entire household on the tips of their
toes, for her brothers' spirit of excitement and desire to
be right on the spot where anything was happening
flowed in her veins too.

She was adored by her older brothers and sister Margaret, who were growing in their independence and maturity. She was the "apple of her father's eye" and the delight of her mother's heart. The practical wisdom gained
by personal knowledge in the rearing of her other six
children was reflected in her mother's influence on this

new little life that God had put in her arms. This knowledge was coupled with the events which composed her own rich background of the minister's home of her parents. She shared with her new daughter all the treasures of a spiritually mature and experienced mother.

With the sensitivity of the very young to feel and love things of the Spirit, Henrietta began to adapt to the heritage that was to be hers in the providence of a great God. Her keen interest in everything around her increased her capacity to receive. It would not be long before Henrietta would sense that her mother's life was different from any other with which she came in contact. Curiosity was a constant companion. Little wonder then that she noted her mother going to her room every morning as regular as clockwork. Curiosity overcame any hesitancy as she toddled along to see what her mother was doing. There were no closed doors in this child's life—boldly she went in. She found her mother on her knees, her hands folded, and her lips moving. Since all children are born imitators, Henrietta copied her mother's actions, kneeling beside her, folding her chubby hands, and making her lips move too. With her arm around her precious little daughter, Mrs. Mears would explain that she was talking to God, and that God loved Henrietta too and would hear her when she talked to him. And then she would pray that the Lord would make Henrietta a good girl that day and always be with her. Satisfied, Henrietta jumped up and was about the many things that filled her busy childhood. But she never forgot her mother on her knees talking to God.

In a few short years it was time to go to kindergarten. Henrietta looked forward with great anticipation to the day when this amazing phenomenon should take place. To one whose natural instincts wanted things accomplished at once, this was a real lesson in patience. But finally the day did arrive, and Henrietta went joyfully off to school. But the joy was short-lived. Upon returning home she confidentially told her mother, "Kindergarten is to 'muse little chillun, and I'se 'mused enough. I want to be edicated." And she continued to want to learn and be educated all through her life.

But her hunger for education did not overshadow her thirst for righteousness. Her self-imposed idea of taking a nap after school had a definite motive behind it: maybe then her mother would take her to the evening meeting at the church. Her mother remonstrated, however, fearing that others would think that she was forcing her child to go—whereas it was the other way around. After much persuasion on Henrietta's part, her mother finally conceded and took the little hassock which was to be placed under her daughter's dangling feet.

On Easter Sunday morning when she was about five years old, Henrietta explained to her mother, as they were getting dressed for church, that she was ready to become a Christian and join their church. Her mother tried to reason with her that everyone would think she was too young to understand what it meant to join church. However, after further conversation which indicated that Henrietta knew what she was doing, her mother promised to talk about the matter with their pastor, Dr. W. B. Riley of The First Baptist Church of Minneapolis.

A few weeks later, young Henrietta and her cousin, Margaret Buckbee, stood before the congregation, responding to questions put to them about their faith with such clarity and frankness that the audience broke out in laughter. Henrietta, thinking she was saying something wrong, turned to her mother for confirmation. Mrs. Mears encouraged her to continue her answers, pointing out

33

that the people were laughing with them and not at them.

Before she could decipher words for herself, Henrietta loved to listen to her mother read the Bible. Sometimes her mother would simplify the words — endeavoring to clarify the meaning—but Henrietta would stop her, asking her not to change them and assuring her that she understood. Strangely enough, little Henrietta's favorite book was Paul's mighty classic, Romans, which became her most frequently taught portion of Scripture in later years.

The Mears household abounded with everyday applications of spiritual truths. Discipline was elevated from an arbitrary parental code to a divine standard of life, which was to prevail in every relationship. The easy and natural transference from a parent-image to a God-image was taken advantage of at every turn, so that the Mears children quickly learned that the obedience and love shown to their father and mother were human analogies preparing them for sonship in the divine family. Forgiveness and retribution, for example, were carefully defined. Whenever a child did wrong and duly expressed his sorrow, he was forgiven; but the issue was not closed, for he had to learn that repentance was not enough—someone had to pay for the wrongdoing.

To bear the penalty for one of her children, Mrs. Mears usually chose to forgo butter—an item, as the family well knew, she exceedingly liked—for a stipulated number of meals. At the dinner table, whenever it was noticed that their mother was not taking butter, a pall of silence and guilt fell on them all, and the culprit wished the ground would open up and swallow him. When the allotted time had elapsed for the fulfillment of the punishment, Mother Mears would ask for the butter—there was of course a flurry to pass it to her as quickly as possible —and she would allow herself half a pat. Such incidents were not lost on impressionable young Henrietta, who was destined to take the lessons in theology she learned around her mother's table to hundreds of thousands of children and youth around the world.

Mrs. Mears frequently visited a home for unmarried mothers. When her daughter was old enough to begin to understand there were tragedies in life, she took her to the Florence Crittenden Home, where Henrietta came in contact with many hapless women. This experience made its mark on her ten-year-old mind; not long afterwards, along with her cousin Margaret, she formed their private social service organization called "The Willing Workers"— the purpose of which was "to do good for unfortunates." Ignoring the jokes made over the title, the two girls went about their tasks with unwavering determination.

One day Henrietta accidentally jabbed a hat pin into the pupil of her eye. Realizing the seriousness of the mishap, Henrietta and her mother discussed the situation. Realizing there was nothing the oculist could do, they decided to ask their friend, Mr. Ingersoll, a member of the Presbyterian church, to call on them and pray for the injured eye. Henrietta knew that God who had made her could also heal her eye. Specialists later agreed that there was a hole in the pupil of her eye, and shook their heads in amazement that she could see anything out of it. It was unexplainable apart from recognition that the Physician from Nazareth had stretched forth his hand and healed the eye, even though the hole remained. From her mother Henrietta learned to accept all Scripture at face value. For God to touch her body simply meant taking him at his word. *Is any sick among you? let him call for the elders of the church; and let them pray over him . . . And the prayer of faith shall save the sick, and the Lord shall raise him up . . .* (James 5:14,15). (This accident was not related to the eye weakness which constantly afflicted not only Henrietta Mears but several of her immediate family.)

When Henrietta was twelve years old, she contracted a painful, crippling case of muscular rheumatism. Many cases were reported in their region that year. One of her friends, having contracted the disease at the same time, died. In constant pain, young Henrietta was almost completely immobile, having to be carried about from place to place. Fear was held for her life. During this siege the weakened girl began to suffer repeated nosebleeds. Once again taking God at his word—*But my God shall supply all your need according to his riches in glory by Christ Jesus* (Phil. 4:19)—her mother asked Henrietta if she would like Mr. Ingersoll to pray for her nosebleeds. The patient agreed. Mr. Ingersoll came and prayed for the bleeding to stop completely. God heard and answered. The bleeding stopped. (Miss Mears in later years would tell her friends, "And do you know, I've never had a nosebleed from that day to this.")

But as the rheumatism became still more painful, she called her mother to her bedside and asked, "Do you think Mr. Ingersoll could pray for my rheumatism?" Within a few hours Mr. Ingersoll was again in her room asking for God's intervention. Suddenly Henrietta was filled with confidence that she was healed completely. The pain was gone. Tears of relief flowed down her cheeks as she raised her voice in prayers of thanks. The road to complete recovery was swift and sure. She regained her strength rapidly, and to build her muscles she energetically took up horseback riding and swimming. Within three months there was no trace of any ill effects, and throughout her life she never had a recurrence of rheumatism.

But as the apostle Paul was blessed with many demonstrations of healing, yet his own bitter affliction—his "thorn in the flesh," which many believe was eye disease —went unchecked by the Master's hand, so Henrietta, though favored with these evidences of God's concern, did not receive healing for her life-long struggle with extreme myopia and general eye weakness and irritation. Paul had cried out three times that his suffering might be abated, but the only response was, *My grace is sufficient for thee* (II Cor. 12:9). So Henrietta called out for relief, but to no avail, finding her only comfort in the sufficiency of her Master's power. In her maturity, Miss Mears often remarked, "I believe my greatest spiritual asset throughout my entire life has been my failing sight, for it has kept me absolutely dependent upon God."

Before entering her first year at the University of Minnesota, Henrietta's vision became further impaired, and her doctor cautioned her that blindness was imminent if she continued studying and reading. Such a tragic warning could have cast black banners of despair across her brilliant and eager mind, but her reply when her mother asked what she wanted to do was typical: "If I am going to be blind by thirty, then blind I shall be! But I want something in my brain to think about!" She chose to enter college and continue her studies. But aware of the dangers, she began to discipline her habits, increasing her powers of concentration during lectures, studying by daylight and not electricity, and learning to comprehend a book when reading it through once. As a result, her ears heard much and her mind retained it—thus saving her eyes. She finished at the university with excellent grades. If it had not been for her mother's illness and the amount

37

of time she had to remain out of classes, she might have received a Phi Beta Kappa key. As it was, because of her high grades she did not have to take any final examinations—and she was still able to see.

Her ability to concentrate on what she was reading, by the way, had been awakened in her many years earlier by her mother, who, seeing her daughter engaged in a book, would come up to her without warning, close the book, and ask her to tell her what she had been reading. The young girl would remonstrate, "But Mother, I've only been reading for ten minutes!" To which Mrs. Mears would reply, "My dear, if you have been reading that long, you certainly should have learned something. Now tell me what you have read."

An amazing footnote to her eye weakness is that God was to call Henrietta Mears into a service which made large demands of her in the area of her greatest weakness. For despite her visual infirmities, she found one of the fulfillments of her ministry in becoming an author!

Young Henrietta gleaned a wealth of knowledge and training from her family as well as from her formal schooling. Her mother's sister, Aunt Henrietta, had been a concert soprano, and she encouraged her niece toward the same profession. Voice lessons were introduced with Mr. Edwin Skedden, an opera coach and director of music at the First Baptist Church. Although Henrietta was not destined for the stage, these studies, along with the few performances she did give, trained her to use her vocal cords to maximum efficiency. Thus as her career as a teacher and lecturer unfolded, she was able to address large audiences with a power and projection that could rival those of a Shakespearean actress.

Through her teens, Henrietta's mother remained the controlling influence in her life. Her saintly devotion and practical wisdom cultivated her daughter's religious sense as well as her social grace. If Henrietta returned home from a party, complaining that it was dull and uneventful, her mother gently asked her what she had done to make it interesting: "Wasn't there some game you could have suggested? Even though it wasn't your party, you should have felt an obligation to help the others have a good time." The same attitude was encouraged when her daughter grieved over an uninspiring church meeting. "But did you give a testimony, Henrietta? Did you offer to help plan the meeting?" Such lessons produced a sense of responsibility and initiative in the young woman, which in later life gave her a restless desire to contribute suggestions and create programs in situations where other people were folding their hands in discouragement.

During her long life Henrietta Mears was an effective personal worker, leading thousands of men and women individually to the Saviour. This ability, too, was fostered by her mother, who took every opportunity to speak to people about Christ. A stack of New Testaments, each marked for verses dealing with salvation, stood near the Mears' front door, and salesmen and other visitors were given one with a gracious word of encouragement to study it. Henrietta's mother would often make some such comment as this to a young man who came to the door to sell something: "I am always so interested in young men. I have four sons of my own, and I am concerned not only with their preparation for this life but for the life to come. I was wondering if you have ever accepted Christ as your personal Saviour." By following her mother's example Henrietta quickly learned a kind and sympathetic approach to people and how to inspire them to seek God.

Another lesson passed on from mother to daughter concerned the economizing of time. Mother Mears strove to use every available moment to its fullest, playing the piano for but a moment cr two while waiting for the family to gather for dinner or reading a page of poetry while resting from housework. She would not allow her children to sleep late, even on holidays; summer vacation was not "running wild all day"—the mornings were spent in reading, memorizing great literature, music practice, or the like. During school Mrs. Mears insisted that Monday morning's lessons be prepared on the previous Friday afternoon, so that the weekend would not be haunted by unfinished homework.

Henrietta Mears showed the effects of this teaching all her life. A distasteful job was not to be put off. If someone needed to be reminded of his duties, she was there to do the job. If a meeting were called for 9:15, Henrietta was there at 9:13 ready to get started. All of this gave a sense of urgency to her life that was infectious. When you were around her you soon found that you, too, were anxious to get things done. In spiritual matters this sense of urgency reached its greatest intensity.

When a senior in high school, Henrietta, along with a good friend, had been attending a series of meetings held in their church. The closing sermon was a great challenge for full-time Christian service, and with one accord Henrietta and Evalyn Camp rose and marched down the aisle when the invitation was given. They felt a tremendous sense of complete commitment to go wherever the Lord wanted them to go and to do whatever work he wanted them to do. The two girls studied and planned and prayed about their futures. Before too long, Evalyn became deeply concerned for Japan and felt the Lord would have her serve him there. But try as she would,

40

Henrietta felt no urge to go to work with the Japanese people. Every young person who has given his life to serve his Lord is keen to know where he is to serve, and Henrietta was no exception. She prayed lest something was wrong in her life that made her not want to go to Japan also. "Is something wrong with me?" went over and over again in her mind. Not one to jump into action without divine direction, as was displayed in later life, she waited and prayed. She abided the Lord's time. She felt her only solution was to search out for herself how she could appropriate God's power, with the hope that in him she would find the direction her life was to take.

For weeks she scoured the Bible for references to Christ's presence, and particularly for those concerning the ministry of the Holy Spirit. She closeted herself with God. The truths of divine revelation began to take shape before her mind like a many-faceted diamond through which a heavenly ray was bursting forth in a multitude of refracted colors. The glory of God shone ever more brightly as the object of her search gained focus in her thoughts. It was God himself she was seeking! It was in him where lay his call. But how to acquire the full measure of his presence, his will, his power? What needed to be done? What discipline to take up? What efforts of mind and will to reach for? Then, suddenly, that which had been a cascading flood of light before her but out of reach, rushed into her soul, illuminating darkened corners, transforming her questions to understanding and confidence, as the controlling insight of her life dawned upon her: There was nothing more she could do to obtain God's presence and power than to receive the Third Person of the Godhead, the Holy Spirit, as a gift: By faith she reached out and took what God had for her— himself.

41

Her life during this time was not devoid of romance. Her vivacious personality, keen sense of purpose, spontaneous humor and immense capacity for appreciation attracted many a rugged and ambitious fellow. However, there was only one young man whom she ever loved and considered for marriage. He was tall, handsome, black-haired, intellectually challenging and a delight socially, a graduate of Dartmouth, and now a young banker, but he was of a different faith. As the friendship developed and love grew, a fear struck her heart, and she knew she would have to terminate this relationship. He tried to make her see that he admired her religious convictions; he tried to persuade her that they could establish their home, and she could go on and believe and do just as she wanted, and she wouldn't have to change in any way. A home had always been very important to Henrietta. She loved children and companionship, she loved entertaining and the social life, and she loved the young man who was doing the persuading. Yet wouldn't she be compromising her faith, her beliefs, to share her life with someone who had a different faith from hers? As the months slipped by, Henrietta could not get away from the thought: It would be like establishing a home and deciding that the husband would eat each night in the dining room, and she would eat in another room. They would both have an excellent meal, but they would have no fellowship together. If in the matter of their faith they could not sit together at the same table and have fellowship, their relationship would be impossible. The conflict was great.

There was only one place she could turn. In the solitude of her own room, she prayed, "Lord, you have made me the way I am. I love a home, I love security, I love children, and I love him. Yet I feel that marriage under these conditions would draw me away from you. I surrender even this, Lord, and leave it in your hands. Lead me, Lord, and strengthen me. You have promised to fulfill all my needs. I trust in you alone." The friendship was terminated.

Years later, looking back on this experience, Miss Mears wrote:

> The marvelous thing has been, that the Lord has always given me a beautiful home; he has given me thousands of children; he has supplied every need in my life, and I've never felt lonely. Since I am a very gregarious person, I thought I would have a feeling I didn't belong. But I've never had it, never! I've never missed companionship. Through one experience after another the Lord has shown me that he had something special for me to do. After I went through that final door, where it was just the Lord and I, into wide open spaces of people and things and excitement, life has been one great adventure. It has been a tremendous thing to see how the Lord has filled my life so abundantly with lovely things, and I want to tell everyone that wherever the Lord puts you—even alone on an island—he absolutely satisfies you. So often young people will say to me, "Oh, Miss Mears, I want to be just like you! You are so happy! I, too, never want to get married." And I say to them, "Nonsense! The Lord intends for you to marry; that is the way he has made us. It just so happens that in my case that wasn't his will." But it has pleased me to know that young people have been able to see my happiness and my complete satisfaction in the life that God has given me.

In considering her single state, Miss Mears, in later

life, delighted her collegians by making the observation that the real reason she had never married was that St. Paul was the only man she could have married, and he didn't wait for her!

Henrietta Mears was destined for Sunday School work. Her religious and secular training all pointed in that direction. At the age of twelve she taught her first Sunday School class, and from that moment on her abilities and ambitions stretched out to compass the souls of tens of thousands of boys and girls, men and women, for Christ. While a freshman in college, she was the superintendent of a junior department. Upon graduation from the University of Minnesota, she entered into a professional teaching career, her first assignment being in Beardsley, Minnesota. She was given not only the principal's chair along with chemistry, but speech and dramatics. She was appalled at the low morals of the high-school students and immediately began to have a positive influence on them. (After her experience in this town she always said, "God made the country, the man the city and the devil the small town.") She enthusiastically entered into the various school activities of her students, coaching plays, organizing choirs, and raising money for new pianos. She also found a coach and organized a football team. She never missed a game, even though it usually meant trudging through sleet or mud. She rooted for the team from their bench, and then her huskies eagerly occupied the first rows in her Bible class and listened to her spiritual coaching.

Everything their Bible class did reflected Miss Mears' enthusiasm. It was a depression year, and even the smallest amount of money was hard to raise. Thus few of the members of the church had much to give to missions when the annual campaign was announced. But nothing daunted Miss Mears. She laid a plan before her young people. "I want you to work and earn as much money as you are able," she said. "Do everything you can to bring in money for our missionaries. And I will match you dollar for dollar." Their youthful eyes bugged with excitement! For the next few weeks her charges ran errands, prevailed upon friends, and saved their money. When Missionary Sunday arrived, it was all they could do to sit still in the pews as the other classes reported their collections: $1.25, $3.00, $15.50. The minister called out, "Miss Mears' Young People's Class." Charlie leaped to his feet and shouted, "One hundred and twenty dollars!" The class was triumphant.

The next year, in North Branch, Minnesota, she was asked to be principal and teacher of chemistry in the high school. Wherever she was she assisted in the Sunday School. While at North Branch, Miss Mears was challenged by an incorrigible imp whom no teacher could tame. Everett's pranks were the scourge of the faculty, who lost no time explaining matters to the new principal. Everett came from a wealthy home, his father being a prominent lumberman and civic leader. Armed with this special distinction, which had always counted in the past, and a pocketful of spitwads, Everett set himself to unnerving the new principal. But to his dismay, Miss Mears, unperturbed by his harassments, refused to single him out in any way, even to giving him notice for his bad temper. She did attempt to introduce him on an equal footing to all the activities in which the students were expected to take an interest. Her friendly and determined attitude began to have effect. One day Everett delivered to Miss Mears an invitation to their home —the brick house on the elevated site with large, sweeping lawns, enclosed by a wrought iron fence—it being the desire of every teacher to be invited inside. But until this moment no teacher had ever been asked to enter. Everett's family expressed their gratitude that Miss Mears had been able to win the boy's admiration and respect. He had also ceased to be such a problem in the family. Invited back to their home time and again, she had many opportunities to talk to them about Christ. Years later Everett's sister called on Miss Mears in Hollywood and exclaimed, "Oh, those wonderful days when you were with us in our home! We will never forget them. You revolutionized North Branch. Our whole family was changed because of your influence on our lives."

The following years found her in charge of the department of chemistry of Central High School in Minneapolis and attending the First Baptist Church. Her sister Margaret had been teaching the eighteen-year-old girls in the church but was in despair over them and implored Henrietta to take them and teach them. The girls called themselves "The Snobs" and would not permit a newcomer into the class. Henrietta set about to teach them, and in a few months they stopped calling themselves "The Snobs." Then when the Sunday School was reorganized, every one of these girls answered a call to serve in the church. There was only one girl left, and Miss Mears began to build the class again.

The Mears sisters began to call on the young ladies of the neighborhood. The first Sunday brought fifty-five new girls to the newly organized "Fidelis Class." This number was quickly doubled, and they kept pushing out the walls of every room into which they were moved. In five years the class grew to over five hundred members, and it was necessary to build a special hall for them. As Henrietta taught, her sister Margaret took up the position of greeter at the church door to invite passing young ladies to come inside and hear her sister teach the Bible. One of these women many years later said, "Margaret invited us in to see her sister's hats, and they were something to behold. But we soon learned that there was more to Henrietta Mears than just her hats, as we found Christ as our Saviour."

As an outgrowth of the Fidelis Class, Miss Mears organized the "Dorcas Group," made up of young married women from the class. Their purpose was to sew and give to missionaries as well as discuss problems of young mothers and spiritual aspects of life. The group met in different homes, soon becoming one of the established fellowships in the church. Both groups still exist today.

One Sunday when Margaret and Henrietta went to the church, they found that their pastor Dr. Riley was out of town and that the pulpit was being filled by Dr. Stewart P. MacLennan from the First Presbyterian Church of Hollywood. His sermon on "The Love of Christ" made a profound impact on the two sisters. This magnificent figure of a man preached eloquently, fearlessly and movingly. It was Margaret and Henrietta's custom to invite visiting ministers to Sunday dinner, but this time Henrietta said to one of the deacons. "I don't think it is fair for us always to have the privilege of fellowshiping with these guests. Why don't you take Dr. MacLennan to your home today?" But the deacon refused, saying, "Now, Henrietta, you know that they always have a better time with you and Margaret." So Dr. MacLennan went to Sunday dinner with the Mears sisters.

After an amiable two hours, Henrietta suggested to Dr. MacLennan that they should drive him back to his hotel so that he could rest and prepare for the evening's service. "Do I have to go?" he asked. "You see, I am writing a new series of sermons on the person of Christ, and I would like very much to go over it with you." And so through the afternoon they listened to this man talk about the Christ whom he knew and loved so deeply. Before their time together was over, Dr. MacLennan told Miss Mears that she and Margaret would have to come to California. The idea was so unexpected that the two women just laughed; but Dr. MacLennan finally made them promise to return his visit if they ever came to California.

Some time later, Dr. Riley, knowing that Henrietta was seeking to know whether the Lord wanted her to remain in public school teaching or if he had full-time Christian work for her to do, suggested that during her sabbatical year she and Margaret travel. "It may give you a vision of this world that will determine the direction of your life." And so she and Margaret left for Europe.

With some of their sabbatical still before them, they returned to the United States and ventured to California to spend the winter there. Of course they looked up Dr. MacLennan and attended his church. They were delighted with all they saw. Dr. MacLennan had taken a little country church near Hollywood and Vine and had built it up to one of the most influential of Presbyterian pulpits. Wednesday evening prayer meetings saw hundreds in attendance. From five hundred to a thousand men met in a special Bible class called "Macsmen." The emphasis of the church' was on the young, and there were some four hundred or more in the church school. The Mears sisters tingled with excitement as they beheld this work being carried on in a city bursting with the strength and bluster of its youth. Dr. "Mac" had Henrietta speak on several occasions, and the response to her messages was immediate. He finally offered her the position of Director of Christian Education. But it was out of the question. All of their ties were in Minneapolis, and whatever successes she might have had were there. Besides, Margaret was involved in business. They owned their own home. And Henrietta was scheduled to return to her teaching post. In a few weeks the two sisters were back in Minneapolis. But Miss Mears' thoughts gave her no peace, and neither did Dr. MacLennan. He wrote—he telegraphed—he telephoned! She had had many opportunities to serve offered to her while in Los Angeles. What if this was God's leading? Letters and telephone calls from Dr. MacLennan indicated that he wanted her for his young people, and he painted glowing pictures of what they could accomplish together with the youth that were pouring into this "city of make-believe." Still not knowing what to do, she returned to Hollywood.

One noon, she and Dr. MacLennan went to the Pig 'n Whistle restaurant on Hollywood Boulevard for lunch. As they approached the door, it silently opened before her. She had never seen a door controlled by an "electric eye." She was greatly amazed and impressed. As they ate their lunch and talked about the possibilities of the work that could be done in Hollywood, Miss Mears, without realizing it, found herself saying, "If I were going to do such-and-such, I'd . . ." She finally saw that her own door had opened as silently and effortlessly as the electric-eye door had opened when she had entered the restaurant.

But there was the matter of her teaching contract, and school was to open shortly. And, of course, there was the home. Property just wasn't selling this time of year, and they wouldn't be able to get their money out of their house. But God had begun to reveal his plan to her. In the years that followed, she would often say to any young person wondering what work God might have for him, "Look to the horizon. Do you see the slightest change? The slightest speck? If you do, follow it." Her horizon had changed, and she must follow that speck to find out whether or not God was trying to tell her something.

She returned to Minneapolis to see what could be done about the teaching contract and selling the home. The home appeared the most improbable. So she decided that as Gideon had laid a fleece on the ground to determine the will of God, so she would lay out her fleece to know his will for her life. Her fleece was two thousand dollars added to the price she would put on their home. The first person to come to see the house dashed through with his head down, apparently seeing nothing. As he left, Henrietta said, "Well, he's certainly not interested." But he was so tremendously interested that he was afraid someone would get to the real estate agent ahead of him, and so he had rushed through as quickly as possible and on to the agent. The fleece of two thousand dollars was met. There could be no question now.

So positive a demonstration of God's leading gave to Margaret and Henrietta their final incentive, and bidding farewell to family and friends, they moved to Hollywood. As her sister worked at establishing their new home—getting the furniture uncrated, hanging drapes, setting up the kitchen, supervising the garden—Henrietta Mears began her work at the First Presbyterian Church of Hollywood, realizing that as she was walking toward closed doors, they were opening by the impulse of an unseen hand. Little did she dream what triumphs there would be! Before finishing her service, Miss Mears was to see a similar portal swing open to tens of thousands of people— some pouring into her Sunday School rooms, others climbing that mountain "a mile nearer heaven," still more picking up dozens of books she was to write, and multitudes in foreign lands turning from dumb idols to the living God because of her influence. An opportunity for effective service was opening through which would march a multitude of redeemed boys and girls, men and women, filling the earth with the songs of Zion and praising and glorifying the one who said: *Behold, I have set before thee an open door, and no man can shut it* (Rev. 3:8).

3

The Sword Unsheathed

The Sword Unsheathed

The work of the Director of Christian Education is too often thought of in terms of output or activity. It is to be admitted that productivity is the logical end for which a director is secured by a church, and it is toward this end that he must apply himself. This cannot, however, be measured by volume of action. It is accomplished only through purposeful action. Only that which is directed toward definite goals, which in turn are founded on sound educational philosophy, can be ultimately meaningful. The principles must always precede the activities.

—HENRIETTA MEARS

In Minnesota she had been a successful teacher, but as Director of Christian Education in Hollywood, Miss Mears would have to organize and train others to teach. With reliance on God and allegiance to his Word, she mapped out the course she was to take. What she often said to her fellow teachers thoroughly characterized her own ministry:

Two things Joshua had to do to qualify him for his great work: To be strong and of good courage, and to make the Book of the Law his continued study. God's Word must be our only infallible guide. In keeping it there is great reward. To reject his Word is to be rejected.

Miss Mears insisted that Christian education must be Christian. Every lesson, each meeting must honor him. And this implied (what she never doubted) that the Christian teacher must be faithful to the Bible. "Christian education recognizes the inspired Word of God," she would say, "not only as its text and the sum of its message, but also as the source of the principles by which successful Christian education may be carried on." And throughout the ensuing years of her career, no one ever thought of Henrietta Mears as being anything but absolutely loyal to the Bible as the authoritative revelation of God.

Admirers were often amazed by her proficiency in teaching the Bible and her ability to quote long passages of it from memory. But they were even more surprised when they learned the simplicity of her study methods, for they were nothing beyond what the most average believer is capable of. She possessed several Bibles in various translations, but her favorite was a leather-bound King James edition, which was well marked and somewhat tattered. It was her friend for almost a lifetime. While listening to others expound a passage, she would jot in the margin their thoughts or her own. And in private study she scribbled ideas that helped her summarize a whole passage at a glance. She usually worked with a notebook at hand, but when one was not available, any sheet of paper would do. Some of her observations were even committed to the backs of envelopes. But the form of writing was not significant; the intensity of concentration was. She must have learned from college days of the possibility of blindness, that one moment of sight might at the next give way to darkness, so let what now could be seen be captured forever! The technique was therefore not the important aspect of her

Bible study; it was rather the avidity with which she devoured every precious truth. The devotional hour was not a routine with her, not a discipline born of fear or habit, for she opened her Bible in the sacred silence of personal fellowship with God with much the same attention as a starving man approaches a banquet. "If you would be pure," she often advised her young people, "saturate yourself with the Word of God." And she showed them how it was done.

Armed, then, with the Sword of the Spirit, and aflame with the love of Christ, Henrietta Mears walked into the first teachers' and officers' meeting she had called at the First Presbyterian Church of Hollywood. They came eagerly, for word had gotten around about the new director, and some had heard her teach and were anticipating great things for the Sunday School. Others were doubtlessly skeptical, thinking, "No one could be as good as they are making her out to be!"

Speaking in soft, friendly tones, her eyes dancing with enthusiasm and good will, she said, "I believe I know just what you are thinking. I think I might feel the same way if I were in your place. 'Another director of the Sunday School—new plans, new ideas, her way of doing things! So everything is going to be changed again! If I have to reorganize my class once more, or try out some fancy new theory, I'll just die! What does she know about Hollywood, anyway?'" Her audience broke out in laughter, more at themselves probably than at their new leader, for she had caught them off-guard. "You don't like changes and neither do I," she continued. "You've been getting along without me up to now, and it would certainly be a great burden for me to have the responsibility of rushing in here to try to reorganize everything overnight. So here is what I thought we might do: We'll all relax for six months and use the time for observation, and then we'll sit down and evaluate the situation and decide together what we need to do. You undoubtedly will have some ideas, and I might just possibly have a suggestion or two myself!" They could hardly wait for her to close the meeting before they rushed to the platform, "Oh, Miss Mears, we can't wait six months! Our department just has to have something done about the teachers. We are having a terrible time. No one wants to teach three-year-olds." And on and on! She had won the first round! Now she had been invited into their departments!

Miss Mears' aggressive and positive attitudes toward her new job ignited the imagination of those about her. "Many of the Sunday School rooms need painting," reported Miss Mears to Dr. MacLennan. And he made the announcement from the pulpit to come on such and such a day, bring hammers and paint brushes, and be prepared to work. On hand to greet them, attired in their work clothes, were Dr. "Mac" and Miss Mears. To the surprise of some, she chose to paint the women's rest room off Fellowship Hall. This showed them that she would never ask them to do something she was not willing to do herself, although no one could ever say that she ever sat down and calculated such thoughts. It was just a matter of a job to be done, and the quicker the better. She soon won their loyalty for any task she asked them to do.

Often after an arduous day of work and counselling, one would see her heading toward her car with an arm-load of books. One young fellow in particular would disengage himself from the group, and without a word take the books out of her arms, while others would call,

"Where are you going with all of those books, Miss Mears?"

"Home to study for those lessons you are going to hear next Sunday and Wednesday," would be her reply.

If any had put up a guard concerning the new director, it came tumbling down fast, as they watched her love and enthusiasm for whatever she did—painting, cleaning, talking with the collegians, or going home to study, with books piled up to her chin.

"I was 'the church mouse,'" recalls Ethel May Baldwin—later to become Miss Mears' faithful assistant, "and no one paid any attention to my comings and goings, that is until Henrietta Mears came out to California for a visit and taught our youth group. She insisted on stopping to shake hands and make me feel at home. This made a great impression on me—to think that a visiting teacher would bother to shake hands with us, and with me in particular."

"Another thing I remember," confides Ethel May, "she was the first leader that I didn't put on a pedestal and then was afraid to go near. It wasn't until years later that I discovered why. Henrietta Mears shunned pedestals. She would never permit a person to place her on one. She was not going to have anyone disillusioned by her falling from some great height."

The Lord had been speaking to Ethel May and had planted in her heart the desire to be a Director of Christian Education, but the fulfillment was not to come in the way that she had planned. Then much later, during a dedication service and the singing of the hymn, "Where He Leads Me I Will Follow," she stood when the invitation was given to indicate her willingness to go wherever the Lord wanted her. About six months later Miss Mears joined the staff. It was during the launching of a membership campaign to get the young business girls into Miss Mears' Tuesday Evening Bible Club that Ethel May overheard Miss Mears exclaim, "I'm just going to have to have a secretary." Without a word to anyone, Ethel May renewed her efforts to find out whether or not this was the place the Lord wanted her. It was! A month after Henrietta Mears arrived to take up her new position, Ethel May became her secretary. The position grew in responsibility, as Miss Mears discovered her abilities, to Assistant Director of Christian Education, companion, cofounder of Gospel Light Press, and a host of other assignments. Many years later Miss Mears said, "If Ethel May should leave at 12:00, I would leave at 12:01." But Miss Baldwin did not leave; she stayed to assist Henrietta Mears to build the work God revealed to her as the years rolled on.

One day Miss Mears picked up a student's manual in the primary department and read the lesson title: "Amos Denounces Self-Indulgence." "What!" she thought. "How can any child grasp that?" Other lessons showed her how irrelevant this Primary Sunday School material was to the six- seven- and eight-year-olds. Then the shocking news came to her ears that the lesson material being used in the junior department was to be discontinued. Moving immediately to find out what could be done, she questioned the possibility of purchasing the type so that a printer could print books for their own use, but the lead had been scrapped. The last resort was to purchase as many lesson manuals as possible, and this resulted in knowing that at the end of three years it would be necessary to find other lesson material for the juniors. The time had come Miss Mears could delay the decision no longer.

Never one to dally, she immediately asked Dr. Mac-

Lennan, "Do you mind what materials we use in our Sunday School?"

"Use anything you want as long as it teaches the Bible," was his reply.

In response to her requests, sample curriculums came to her desk. Then she gathered the educators of the church together to make a survey of Sunday School literature on the market in 1929. Most of the materials were Biblically sound but were unattractively presented with no pictures for the children, and certainly not graded for any particular age—all would have to be adapted. Moreover, there was no chronological presentation. One Sunday the child would study about Saul, the king, and the next week about Saul of Tarsus; the lessons jumped from the Acts of Abraham to the Acts of the Apostles. This latter presentation Miss Mears termed the "grasshopper method." And in the most widely used curriculum it was discovered that only once in years was the lesson of the story of creation presented. If you missed that Sunday, you had to find out elsewhere than in your Sunday School class how the world began! Miss Mears had sat on the curriculum committee for the public schools of Minneapolis and was keenly aware of the necessity to grade materials to student's abilities. She was therefore appalled to find that Sunday School literature was woefully deficient in this regard. As the supply of the old curriculum for juniors was used up, the new books arrived on Miss Mears desk; she opened the package and looked the materials over. "Paul survived his shipwreck because he had eaten carrots and was strong," revealed one lesson. She wrapped up the books and sent them back, explaining that she could not use any material in her Sunday School which denied the miraculous in Scripture.

Motivation by the impression that the Bible was the

most poorly taught book in the world, she faced the task before her. Two incidents constantly remained vivid in her thinking. When she had first come to Hollywood, a young junior boy had said, "I don't wanna go to Sunday School anymore. All they do is tell you the same old story over and over and over again; only it just gets dumber and dumber." And a young man with a Phi Beta Kappa key asked her, "What's wrong, Miss Mears? I've gone to Sunday School all of my life, but if I had to take an examination on the Bible today, I'd flunk." Armed with these illustrations of glaring weakness, Miss Mears and her educators worked out a prospectus, determining the accomplishments expected at each age level. The die was cast and the writing begun. There was absolutely no thought of ever printing and selling the lessons. Miss Mears just saw a need in her own Sunday School and answered it to the best of her ability. To keep ahead of the week-by-week demand for lesson materials for a Sunday School that was growing out of all bounds of anyone's experience or the realm of reason was a full time job in itself. But the administrative tasks also remained constant in their demands, to say nothing of speaking and teaching responsibilities, which consumed hours and hours of preparation. True, it was not humanly possible, but God intervened and was lavish with his might and power and strength. This can be the only answer!

As page after page of Bible lessons came from the pen of Henrietta Mears, they were taken by her secretary, Ethel May Baldwin, typed, mimeographed and stapled. Only four lessons could be produced at a time, rather than the usual thirteen for a quarter, due to the amount of space needed for typewritten copy and the thickness of the books. Desiring to make them as attractive as possible, numbers of out-of-date religious calendars were collected, and the beautiful Biblical pictures cut out and pasted on the covers. Because mimeographing rubbed off on Sunday clothes, fancy fonts of type were purchased for the old multigraph, and handset titles run on the covers in printer's ink. Today these first books don't look like much alongside the beautiful Sunday School books that are on the market, but in their day, they were way out ahead of anything available, even though "homemade." As the mass of production increased, Miss Mears kept inquiring of those with experience in printing magazines and books, but she was constantly told that costwise these were completely out of her reach. So she was resigned to closely graded, Biblical, mimeographed lesson books put together as attractively as possible.

They stand not alone, those who build kingdoms; God does not leave us alone when we undertake beyond our strength to obey his will. While teaching in a junior high school in the Los Angeles public school system, and superintending the junior department at the church, Esther A. Ellinghusen, a courageous Christian visionary, locked arms with Miss Mears. She, too, took pen and paper to write and meet the demands of the juniors. Miss Ellinghusen interviewed the head of the remedial reading department of the Los Angeles public school system, studied vocabulary charts, and compared school textbooks for size of type, vocabulary, sentence structure, and illustrative material. She wrote constantly, consumed by one thought, "How can I best teach these children about God's love?" Many whom she enlightened, reflecting back from later years of maturity, never doubted that God's love had been taught them well.

The demands on the "production department"—Ethel

May Baldwin—increased as the writers covered more and more pages with their Bible lessons. But always one to organize, Ethel May increased the production department "staff" to include her father and mother. Growing concern on the part of her mother that her daughter would develop cancer of the hand from stapling the hundreds of thick books, meant that Ethel May's father took over this job.

During 1930 the Great Depression was rampaging across the nation. It was necessary for the church to cut every possible corner when making up the budget, and so naturally Sunday School papers were among the first items to go. To compensate for this loss the ingenious ladies improvised word puzzles, mazes and crossword puzzles, which were not included in the mimeographed lessons. And the work grew.

"You know, I believe everyone gets to California at least once in his lifetime," Henrietta Mears used to say. This seemed to be the case as visitors from far and near were forever dropping by the Sunday School to see what was being done. As they listened, they began to realize that the children knew a great deal of Bible and were answering questions intelligently and with enthusiasm and a grasp of the situation. The most natural question would come, "What lesson material are you using, Miss Mears?" With a toss of her head and a slight shrug of her shoulder, she would unconcernedly reply, "Oh, just some mimeographed material that some of us are writing and putting together here." But this simple reply was the reason that parents were driving their children from neighboring towns, some driving as far as fifty miles, passing up many churches on the way. This was around 1931 when there was no thought of freeways, but distance made no difference—they wanted their children to study the Bible. It was Henrietta Mears' principle at work—"Give them something to come for and they will come miles to get it." She never sat down and said, "Now, I'll do this, so that will happen." Never! But results made them come and see for themselves. Some of the visitors would mildly ask if they could get this lesson material, but Miss Mears patiently explained, "Such a thing would be out of the question, as we are hardly able to produce it fast enough for our own use." But some were undaunted by such obstacles as production, which they probably did not fully understand, and many continued to request the literature, even though Miss Mears kept answering, "I'm just producing it for my Sunday School and have no way to do more."

As Miss Mears was invited out to various churches to speak, she felt that she must accept and do her part so that she could in turn invite pastors and workers to come to Hollywood. And so in the course of this exchange of speaking engagements, a Mr. Marion Falconer, a druggist in Anaheim and superintendent of the Sunday School of a Presbyterian church, invited her to speak to his teachers. Through this initial introduction he and Miss Mears became well acquainted, and their paths crossed as each attended any workshop for teachers held within the area, so eager were they both to bring the best to their Sunday Schools. Then one Sunday morning Mr. Falconer came to visit Hollywood. Before leaving home he had decided to ask Miss Mears to publish the lesson material she was writing for her Sunday School. While waiting for Miss Mears to finish her responsibilities, he went to various departments to observe. Whenever Miss Mears was confronted by something bordering on the impossible to her way of thinking, she had a gay little laugh of incredulity to turn aside the inquirer. In most cases this was all that was necessary to bring about a change of conversation. But not so in Mr. Falconer's case. No doubt he envisioned his own Sunday School struggling away with poor lesson materials, and here right at hand was a curriculum in the process of production which was actually attaining the very results he longed to have in his own Sunday School. After much talk and strong persuasive reasons as to why this lesson material should be printed and made available for many Sunday Schools, Mr. Falconer finally extracted this promise, "Well, I'll tell you what I'll do, Mr. Falconer. I could not possibly say that I would print the material as of this moment, but I will look into the matter of printing once again." Many were the times in years to come that Miss Mears would say, "Thank Mr. Falconer for making me print the Sunday School lessons. He just wouldn't take no for an answer."

Sparked by a commitment to check printing costs, her mind began to turn over ideas. "I wonder how Harry Rimmer gets those scientific paper-covered books of his printed. He doesn't have a lot of money. Ethel May, let's call up Harry Rimmer." They were old friends from Minnesota days, and when he heard her request, he said, "Henrietta, go see my printer, Cary Griffin. He'll take care of you." It was as simple as that! Mr. Cary Griffin threw in his lot with "the ladies." Never one to rush into anything without counting the cost, both in time and money, Miss Mears asked Mr. Griffin what would be involved financially, suggesting that possibly the books could be sold and then the bills be paid. To have engendered such confidence in a stranger is to the credit of both Henrietta Mears and Cary Griffin, for he agreed to hold his bills; but where he had to make a layout of cash, as for instance the engravings, he would have to have money. Miss Mears liked to tell how Mr. Griffin would sit on her davenport and "educate" her to the problems of printing—with patience and understanding. There was an area of printing, however, to which neither she nor Miss Ellinghusen ever got "educated." The composition of a page was never grasped, so Mr. Griffin finally gave up. The ladies wrote and he paged. If there was too much copy, another page was added, or the copy was cut. Writing and editing nine books a quarter, in addition to manning a growing Sunday School, played havoc with that thing all printers call "schedule," but the ladies wrote as hard and fast as they could, and Ethel May proofread as quickly as she could. It was decided not to date the material. The courses were to be repeated each year for each particular age, so by not dating the material the churches could use it the next year instead of having to throw it away, as Miss Mears had had to do with cupboards full of outdated books when she came to Hollywood.

Esther Ellinghusen always caught everyone up in the thing she was doing, so naturally her teachers in the junior department heard about the lesson material often. This being the case, no one thought it odd when one Sunday morning D. Stanley Engle, one of her teachers, asked, "Esther, who is going to ship these books and take care of the accounting?" Mr. Engle was an accountant with the Union Oil Company, so naturally he'd think of these things. That was a good question! Who was? And so Stan Engle joined forces with the ladies! His garage became the warehouse. Mr. Engle recalls that when Esther Ellinghusen wrote a check for $84.74 to pay for the engravings in the junior pupil's book, the first one to come off the press, her mother said, "Well that's money down the drain!"

When Miss Mears saw the first book actually in print,

she was so excited that immediately she decided to print a junior high book, paying the costs as Esther had done. There was one problem. It was June, and the book would have to be finished and printed by mid-September so as to be in the hands of the Sunday School users for the quarter starting in October. She had wanted a course on the Christian life to ground the new junior highs and confirm their faith, since many had received Christ in their junior years. She whipped both pupils' and teachers' books into shape. Over the years Miss Mears tried to get back to redoing those books—feeling they were too simple—but it seemed each time she thought of revising them, some mother would come to her with a story of how she had found her son on his knees beside his bed, doing exactly what was asked of him in the lesson. To Miss Mears this was God's seal on the book.

Orders were now coming from numerous churches; by the end of 1933, twelve courses had been published, and 13,366 copies had been sold to 131 Sunday Schools in 25 states. It was this widespread coverage which surprised the ladies. By the end of 1934, sales tripled, and new books were continuing to be added along with flannel-graphs. The Engle's home was now the annex to their garage, with books piled high in corners and under tables. Mrs. Engle was constantly on the telephone taking orders or opening mail, while her husband kept accounts in the evening, tied bundles and shipped the literature to an ever increasing number of churches in many states.

The writers and the printers continued to operate like one, a seldom-to-be-expected situation in a world where customarily every man is out to get all he can for himself. Cary Griffin made Gospel Light Press. But likewise Gospel Light made Griffin-Patterson Printers.

Ethel May Baldwin recalls, "One day when Miss Mears

was writing a lesson, she put down her pencil, leaned back in her chair, and said, 'I can't write another word! What's going to happen to it after it is written?' It could only have been through the Spirit of God that I replied, 'God only asked you to write. He will promote the literature.' And the thing that always baffled me—she believed me!"

As 1935 approached, Miss Mears decided that she would like to take a trip around the world, but the question was, how to get that mass of books written and take three months out of her writing and editing schedule? She finally voiced an opinion, "What's wrong with publishing half a book?" This was such a momentous, unheard of request that Cary Griffin had to come over to talk to "the lady." He took out his pencil and began to figure, "Well, now, as far as I can see, it would cost you an extra cover for the run." As Miss Mears and Miss Baldwin walked up the gangplank, the galley proofs were put in their hands to be read and sent back. Fearing to mail it from a foreign port, they hurried through the proofreading so as to send it from Honolulu. There had been such a problem finding wrapping paper and string that they could not resist writing in the corner of the package where the return name and address appears, "Paper and string have we none, but such as we have send we unto thee! Hezekiah 3:2. HCM and EMB."

The country was staggering with poverty, but Gospel Light Press continued to show an increase in sales each year. It had started with no capital, and for its first three years had no rented facilities or full-time employees. But by 1936 it was a case of either finding a store for Gospel Light Press or moving the Engles into another house. On Thanksgiving day the four partners—Miss Mears, Miss Ellinghusen, Miss Baldwin, and Mr. Engle—held a special thanksgiving service in their new location, 1443 North Vine Street, two blocks away from the flashing lights of the film capital's most famous corner, Hollywood and Vine.

Mr. Engle then discovered that Campbell's Soup boxes were just the right size for shipping the books, and was often accused of walking to work through the alleys to find these cartons. Before long all the employees—clerks, typists, shippers—were caught up in the game of "Find the Campbell's Soup Boxes."

Miss Ellinghusen took a year's leave of absence from public school teaching in order to finish several new courses she was preparing. Completing these early, she spent the rest of her leave traveling through the Pacific Northwest, holding workshops, visiting churches and demonstrating the curriculum. Thousands of pupils were put on Gospel Light materials, and sales rose significantly through her efforts to acquaint pastors and church educators with the new Sunday School curriculum. She demonstrated what personal contact could do.

By the end of 1937 over a quarter of a million books had been sold.

"Little did I realize," one of her college boys recalled years later, "when I saw Miss Mears writing away on lessons in those early morning hours at the church, that one day these lessons would be distributed by the millions around the world. Her dedication in giving out the Word has brought blessings and hope to multiplied thousands." Little did this seminarian, now Dr. Cyrus N. Nelson, think that one day he would be President of Gospel Light Publications, which was the organization that evolved from the new materials.

In 1938, to meet the increasing demands for leadership training, Miss Mears, with her associates, launched a

Christian Education Training Course at Clifton's Cafeteria, in downtown Los Angeles. Reservations for the first meeting were optimistically made for two hundred people. When Miss Mears arrived, she could hardly make her way through the crowd—so large that many of the guests ate while standing. From all over the city Sunday School teachers had come to learn how better to teach God's Word. These classes were held for several years, meeting on the second floor of Clifton's for a series of Monday night workshops. But when over five hundred people began to crowd into the cafeteria for each session, the manager found it necessary to ask Miss Mears to find another location. Eventually these teacher training workshops grew to such dimensions that they were moved to the Forest Home Christian Conference Center in the San Bernardino mountains, where teachers and pastors from all over the country were invited to come for a week of intensive instruction and exchange of ideas.

It is important to realize that what we take for granted today was a generation ago a unique phenomenon. After the First World War interest in spiritual matters in America reached low ebb. This lethargy depleted the Sunday Schools of teachers and students alike. As far as many were concerned, the Sunday School had seen its day and could not be revived. Miss Mears and her co-workers, along with others, were used by God to fan these dying embers into a flame of revival. The meetings that began in Clifton's Cafeteria developed into conferences, rallies and Sunday School conventions across the North American continent. Miss Mears' reputation as an author and leader grew, and it was her privilege to address tens of thousands of people every year on the "romance" of the Sunday School. Conservative Christians found in this movement what they had missed for decades. Many of them knew how at the turn of the century such conventions were commonplace, even to the point where Congress and the President would adjourn their duties in order to attend Sunday School rallies in Washington. But liberalism had taken its toll. Now, in the 1930's and 40's, with Miss Mears and many others in the lead, Christians were again inspired to take the gospel to the youth of the world.

Miss Mears became a cofounder of the National Sunday School Association, and her appearance on convention platforms in America and Canada struck courage in the hearts of thousands of leaders from every denomination Innumerable churches regained their composure after the onslaughts of debilitating liberalism and stood with conviction while presenting the message of salvation to the oncoming, questioning ranks of youth

Statistics can be exciting if behind them are seen transformed individuals. Twelve years after Dr. Mears came to the First Presbyterian Church of Hollywood, Gospel Light Press was one of the four largest independent publishers of Sunday School literature in America. Orders were being received from every state in the Union but one. To expedite shipments, 13 depositories were located across the country, with 53 bookstores handling the literature. Gospel Light serviced 2,126 churches directly, with 736 of them in California. From 1933 to 1940, Gospel Light Press increased its sales 120 times over the first year's record. Hundreds of thousands of youngsters were being taught that God had a plan for them. Men and women who thought that they could never teach were now being trained and equipped. Sunday Schools in hundreds of churches multiplied far beyond expectation. Pastors took heart, parents were won to the Faith by converted children, and young men were once again looking upon the ministry as an honorable calling. The Sword was unsheathed.

Wherever Miss Mears went, her message was the same:

We are standing on holy ground. The Lord said to Moses: *Put off thy shoes from off thy feet, for the place whereon thou standest is holy ground* (Exod 3:5). This is the place where God meets men, and today he is looking for those who will do his will Does not God want us to be concerned with the youth of our age? What am I to do about taking the gospel to them? I must stand at attention before the Lord of Israel. I can hear him speaking to me, as he did to Moses: Go, deliver my people. What does God want you to do? Meet him face to face, and you will find out.

4

Sunday School Is Big Business

Sunday School Is Big Business

Dreams do come true. The first thing I did in Holly-wood was to write out what I wanted for my Sun-day School. I set down my objectives for the first five years. They included improvements in organization, teaching staff, curriculums, and spirit. I wanted a closely graded program, a teaching material that would present Christ and his claims in every lesson, a trained teaching staff, a new education building, choirs, clubs, a camp program, a missionary vision, youth trained for the hour.

—HENRIETTA MEARS

Miss Mears was a blend between the abstract dreamer and the down to earth doer. Visions were quickly trans-formed into plans. The primary objective was not num-bers, but quality. Miss Mears knew that people would come if there was something worth coming to.

In 1928 the Sunday School of the First Presbyterian Church of Hollywood had 450 enrolled, and there was no education building. In two and a half years the en-rollment grew to 4,200. Back in 1923 it was planned that when the present church edifice was completed, construc-tion would begin right away on an education building. But this project had to be set aside because of the de-pression. Miss Mears used to say, "I guess the Lord didn't give us an educational plant for years, in order to prove that it isn't buildings out of which a Sunday School is to be created, but rather a program that presents Jesus Christ. If the children and youth and their parents are coming, you'll find some place to hold the classes." And so for twenty-two years the Sunday School grew and thrived, and a generation went out never having had the advantage of the facilities of Education Building No. 1, which was erected in 1950.

"God closely graded children, I didn't," Miss Mears could be heard saying. From the moment she came to Hollywood, one of her dreams was to have a department for each age, up at least through eight-year-olds. The varying scale of maturity in these beginning years means real development every three-four-six months. In these years to be able to separate children every six months would be best, and this was accomplished as the years moved along.

One June the superintendent of the kindergarten department explained that the four-year-old (or-almost-four) graduate from the two-and-three-year-old department was not sufficiently prepared for her age group. Of necessity the two-three-year-old program had had to be geared down and the three-year-old was not learning all that he could. Four months before graduation the next year, the older ones who were to graduate were taken to the bedrooms upstairs in one of the houses and a program implemented just for their age. The difference in their comprehension and grasp of things was so tremendous that Miss Mears was determined to continue to do this—at least for four months—until a place could be found to create a new department. And so a step was taken toward forming a department for each age.

Naturally, with such unusual Sunday School growth the incidents which took place were laughable—not at the time, but in retrospect. Over the years Miss Mears and the Craig family, wonderful Scottish custodians of the church would laugh about the many times she had chased them out of their home. The five nice big square rooms, which they once occupied, looked so inviting for Sunday School rooms, clubs, Vacation Bible School, and so on. And so the chase was on! The Craigs moved from the "Bungalow" to a place next door, and occupied one-third of the building. Before long two-thirds of that apartment house was converted into the junior department, wire and drapes forming class space after the worship service, and the bedrooms upstairs making excellent classrooms. The juniors soon discovered that it was an easy jump from the upstairs porch of the Junior House to the roof of the "Bungalow," so a chase of one sort or another was always the vogue. When it was necessary to take over the Craig's third of the house, this time they out-foxed Miss Mears. They got out of the line of chase and onto another street! But she was always close on their heels. After giving them time to settle in, catch their breath, relax and think, "Well, I guess that's that," the telephone would ring, and a familiar voice would say, "Mr. Craig, do you think you could move upstairs? You know that apartment would give you an extra room." The never-complaining Craigs moved upstairs. And that downstairs apartment just north of the church became the department for the two-year-olds; then it was needed for a club; the junior highs held their meeting in it on Sunday evenings; it was turned into offices for two of the ministers; and when we could finally get Miss Mears to move out of the main church building, it became the Christian Education Department. (Miss Mears always felt that when a person came to the church to see a minister, or the director of Christian education, the individual should be found in the church building. Also she wanted to be in the "main line of traffic." How would they ever know to come to a "house" for an office? Well, they found her all right. The office the entire time she occupied it became "Grand Central Station," and there was always "room for one more." By the way, this "multiple-unit" is now the church library, and the space is still functional.) Is there any wonder that Thomas Craig's theme song became, "Once again the scene is changed"?

One morning the Christian education staff arrived, Miss Mears and Miss Baldwin, to hear sawing and hammering. Since they were usually the ones in the thick of such occupations, they wondered what could be going on. To their horror a big chunk of the kindergarten department was being taken off to give a larger space to the church office. Now no one questioned that the church office needed to be larger, but what does one do with a circle of 125 kindergarten children who are present each Sunday morning? (For those not in the know, a circle of twenty-five is considered too large.) But the very fact that there was not another room large enough to hold the kindergarten department, including four-and-five-year-olds, made it necessary to divide the group, and so another step was taken toward Miss Mears' goal of a sepparate department for each age.

During these early years the second floor of the church was occupied by the primary department—first through third graders. This room had been designed as a ladies' parlor—long and narrow. It was always a question whether to arrange the chairs the length of the room with the children facing the doors and being disturbed by the late-comers, or to turn the chairs the other way and face the bright light streaming in through the windows. Of course, if the superintendent could hold the attention of the children in the last rows—about fifty-six feet away—the room could be turned lengthwise. Then the primary department was pushing out the walls of their room, and it was necessary to take the third floor of the church (same type of room), and eventually the fourth floor. Of course, other departments had been occupying these floors, and it was necessary to find space for them, but it was good to get high schoolers off the fourth floor! But, whoever heard of primary third graders—eight-year-olds—on the fourth floor? The superintendent and assistants cocked their heads in that "well-I-don't-know-about-that" angle, and it was the first time they felt they faced an impossible situation. In case of fire how would they get out? The fire escape was too scary! Solution: an enclosed outside stairway was built, and children from all three floors had to use this outside stairway and meet their parents at the foot of it, so as not to get mashed in the crowd of adults who would be pouring out of the balconies at the close of services.

After many Sunday mornings, Miss Mears wondered what kept the superintendents and teachers from descending upon her in a body to turn in their resignations. To their credit they were not serving Henrietta Mears, but as she herself was serving the Lord, so they were serving him, and he ruled and overruled in each situation.

There were never "opening exercises," but there were "worship services"—a far more elevating term. Even the youngest child was being taught and trained to WORSHIP the Living God, not do some "opening exercise." It was perhaps a blessing that there was never a place where every man, woman and child could be gathered for the first half-hour, or the worship service—it would never have happened anyway! Miss Mears was always thinking of the teenager who wouldn't be caught dead in Sunday School with a lot of babies (any age under them) and adults. And the priceless children needed to be considered, too. Her hue and cry was, "If you are having problems at the junior high level, BEGIN YOUR TRAINING EARLIER while the mind is eager to grasp new thoughts and everyday living can form good habits easily."

As the classrooms in houses and buildings petered out, some "rabbit hutches" were built. This nickname clings to this day when an old-timer is referring to them. As homes began tumbling down to make way for progress, it was imperative that classrooms be built. Naturally, they must be temporary, for big plans were afoot. The building code people looked favorably on the church—after some persuasion, that is—when they became acquainted with the indication of growth and good intention on the part of the congregation to build. So permission was granted for temporary classrooms to be built. (It was often wondered if they had known how "portable" these classrooms were to become, whether or not permission would have been granted for their building.) The Sunday School leaders had no idea either, but these "rabbit hutches" were moved from spot to spot as they got in the way. Eventually, there was no place to hold the junior department. What to do? The board of education of the public schools came to the rescue, and rented to the church a grammar school auditorium and as many classrooms as possible. This was two blocks away. Even with these magnificent accommodations, after the worship service several classes had to hike to the church property and to the famous "rabbit hutches" for their sessions. But this was all temporary.

During Miss Mears' ministry three large education buildings were erected, a successful Sunday School curriculum was developed, and tens of thousands of students were reached with the gospel and built up in the faith.

Many observers believed that Miss Mears possessed some kind of a magic formula for such phenomenal growth. Visiting teachers, Christian education directors and pastors implored her to divulge her secrets. Letters requested information on how similar successes could be repeated in other churches. Her answer may have been a disappointment: "The key is in one word—*work*. Webster spells it, W-O-R-K, and it means just what he says it does. Wishful thinking will never take the place of hard work!"

Henrietta Mears seemed to thrive on work. She always told her young people, "You don't know what you can do until you try it." The more she undertook, the more she could do. Ted Cole, one of her collegians, once recalled, "It didn't matter how youthful or athletic one was, no one could keep up with Miss Mears!" (And she had been going strong for years before he appeared on the scene.) Miss Mears was capable of exhausting those who worked with her while she herself remained willing to go on, tired but gripped by uncontrollable enthusiasm. When her position as Christian education director had to leave her hands, no one thought it strange that her tasks were divided to several people. Always seeking to build a better Sunday School, and not a bigger one, the matter of what the pupil was learning became pre-eminent, but a curriculum could not be developed at the sacrifice of teacher training, student visitation, classroom preparation, office management, teaching and directing the college department with over five hundred on an active roll, and the endless speaking and teaching preparations she had as administrator and teacher. To be willing to add writer to administrator and teacher took courage and forethought, because she had been reared to finish whatever she undertook.

All this energy was activated by a dynamic faith in

the power of God. "If a church is really determined to increase its Sunday School," to quote her, "it will find ways and means to accomplish its purpose. The need is primarily for a greater faith in a wonderful God. Jesus said that he could not do many things among those of his day because of their unbelief. The building of a Sunday School is a long road, and there are many turns and climbs, but the rewards are worth the effort." And so Henrietta Mears and her colaborers adhered to the principle of the old-fashioned trolley car, keeping the grooved wheel at the end of the pole pressed upward in rolling contact with the overhead wire to take off the current. This permitted them to ride on God's omnipotence, his everlasting power.

In the initial stages of her work she formulated objectives that guided her throughout her career, and which time and again she shared with teachers across America:

1. *Canvass your neighborhood.* What is the potential of your city? Let us believe that any church in the United States can grow. How many unchurched boys and girls are in your community? Start where you are with the youth nearest you. Are they being reached? Don't be afraid to count numbers! Gather figures and discover how many unchurched youth there are in your community. Many of these you could have in your Sunday School.

2. *Teach the Word.* The Bible is the living seed that brings life. We are born, fed, enlightened, equipped for service, and kept by the Word of God. Youth must know how to use this chart and compass. Other things may be good, but this is the best. Always specialize in the best.

3. *Win people to Christ.* Are children introduced

to a living Saviour in your Sunday School? This is paramount. Eighty-five percent of the boys and girls attending the Sunday Schools of America do so without ever taking Christ as their Saviour. If they are not won for Christ and built into the life of the church, they will leave God's house and be lost forever. Carry out every means of winning them to Christ. All programs that deepen the spiritual life and strengthen the faith of youth enrich the church. When a young person has been allowed to go through the Sunday School and reach college without taking a stand for Christ, it is difficult to win him back to the church. He has learned to live without Christ. Childhood is the time when God has made the heart tender. Fill the child then with the knowledge of a personal Saviour who has a plan for his life. The high-water mark of conversion comes between eleven and thirteen. After twenty, one in a hundred becomes a Christian, and after thirty, one in a thousand.

4. *Enlist for service.* Let each child know he is accountable to the Lord for his life and that God has a job for him. What is more exciting than discovering God's plan in one's life? Find a place for every student to work.

(Miss Mears' genius lay in her ability to get others to work. She never waited for teachers to come into her Sunday School from some other church to assist her. Her principle was to train her own leaders. Her enthusiasm and challenge and drive influenced most ardent objectors. During the early years in the college department there was in her estimation only one hope for a song leader. Miss Mears told him that he was to lead the singing for the meeting that evening. The lad was panicked by the thought and said that he absolutely would not do it. Miss Mears told him that if he didn't, no one else would. As he continued to protest, she pushed him out of the office and told him to go practice and learn how to lead singing. Through the closed door could be heard, "I won't do it! I am not a song leader! I don't know how!" But he led the songs, and eventually went into the ministry. Years later, Dr. L. David Cowie wrote of the incident: "Teacher puts you on your mettle to produce. You had to do it, and she wanted you to be able to do it, and to feel the sole responsibility, and not to have any feeling that she would do it for you. She literally forced me into being a leader. She pushed me into responsibility!")

5. *Look over your building.* Are the rooms attractive to the youth in your community? Sometimes a can of paint will work wonders. Curtains will divide a large room into individual classrooms. Basements can be converted into department rooms with a bit of carpenter work. Look over what you have and be daring in your thinking. When our Sunday School grew from about 450 to 4,200 in the space of two and a half years, we had to build screens, use curtains for partitions, discover every available space under steps, in closets and offices, and buy adjoining apartments and houses, making a Sunday School out of what was at hand. Nothing is as thrilling as to have to knock down partitions to build an annex, or change a porch into a room, or pitch a tent. Anything that indicates growth thrills people.

6. *Study your program.* As you study the program of your Sunday School, ask yourself if it is merely an assortment of ideas, or do you have a comprehensive, long-range plan? Every successful

leader must plan his work and work his plan. Plans must be sound. Christ left his disciples with a definite plan. A leader who moves by guesswork without practical, clear-cut plans is like a ship without a rudder. Sooner or later he will crash on the rocks. Master the art of program making. Visit a radio broadcast and note how each minute counts.

And balance your program. Don't run to extremes. See if you are putting due emphasis on attendance, worship, teaching, stewardship, missions, social life and evangelism. Strive always for a successful program, remembering that nothing suceeds like success. Everyone likes to belong to a growing concern.

Dr. Mears applied all these principles to her own Sunday School.

Having a positive attitude toward the requirements of today's youth, she was never one to bemoan their delinquency but rather had a program to meet their ambitions. She never blamed the youth for not wanting to come, but rather looked to see what was lacking in the program to attract them. She knew the necessity of having more than just the Sunday morning Bible hour to compete with the attractions that would draw them off. Youth have to be kept busy; they must have a total program to satisfy their total personality. Miss Mears knew this well. Of course, it all began with the teaching of the Bible, but enormous value was placed on week-day activities, clubs, interest groups, socials, camps and choirs.

Her awareness of teenage interests was revealed early in her career, before she came to Hollywood. When Miss Mears first began her full-time teaching in Minnesota, she was assigned to a small town. Her landlady allowed her to have a Bible class in her room. At first she had only one pupil, but the class grew until the young people were occupying the parlor and dining room and were listening in at the open windows. However, she knew there must be something to hold them other than the Bible, and so Miss Mears secured a coach and formed a basketball team. What she didn't know about the sport, she made up for with enthusiasm. The newspapers would announce that the visiting team had outplayed the local boys, but that the latter had won by a large margin of points.

And so when she came to Hollywood, a place in which to gather and the type of activities to meet the physical and social needs of youth occupied much of her thought; and leadership was always secured to handle this phase of the program. In her college department Miss Mears constantly took stock of the plans of the social committee. insisting that parties and recreation always be on a high plane and full of good fun. The program was alway; geared to meet every need of the youth—Bible study. worship, social life, friendships. The principle behind this was that school friends move away and change, but church relationships grow and grow. This kind of pro graming brings in parents, too. The object was to mak; the program so attractive that it could be said, as on; fraternity fellow expressed it, "I'd rather bring my friends to a social function at the church than at the fraternity, because they are always so much better."

And then more than twenty years had passed and the day came when Miss Mears was asked to present what she wanted in the way of an education building. "What shall I include?" she asked Mr. William S. Porter, chairman of the building committee. "Include everything you want," was the instant reply, expressing confidence in her and the program. She often remarked, "And I did that very thing. I included all the dreams we had had for the junior highs and high schoolers. And do you know, they gave us everything we asked for!" Dream big was always her theory! And so hammers pounded and saws buzzed until Education Building No. 1 stood as a living testimony to a faithful congregation who had erected a building for their youth. This was the year 1950.

Six years later two magnificent buildings materialized to meet the needs of the preschoolers, 2-3-4-5-year-olds, primary and nursery. Flags waved, horns blew, and drums beat as members of these age groups marched to the ground breaking ceremony. They could be heard long before they could be seen! The congregation thrilled to every sight that greeted their eyes as this precious future generation came into view. As the work proceeded and the remaining houses along the block were either razed or moved, the long awaited moment arrived when the "rabbit hutches" had fulfilled their purpose, and building chairman Robert T. Hunter could order them demolished. On Sunday morning, September 16, 1956, a service of thanksgiving and dedication was held to express thanks unto God and to humbly dedicate this house in the Name of God the Father, God the Son, and God the Holy Spirit, for the teachings of his holy Word, the practice of prayer, the joys of Christian fellowship and the missionary advance into the world for the winsome presentation of Jesus Christ to all, for the Christian enrichment of community and world, for the eternal purposes of God as they include all children who serve and are served. Miss Mears' dreams were coming true.

But the reason new buildings were going up and classes were growing lay in the high standards of excellence she demanded of her teachers. Miss Mears frequently spoke about standards of excellence:

Our Sunday Schools must become vastly more efficient institutions. Their sessions must be carried over to a weekday program, for no child can receive all the Christian instruction and training he needs in one hour on Sunday morning. The church must be prepared to reach out and get the many millions of boys and girls who are still without religious instruction of any sort. And to meet this challenge we must have educational plants that are adequate. Compare the glazed halls of our modern school buildings with the worn-out carpets of the Sunday School department; the up-to-date, well-bound books on every school desk with our ragged songbooks and Bibles; the fine hardwood study chairs with the dilapidated ones so often relegated to Sunday School departments. No wonder young people feel that the three R's are more important than the fourth—religion! When the student goes on Sunday to a room poorly lighted and miserably furnished, what else can he think? He sits at the feet of teachers five days a week who have had the finest training for their work, but on Sunday the lesson from God's Word is taught by a teacher who has accepted the class because there is no one else to take it. Sunday School is in fact the only teaching a person will undertake without training. We must change our standards. Everything we offer youth must be excellent. Their associations with the gospel must be of the very finest in every way.

And it was this last emphasis—the training of teachers —that became one of the compulsions of her life.

Miss Mears knew what made a good teacher To translate her knowledge gained through public school teaching into the life of the Sunday School was her determination, so that teachers might be adequately prepared for their tasks. She did not wait for the "natural" teacher to come her way to take over a vacancy; Miss Mears trained whom she needed. She emphasized:

Teachers are not born; they are made. However, a person must have the natural desire to be taught. A good teacher is first of all teachable himself. We must train workmen in our Sunday Schools that need not to be ashamed. A teacher must know his subject, observe his pupils, and then do something about them. The more a teacher depends upon the Holy Spirit, the more will he wish to make himself an instrument fit for his use. He will want to know how God made the human mind. He will desire to probe the depths of the human heart. He will seek to know the laws that govern his approach to this pupil, who was created to be a temple of the living God. But failure to work according to God's laws and lack of definiteness have characterized much that has been done under the name of Sunday School teaching.

Miss Mears was not hasty in choosing teachers for her Sunday School, and wholesale announcements regarding needs for teachers in such and such a department were taboo. One bad choice might take years to undo, but a little cautious foresight could avoid such a situation. She sought certain qualifications: An evident and productive relationship with Christ was the first. Miss Mears did not want to have teachers who habitually failed in other areas of life; just the opposite was her policy—she sought after busy men and women who were already putting out for the kingdom.

One day she called up one of the elders of the church who was a successful automotive salesman in Los Angeles and was involved in a myriad of other activities. She asked him to take over a twelfth-grade class of boys.

"But, Miss Mears, I am already so busy with my other tasks that I wouldn't know how to squeeze this class in," he argued.

"That's the very reason I am calling on you, George," she answered. "I want you in my Sunday School because you know the value of time and because you have proven yourself in other fields."

A second requirement was the willingness to spend time in lesson preparation and training classes. Miss Mears was herself an excellent example of her own demand. She spent an extensive number of hours in preparation of each message. "Don't display your ignorance and bring disrepute upon Christianity by speaking out in your university classes," she would admonish all. "Study, and know whereof you speak, and then open your mouth." While Dr. William Evans was the church's interim pastor, he gave her the following suggestion: When you are preparing a lesson, first list various members of your class on one side of a page, and under their names write out their spiritual needs. Write down on the other side how you are going to meet those needs in your lesson. This method was always evident in her talks, whether she had actually written it or her contacts had produced it. Her lessons were a part of her personality, the expression of her heartfelt concern.

Even after long periods of preparation, she would rise early on Sunday mornings to meet the Lord in prayer and in reading of her Bible. This availability to the Lord for new instructions or strengthening of other thoughts gave her a spiritual authority for which her teaching became known.

The Life Work Recruit meeting was the only thing that she permitted to alter her rule to do nothing on Saturday night but prepare herself for her Sunday responsibilities. In the early days of her ministry she was challenging her youth to expose themselves to the will of God for their lives, whether it was to be a Christian in the business world, or the professions, or the ministry. And so the Life Work Recruit group came into existence. One particular Saturday evening meeting ran very late and she dropped into bed exhausted. Her secretary, Ethel May Baldwin, was spending the night. To Ethel May it seemed as though they had just gotten to sleep when the alarm went off. Risking an eye to see what really had happened, she knew it was still dark outside because by the light of the street lamp she could make out a ghostly figure reeling, dizzy with sleep. Out of the depths of Ethel May's pillow came, "Get back into bed. If you don't know the Book of Romans by now, you never will!" And soon deep breathing came from Miss Mears' side of the bed and she knew that she had been believed. "I never got by with that but once!" Ethel May later said. "Wasn't I lucky she was teaching the Book of Romans that she had loved to have her mother read to her as a child and she had taught so often?" Teacher laughed the heartiest, realizing in the morning what had actually happened.

Her spiritual preparation continued right up to the moment she stepped onto the platform. The college department always had a pre-prayer session a half-hour before each meeting. Teacher made it the unfailing habit of her ministry always to be present and participate. With twenty or more collegians kneeling and praying with her, she would ask the Lord to bless the lesson and sometimes included its points in the supplication.

Someone has said, "Childhood is like a mirror, which reflects in afterlife the images first presented. Children have more need of models than critics."

Miss Mears knew that religious training involved a man's will, his emotion and his mind. She wanted teachers who would instruct their pupils not only to know, but to feel, and finally to do. She would say:

> Every child is born with a great capacity for knowledge. We cannot make capacity, but we can cultivate that thing which is God-given. We grieve because children remember so little of what we have taught them from God's Word. There is a reason for this. Not enough attention is given to other phases of religious education. Learning is more than the ability to repeat the ideas or writings of another. There are real evidences of learning. We must face this fact. When a child has learned, we find there is a change in his behavior. His life is different. He places different values upon things. To tell him the story is not sufficient. The purpose of the teacher is to "draw out" not to "cram in." We must create an interest in the heart and mind of the child that will make him reach out and take hold upon the things that he is taught. Whenever an interest is created, there is at the same time a great desire to learn as much as possible about that thing.

Since by association the child begins to see lived out in his teacher's life something that he has been trying to tell his pupils, the teachers were urged to do whatever was possible in the way of "extracurricular" activity, or to share themselves with their pupils. One of the ninth grade teachers was an officer on the police force, later to become an inspector. In addition to his Sunday morning lesson, he frequently took his pupils swimming in the police center's pool and escorted them through its various buildings, explaining the functions of each one. His students greatly loved this Christian man, and the association he built up in them between living a godly life and respect for law deeply influenced their young minds. An instructor in Miss Mears' high school department was a leading researcher in an aircraft plant. His scientific training spilled over into his teaching of the Bible with the result that his students, beset with intellectual problems, felt confident in taking their questions to him, for he spoke with a precision that they admired.

Public school teachers were always eyed for their potential, and some of Miss Mears' most gifted associates were instructors, principals and counselors in the Los Angeles system.

Here again Dr. Mears' high standards for the church school are evident:

This whole process is called Christian education. It is a very comprehensive field, indeed, and cannot be run by the inexperienced. We are too willing to let the Sunday School be managed by a few willing but untrained enthusiasts. It is a hard task, because it is endless. We can never rest from this gigantic evangelistic and educational program. It means a marathon of physical endurance, of mental acumen, of moral courage and spiritual strength. It is a task for strong men, not babes. There was a day when men like the great merchant prince John Wanamaker devoted every moment outside of business obligations to the Sunday School. That kind of investment made spiritual history.

How seldom the Sunday School teacher is asked for his credentials! A public school teacher is not questioned as to whether he will teach, but rather, can he teach. Our request in securing Sunday School teachers is invariably, "Will you take a class?" And goodnatured men and women, much against their wills, answer, "I will keep the class going until you can find someone else." If an algebra teacher is absent, can you imagine the principal going out in the neighborhood, ringing doorbells and asking a housewife, "Will you come over and take a class in mathematics because the regular teacher is sick?" Absurd! He notifies the superintendent's office of his need, and a trained person comes.

Many an untrained person had potential though, and Miss Mears involved him in the leadership training program. These programs were not isolated from the overall dynamics of the Sunday School, for anyone enrolled in a leadership class found himself immediately at work. A major part of the teacher's learning process was to be active in the job for which he was being instructed. During her teacher training sessions, Miss Mears emphasized over and over again the following qualifications of leadership, passed on here in their entirety:

1. *Definiteness of purpose.* The apostle Paul said, *This one thing I do* (Phil. 3:13). What is the primary objective of your life as a teacher?

2. *Definiteness of decision. Choose you this day whom ye will serve* (Joshua 24:15). God is constantly asking men to decide. One who wavers in

his decisions shows he is not sure of himself. He therefore cannot lead others. Be definite. Many people are afraid to decide something because they may be wrong. Don't let this fear slow you down. It is better to decide and to be wrong, than to make no decision at all.

3. *Burning desire. He shall give thee the desires of thine heart* (Ps. 37:4). Set your desire on God. A leader must be consumed with a desire to achieve his purpose, and purpose and decision must be motivated by spiritual ambition. There is energy in such desire. What do you really long for as a Christian leader?

4. *Unwavering courage. Be strong and of good courage* (Josh. 1:6). No follower wishes to be dominated by a leader who lacks self-confidence and courage. *Be ye followers of me, even as I also am of Christ* (I Cor. 11:1) was Paul's plan of leadership. His conviction and courage sparked the enthusiasm of others. This Christ-centered courage must conquer fears of failure. Many people believe themselves doomed to failure, or mediocrity. But there is no such word as "failure" in the Christian's vocabulary. This courage must help the leader to cultivate qualities of decision, promptness, action, and the habit of finishing what he begins.

5. *A keen sense of justice.* No leader can command and retain the respect of others without impartiality and a feeling for equality. Christ gave his life that he might demand our lives from us. The leader must be willing to do what he expects others to do.

6. *Definiteness of plans.* Plans must be sound. Think, do not guess. Write out your plans. Do you

cut your program into workable units so others can carry out your plans? Your achievement can be no greater than the soundness of your plans. As a Sunday School teacher you are engaged in an undertaking of major importance both for time and eternity. To be sure of success, you must have plans that are faultless. If your first plan does not succeed, find another that will.

7. *Plan with others.* Don't try to go it alone. Christ chose twelve men to be with him. Every plan you originate should be checked and approved by members of your department. No individual has sufficient experience, training, or native ability to insure great success in spiritual things without helpers.

Some years before coming to Hollywood, Miss Mears attended a Sunday School convention where she heard an address on the accountability of the Christian educator. She returned to her hotel room, profoundly impressed with the challenge. The hour was late when she finally began to fall asleep. Suddenly she awakened with a flash of thought: "Why have I come to this convention? To let an inspiring message like this go by without response?" Her career stretched before her like a broad but unmarked highway. "Where am I going on this road?" So she recast into her own words what she had heard that night, making these resolves her guideposts for the rest of her career:

1. *I will* win the personal allegiance of every student in my Sunday School class to the Lord and Master, by talking, writing, and praying. I will expect a decision on the part of each one, and I will make sure that that decision is based on facts. No

boy or girl will I ever give up as unreachable.

2. *I will* not think my work over when my pupil has made his decision for Christ. I will help him to realize how necessary daily Bible reading and prayer are. I will also put helpful books in his hands, and will encourage him to unite with God's people. I will show him the importance of church work. In all this, I will stay close until he is established, remaining at all times accessible to him.

3. *I will* see that he finds a definite place in some specified task. I will not rest until every student is an out-and-out aggressive Christian, for God has a place for each one to serve.

4. *I will* bring Christianity out of the unreal into the everyday life. I will show my students the practical things they should be doing as Christians. The ministrations that the world needs so much today—meat for the hungry, drink for the thirsty—are judgment-day tests of genuine Christianity (Matt. 25).

5. *I will* try to help each one discover the will of God, because the Master can use every talent. I will try to see in them what God sees. Michelangelo saw the face of an angel in a discarded stone. Christ saw a writer in a tax gatherer, a preacher in a fisherman, a world evangelist in a murderer. He takes the foolish things, and weak and despised, to work his purpose.

6. *I will* instill a divine discontent into the mind of everyone who can do more than he is doing, not by telling him the pettiness of his life, but by giving him a vision of great things to be done enthusiastically, passionately.

7. *I will* make it easy for anyone to come to me with the deepest experiences of his inner life, not

by urging, but by sympathy and understanding. I will never let anyone think I am disappointed in him.

8. *I will* put the cross back in the Christian life. "It is great to be out where the fight is strong, to be where the heaviest troops belong, and to fight there for God and man."

9. *I will* pray as I have never prayed before for wisdom and power, believing God's promise that *if any of you lack wisdom, let him ask . . . and it shall be given him* (James 1:5).

10. *I will* spend and be spent in this battle. I will not seek rest and ease. I will not think that freshness of face holds beauty in comparison with the glory of heaven. I will seek fellowship with the Man of Sorrows, acquainted with grief, as he walks through this stricken world. I will not fail him.

5

Winning Men to Christ

Winning Men to Christ

*Personal work is one person finding another person
and bringing him to the personal Saviour.*
—HENRIETTA MEARS

One afternoon while calling on members of the Fidelis
Class—the Bible class at the First Baptist Church in Minneapolis which she taught for many years—Miss Mears
stopped in front of a large brown house. She secretly
hoped that Virginia would not be home, or would be
busy, for this young woman seemed so uninterested in
spiritual matters. Miss Mears was greatly relieved to find
that Virginia's fiance was with her; so Miss Mears thought
to herself, it would not be appropriate to talk with her
about the gospel. After a few moments of pleasantries,
she left the couple. As she began to drive away, she
felt that God was speaking to her: "Henrietta, why didn't
you talk to Virginia about me? Wasn't that why you
came here in the first place?" She drove around the
block, parked her car, and once more rang the bell. Virginia and the young man were amazed to see her again
and asked if she had forgotten something.

"Yes," replied the Bible teacher, "I failed to do the very thing for which I came here in the first place—to talk to you about your relationship to Christ."

"Oh, Miss Mears," Virginia exclaimed, "George and I were just saying how we wished you had stayed, so you could talk to us about God." Within half an hour the young couple met the Saviour.

Henrietta Mears believed that men and women should be won to Christ one by one. This was the foundation of all her work, and thousands of people in the Sunday School of the Hollywood Presbyterian Church were evidence of her commitment to this principle. No group was more important than the individuals in it. Programs, drives, committee meetings, office routine—all had the goal of winning men and women to Christ. And what made her remarkable in this field was her total love for every person who came her way. She did not love people merely in the abstract, for Christian love was not simply a doctrine with her; it was rather a part of her character, radiating in everything she did.

The wife of a famous preacher was invited one afternoon to attend the Hollywood Christian Group (the fellowship Miss Mears helped to organize to introduce Christ to film personalities), which was meeting in the home of a top actress. As Miss Mears and the guest sat together on a small sofa, the actress was called upon to give her testimony. The preacher's wife thought to herself, "How can this woman, who plays such questionable roles on the screen, talk this way about Christ?" But she was suddenly aware of Miss Mears muttering under her breath, "Bless her heart! I just love that girl! She is the dearest person!" Some time later the guest wrote to friends, "It was a good thing that Miss Mears couldn't hear my thoughts when that actress was giving her testimony. I was raised in the Orient, where if one was built like a woman she overcame it the best she could. I sat there looking at this movie star like the chief of the Pharisees; but Miss Mears was encouraging her. Some of us talk about love, but Miss Mears loves. No wonder God uses her!"

There was a lonely, rather nondescript fellow in the college department. His chief talent was making a nuisance of himself. Most of the other members of the class tried to ignore him, usually without success. But Miss Mears went out of her way to be nice to him. He did not have much money, and frequently he was in dire financial difficulty. But during one of her illnesses he sent Miss Mears a dozen roses and a box of candy. He had found someone who cared for him. When the roses arrived, Teacher said, "Bless that dear boy's heart! He is such a wonderful fellow!" And she meant every word. It was little wonder that people were constantly beating a path to her door of friendship, counsel, and prayer, for she had a wonderful gift of listening, not just talking.

Henrietta Mears allowed Christ to love others through her. Although she had no trouble comprehending and explaining difficult points of doctrine, this was not her approach in winning men to the Saviour. She was fond of saying:

If you talk theory, self does not see where self is concerned, or where self is going to benefit, or where self is in danger; so interest is lost. A sermon on the deity of Christ might not arouse the slightest interest. But it will if you begin with this question: Had you been the thief on the cross, what would your reaction have been to Christ's death? And if He had

105

said to you, "Today thou shalt be with Me in paradise," what would you have thought?

Miss Mears always tried to discover what interested the person with whom she was talking. Her ability to empathize with the joys and sorrows of others was boundless. She was usually the first to hear of someone's new job, the birth of a baby, or a success at school. And her unselfish interest in other people was genuine.

Her assistants were often quite amused when someone would burst into Miss Mears' office with some news which she had already heard but which she would listen to all over again as if for the first time. When asked why she didn't tell a person that she had already been told what they were about to say, she explained, "It would be like pricking a child's balloon. I want people to feel that it is fun to tell me things. In this way I can keep my contact with them."

Miss Mears saw potential in everyone she met. She knew what Christ had done in her life, and she thoroughly believed that with God all things are possible. She loved to emphasize what Jesus did for the woman of Samaria:

This fallen woman was the most unlikely candidate for anything spiritual, but the Saviour saw her potential. Her salvation was evidenced by her running off to tell others of the Messiah. This one revolutionized life started a revival in Samaria. It came about by her carrying Christ's power to everyone she met. She was magnetized for service. Jesus had a way of touching and changing a man, then using the changed man to touch and change someone else. The change that came to the village of Sychar came first to one person in that village. The Reformation that shook Europe first of all shook Luther.

Miss Mears never underscored a person's weaknesses. Instead of stressing the don'ts of the Christian walk, she presented the do's. She delighted in pointing out that the children of Israel were saved out of Egypt unto Canaan. "I don't want to talk about Egypt," she would say, "for that is only what we are saved from. I want rather to discover all the privileges God has for us in Canaan, the place of blessing."

This emphasis was graphically illustrated one evening at Forest Home when a college fellow, standing before the fire to give his testimony, pulled a package of cigarettes out of his pocket and threw them into the fire, as he said, "Well, I guess Miss Mears wants me to get rid of these." To the astonishment of all, Miss Mears reached into the fire and handed the cigarettes back to the startled youth. Then looking him square in the eye, she said, "Harry, God doesn't want your cigarettes. What would he do with them? He wants you." Her logic was simple: Once Harry found Christ, smoking would no longer be a problem.

Miss Mears was accessible to people It did not matter what time of day or night, she could always be reached. At Forest Home she allowed her schedule to be filled up far past midnight with those who wanted counseling. This did not hinder her rising for the faculty prayer time before breakfast. Whenever she became ill and needed rest, it was almost impossible to persuade her to unplug her phone so that people could not use up her strength before she had time to regain it. On one occasion she obeyed her doctor's order to stay in bed, but she allowed her college department cabinet to hold their meeting in her room. Then, as they knelt, she placed her hand on each one's head, praying for him.

Dr. Mears was always mindful of the needs of the sick and tried to visit in their homes (or at least by telephone) to pray for them. One Sunday afternoon, after she had taught twice and had presided through a long committee meeting without eating since early morning, she was obviously weary. When one of the college boys volunteered to drive her out for a late lunch, she asked him to take her instead to the home of an old friend who was bedridden. "Mother Atwater hasn't been able to come to church for several weeks," said Teacher, "and I want to pray with her and let her know we've been thinking about her."

Miss Mears' friendship with "Mother" Atwater illustrates another aspect of Teacher's personal work. When Miss Mears took over the college department, Mother Atwater was superintendent of the group. "I am no superintendent," Mother Atwater confessed, "but if I can help in loving these dear young people and being a 'mother' to them, I'll do it." Miss Mears and Mother Atwater became close friends, and Teacher leaned on this saintly woman for encouragement, especially for prayer. Miss Mears would frequently phone her concerning some urgent spiritual need and ask her to intercede. Besides prayer, the two of them spent every Thursday afternoon calling on students and winning them to Christ. Come rain or shine, they consistently devoted this one afternoon to calling, with the result that the college department grew rapidly, not because of one or two big membership drives a year, but by the weekly influx of new collegians who had been introduced to Christ. Mother Atwater was on her knees at five every Sunday morning, praying for two hours or so for Miss Mears and the college department. Her ministry continued throughout Miss Mears' thirty-five years at the church, and the two of them died within a year of each other.

Miss Mears won men and women to Christ by her life. In a city known for its moral corruption and superficiality her zeal for all things good was an open window on the holiness of God, through which many frustrated souls saw beyond the shallow materialism of their empty lives. She was loyal to the highest virtues of the Christian faith and could not tolerate in her own life anything discordant with her Lord's commands. But all of her godliness was crowned with love; it never degenerated into a stifling legalism. Christ's law for Henrietta Mears was to be obeyed, because it was the will of the one whom she loved with all her being. This purity and nobility of character was her strongest appeal when people around her were looking for something in which to believe. Her devotion to Christ was the essence of her personal work, and she radiated him to those about her. She knew that it was not some *thing* they were looking for to believe in, but some *one*.

This loyalty to Christ was highlighted by a healthy sense of humor. Henrietta Mears knew how to have fun. Once, while sailing the Caribbean, she was invited to a costume party. Whether or not she ever thought of herself as such, Miss Mears was a natural actress. Entering a room, she claimed attention. On this particular occasion her fellow voyagers were decked out in gay and ridiculous costumes. The party was well under way when the Sunday School teacher made her appearance, from head to toe dressed as a zany roaring-twenties character. Several ostrich plumes floated over a large picture hat. A brilliant red frock, with several feet of beads hung around her neck, completed the outlandish ensemble. Everyone roared with laughter. She immediately entered into the gaiety of the party with her usual gusto. Finally, one of the passengers could stand it no longer, and said to her, "This is utterly amazing, Miss Mears. I know you don't drink liquor, and yet you are having more fun than the rest of us!" And that was Teacher's point—a Christian can have more fun than anyone else.

Her ability to make people laugh was contagious with all ages, but especially with college folk. During fellowship times at Forest Home, the students often urged her to give her famous sermon, "Old Mother Hubbard," from the "Book of Numbers." When she could be persuaded to do it, someone would run for the nearest telephone book, another would find some old hat, and a third would offer his coat or jacket. With her glasses pulled down to the end of her nose, and with the coat turned backwards, she would stride in, hat down over her eyes and the telephone book under her arm. Bending low over the text, she would read along with her finger supposedly on the passage: "'Old Mother Hubbard went to the cupboard'—I want to read this passage clear through, so you can get the full meaning, and then I will come back and we shall look at it statement by statement." And on she would go, her explanations prostrating the audience with laughter: "'Old Mother Hubbard went to the cupboard.' Can't you see the pathos of this o-l-d, o-l-d woman going to the cupboard? 'To get her poor dog.' No! She didn't go to get her poor dog, but that's the way some of you read Scripture. You stop right in the middle of a thought. What did she go to get? What is the object of her 'wenting'? You've all seen an old woman 'wenting' haven't you? She's all bent over low, with furrowed brow." And so the nursery rhyme was expounded, until the collegians were limp, tears rolling down their cheeks.

Miss Mears' vital and vivacious personality, radiating good will and zest for life, appealed to the citizens of the movie capital, as it did to other alert and energetic people. But along with this, she was a well-trained personal worker, who studied the art of winning the lost. She led many classes and institutes on becoming more effective witnesses for Christ. Sometimes these classes had as many as three hundred people enrolled. She had syllabi mimeographed for her students' use. Each person was required to talk to others about Christ during the week and then be prepared to report at the training sessions. This dynamic approach involved everyone in practical experience, and many were the joyous testimonies week after week as people who had always considered themselves incapable of leading someone to Christ told what success God had given them. But the great adventure of these classes lay in the new Christians enrolling in the course and then bringing their own converts. It was not unusual to see at the end of a personal workers' series several generations of new believers sitting side by side.

There were three fundamentals underscoring Miss Mears' classes: First, a *personal worker must thoroughly understand what the gospel is and is not.* "A religion," she would say, "is what man does for his god; Christianity is exactly the opposite: it is what God has done for us." To emphasize her point, she would expound the doctrines dealing directly with salvation: the holiness of God, the effect of sin, the atonement of Christ, faith, regeneration, etc. She did not want people going out as personal workers who had an inadequate comprehension of what they believed. "Christians are salesmen for Christ. A salesman

111

must understand his product." Second, *the personal worker must be absolutely committed to God.* He must be a channel through which the Holy Spirit can flow. "God converts people; the personal worker is merely his instrument." Third, *the worker must have confidence in his product.* "If I put wheat into the ground, I must have confidence it will come up; so I must believe that if I put the gospel into a pair of ears, it will bring forth its fruit." One of her picturesque illustrations was: "If you come into a room and sneeze, everyone will get your germs. The gospel is contagious; go out and sneeze in people's faces!" Faith in the effectiveness of God's Word was at the heart of her work. One of her most frequently quoted passages was Isaiah 55:10,11:

As the rain cometh down, and the snow from heaven, and returneth not thither, but watereth the earth, and maketh it bring forth and bud, that it may give seed to the sower, and bread to the eater: so shall my word be that goeth forth out of my mouth: it shall not return unto me void, but it shall accomplish that which I please, and it shall prosper in the thing whereto I sent it.

Her confidence fed on this promise; and every time she learned of someone finding Christ through her ministry, she was spurred on more than before to reach the lost.

Some of the guidelines she used to help others get started in personal work were:

Ask a man if he is satisfied. Most people are not content with their lives. A person must understand that he is a sinner. After he sees this, show him what he must do about his sin. Give him the facts about salvation. The sinner must come to the Saviour. There must be a personal encounter. Never pronounce a person saved. Show him that everything is based on the Bible, and let him draw his own conclusions. Point out that his salvation depends on God's ability and faithfulness. And make sure that he realizes that God will not cast him off if he sins. Also, show him what to do when he sins as a Christian. Urge him to begin confessing his faith before others immediately. Point out that Christ demands all of his life. The Lordship and Saviourhood of Christ should go hand in hand.

Of course, Dr. Mears illustrated each point from the Bible, and she urged her students to know key verses by memory. One of her illustrations in dealing with men and women about salvation was that of enlisting into an army:

A soldier is not inducted on the basis of feeling, but of absolute allegiance. The new convert must realize that anything less than total surrender will not do. Secondly, the soldier is required to make his enlistment known. He is fighting for a public cause. So the Christian must not be afraid to tell others about his faith. Thirdly, the soldier is called unto a job; so the Christian is supposed to get busy in God's work. Our faith must put on shoes.

Dr. Mears' favorite text in dealing with young people was, *Lord, what wilt Thou have me to do?* (Acts. 9:6). This question implied the absolute commitment to the Lord Jesus which she considered to be the necessary ingredient for spiritual success. This surrender must be in every area of life; nothing can be withheld from the Saviour's control.

Surrender also meant work for Christ. Salvation as an end in itself had no meaning for Henrietta Mears. Frequently she would ask Sunday School workers at training conferences, "What is the goal of your Sunday School?"

Almost invariably someone would answer, "To lead boys and girls to Christ."

"No!" she would reply emphatically to her startled audience. "That, of course, is part of it; and you know the emphasis I place on evangelism; but if your task stops there, you will never be successful. Our job is to train men and women, boys and girls, to serve the Master. They must feel that there is a task for them to do, that there is a place marked X for every person in God's kingdom. Here is my X; no one can stand on this place but me. Now I must help others to find their place. God has a job for every Christian, and no one else can fulfill it." Growth came quickly in new Christians when these ideas took hold. Christians discouraged and aimless for many years sought her for counseling. She would tell them that their Christian walk had lost its stride, because they had not realized Christ's plan for their lives. When this purpose began to catch fire in their hearts, everything took on a new glow. Many were the professional people —doctors, teachers, lawyers—who found out that they were called to be witnesses and missionaries right where they were.

A highly successful car salesman in the church came to the realization that he had an obligation to be a lay witness for Christ. He began to study his Bible with increased enthusiasm, and he even spent a year in seminary. Eventually, he took over some of the teaching responsibilities in the adult classes. Every weekday morning he would come to the church and study for three hours in preparation for his classes. He never felt called to give up his secular work, but in his capacity as a lay teacher, he had great influence among the businessmen of the community.

In training others to be personal workers, Dr. Mears stressed these points:

1. A soul winner must be a Spirit-led man or woman, not only in the matter of soul-winning, but in all things.

2. A soul winner is made, not born. Anyone can do it if he is willing to make the effort.

3. The place to start is right where you are now. Don't think about becoming a missionary across the sea if you are not a missionary at home.

4. Let the Holy Spirit guide you to people; be sensitive to His leading. Never rush ahead of His initiative.

5. Realize also that He is working not only in your heart but in the person to whom He is directing you.

6. Whenever possible, deal with a person alone; and never interrupt when someone else is working with a person.

7. Start where the person is—with his interests, his knowledge.

8. Hold him to the main point of receiving Christ as personal Saviour; don't let the conversation wander.

9. Allow him to talk about his problems so that he will see his need. Don't jump into your own ideas about what he should do. Your job is to lead him to Christ.

10. Do not try to convince by argumentation. He is not to accept a creed, but Christ; just introduce him to your Friend.

11. Tell what Christ has done for you; no one can argue against your own experience.

12. Don't force a person to accept the whole Bible right off. Lead him to Christ, first of all, and let the Bible's truth become self-evident.

13. As you explain salvation allow him to read the passages of the Bible for himself.

14. Don't be impatient; let God work in his heart.

15. Encourage him to pray with you and to pray aloud.

16. Let your reliance be wholly on the Spirit of God and the Word of God and not on yourself.

When Billy Graham was in New York's Madison Square Garden, Miss Mears flew back to see what amazing things God was doing. Upon entering the packed hall, she was immediately recognized and ushered to a front seat. In the same audience was a friend, who for many years wanted Miss Mears to talk to her unconverted sister about Christ; but because the sister lived in the East, the friend was resigned to the fact that Miss Mears would never meet her. Unaware that the two women were in the garden, Miss Mears sat back to take everything in. She reveled in what the Lord was doing through Cliff Barrows and the huge choir and thrilled to the singing of George Beverly Shea. But as Billy began to preach, the realization that she had taken the attitude of a spectator jarred her. "No matter where I am," she thought, "the Lord never intended me to be a spectator." And immediately she lifted her heart in prayer: "O Lord, don't let me sit just as an observer. I want to be a participator.

Use me here for your purpose." As the invitation was given, the friend spotted Miss Mears and quickly brought her sister over to meet her. Miss Mears took the woman into the Inquiry Room, and in a few moments introduced her to Christ. And as the days and nights rolled on, Miss Mears led many others to the Saviour. She frequently shared this experience with her collegians, pointing out that God does not call us to sit on the side lines and watch. He wants each one of us to be playing in the game.

And wherever she went—New York, London, Athens, Galilee, or Hollywood—Henrietta Mears played in the game, finding the lost, bringing them to Christ, training them for his service, and encouraging them to go to others.

6

Beloved College Department

Beloved College Department

As I travel around the world, I meet scores of people who say to me, "I love that old pile of bricks on the corner of Gower and Carlos: It was there I met my Saviour, my friends and my wife, and there I found my life's calling." I have tried to create in our college department an atmosphere that God could use to draw young people unto himself and to train them for his service.

—HENRIETTA MEARS

When Dr. Clarence Roddy, professor of homiletics at Fuller Theological Seminary, was once asked whom he considered to be the best preacher in Southern California, he immediately replied, "Henrietta Mears."

Miss Mears did not like to be thought of as a preacher or minister, however. She believed these roles were for men. On the other hand she loved to be called "teacher." She had a reverence for the title, giving glory to Jesus, The Teacher, and this became the name by which she was called by thousands of college students who sat under her teaching at the First Presbyterian Church of Hollywood. It was not uncommon to see three hundred university students from the campuses of greater Los Angeles listening to Miss Mears in the college department on Sunday morning. They came because they were fed with the Word of God.

When Teacher stood to teach, she commanded attention. She began each lesson with a prayer encompassing the nations. She would invariably remember by name several of the alumni of the class serving in the far corners of the world. This prayer would lead her students to the very throne of God, and somehow, right at the beginning of the lesson, God commanded their minds and hearts.

Her lessons were challenging, informative and logical —and always biblical. Certain books of the Bible were her favorites, perhaps the chief of these being Romans. Her mind thrived on the great doctrines Paul presents. She loved to emphasize Christ's death for sinners, the power of the Holy Spirit, and the majesty of God. When she came to the ninth chapter of the Epistle (the blackboards overflowing with Scripture references), Teacher's powerful voice had thunder in it as she would say, "People ask me if I believe in predestination. I must admit that I see many problems with this doctrine. But the great question is, what does the Bible say? If St. Paul teaches predestination in these chapters, then I must believe it. One thing I do find in this passage, and that is the greatness of God. I believe in a sovereign God." And for the collegians listening to her, their college chapel was filled with the glory of the Lord. When Teacher talked about the greatness of God, they heard the angels' hallelujahs.

When Miss Mears expounded Romans, she stressed the doctrine of justification, but not as a mere intellectual inquiry. "Paul says that we are not justified by our own works but by faith in Christ," she would say. "Now, students, have you been trying to earn God's favor? You can't do it. You must believe in Christ." And she was fond of presenting Paul's sense of indebtedness to preach the gospel and his love for his countrymen that they might know Christ. It was easy to see Paul's enthusiasm becoming a part of Teacher's excitement as she taught Romans. It was no wonder then that Romans became the favorite book of many of Miss Mears' students who went on to become Bible teachers themselves.

Other series she taught were on the Gospel of John, the Acts of the Apostles, Genesis and Isaiah. She also had a course which took the better part of a year, which was a grand sweep through the entire Bible and included a general introduction to each book.

Miss Mears was also a serious student of prophecy. She had several series on the subject and time and again took her students through the book of Daniel. Once, when she had just returned from a trip to Israel, she was filled with excitement about how the Jews were coming back to their ancient homeland, and she spent many weeks exploring the prophecies dealing with Israel's restoration. But again this was not irrelevant to the practical needs of her audience. She saw in prophecy the actions of a divine Christ who was controlling history. He was always at the center of her lessons.

Henrietta Mears had a bold approach to God, to people and to ideas. She had courage to venture out into difficult realms of thought and doctrine even if she couldn't fully comprehend them. This courage attracted the growing minds of her young people. One day she sat in her office with a college student talking about the Bible. Teacher asked the student what Paul meant in the first chapter of Colossians where he says, . . . *to reconcile all things unto himself* (Col. 1:20). The student gave an initial answer, but Teacher replied, pointing again to the verse, "You still haven't taken into account the word *all*. What does Paul mean, *to reconcile all things?*" The student was taken aback by her emphatic query and admitted he didn't know. "I am not sure I understand either," Teacher responded. "But I thought we could come to some conclusion together." This adventurous attitude toward the Bible and her willingness to share questions with her students awakened the imagination of many a young man who later went on to seminary.

Her boldness with students sprang from her confidence in Christ. "I may not be able to answer all their questions and doubts," she would share with other teachers, "but I can introduce them to the One who can." There was one rugged chap, who had grown up in the Sunday School, and who was now coming to the college department. He was a star football player and an "A" student. He used to bring question after question to Miss Mears about the Bible and science. Miss Mears was at no loss to answer perplexing questions, for she had a science background and was abreast with most of the current intellectual problems of her collegians. But as soon as she would answer one question, this young fellow would raise another; and this went on and on, without hope of meeting his needs. Miss Mears finally said, "Bob, as soon as we finish discussing one question, you raise another and you have hundreds more. This is going to get us nowhere. I want you to meet a Person who can answer all your questions and do much more than that for you." Shortly after that Bob accepted Christ and today is pastoring a Presbyterian church. Everything in the college department was for this end—to introduce students to the one who could answer their problems.

At the center of the college department's activities was the midweek meeting, held on Wednesday nights, at which Miss Mears most clearly presented the claims of Christ and invited students to accept him as their personal Saviour. These Wednesday night meetings were first of all for prayer, and Christ was always the unseen but very real Presence who walked up and down the aisles. They were also for Bible study, and thirdly for sharing. (*"Let the redeemed of the LORD say so,"* admonished Teacher, as she encouraged young men and women to give testimonies about Christ.) The devotional aspects of the Christian walk were always stressed on Wednesday nights. The songs, the mood of the meeting, the Bible passages to be discussed were all chosen with the Christian's practical needs in mind.

Prayer was the essence of these meetings, and at least twenty minutes were devoted to it at the end of each meeting, as the collegians knelt on the asphalt tile with the lights turned low. As the sentence prayers came from now one side then the other side of the darkened room, Teacher would often suggest what should be prayed for —helping some frustrated young person to find Christ. Sometimes she would begin singing a familiar chorus. Her favorite was, "All of my heart, all of my heart, take all of my heart, Lord Jesus." She would lead out with her low, sonorous voice, and once the others took up the melody, she would slip into the harmony. Her kindly voice moved some to tears as God spoke through her gentle prompting.

Prayer was not only the climax of the evening, but for the leaders of the department, it was the beginning of their tasks. An hour before the rest of the students came to the meeting they met in Teacher's office. Sometimes as many as twenty-five were appointed to teach the individual groups into which the Wednesday evening meetings were divided. After reviewing the passage to be discussed, these leaders with Miss Mears got down on their knees, exalting the Lord, confessing their weaknesses and imploring the Holy Spirit to empower them. They asked God to help them as leaders to understand their responsibilities and to clarify the passage of Scripture they were to teach. They prayed for the visitors, that they might accept Christ. They prayed that their department would experience a deep moving of God's presence. Teacher was always there, and the greatest effectiveness of her ministry was generated in these and similar prayer times. These group leaders, after prayer, entered into the main meeting with a sense of expectancy and confidence, for God had revealed to them what he wanted them to do.

Bible study on Wednesday nights was different from the lessons Miss Mears presented on Sunday mornings. Her approach on Sunday mornings was straight lecture, without discussion. Wednesday evenings were based on discussion, for she wanted to get the collegian himself involved in the Word. After a brief song service and opening prayer, the students moved into small discussion groups with not over fifteen people in each. Sometimes they would meet around tables. During one series on the book of Philippians, Teacher sat at a special desk at the front of the room and set the tone by going over the general outline and discussion questions which had been distributed to everyone. The discussion leaders took it from there.

The leader was to get the students in his group to find the answers in the Bible for themselves. The students were to do the digging, the discussion leader being instructed not to give little sermons of his own. This rule was hard to follow as many of the group leaders were pre-seminarians who wanted to share their own views. But the better leaders were the ones who did not have a great deal of confidence in their own abilities and thus were more willing to listen to others.

An example of a successful group leader may be found in Ray, not a pre-seminarian but a television executive. Ray knew Christ in a practical way but was not much interested in the finer points of doctrine. When asked to lead a Bible study, he was stunned, protesting that he was completely ill-equipped. It was with much fear and trembling that he finally accepted and began with his first group. His fear changed to confidence, however, when he learned that all he had to do was to get others talking. From his business experience Ray knew how to draw people out. It wasn't up to him to have all the answers, but for him to keep a discussion going on a given passage which would help his students learn for themselves. Ray's group became too large and several times had to be split in two, while some of the groups led by fellows studying for the ministry who were constantly sharing their views remained small. Miss Mears' principle was: Get people involved for themselves in the Bible; get them talking about God's Word.

She devised several techniques for keeping the discussions going: Have someone read the passage and give a summary of it. Have someone give a brief outline of the passage. Ask what the passage teaches about God, Christ, the Holy Spirit, man, and his responsibility. Find the key verse. Read a favorite verse. Read another passage that sheds light on this one. Have specific questions on the passage itself. No leader who understood how to use these devices ever complained of not having an interested group. Most of the discussion leaders were distressed that they did not have time to let their people finish everything they wanted to say.

When the forty minutes or so were finished for the group studies, Miss Mears would call for everyone's attention and would ask for the leaders to stand and summarize the essential points their group had gleaned. This led naturally into an inspiring testimony time. Testimonies were the third purpose of Wednesday nights.

The testimonies evolved out of the Bible study and thus avoided incidents which reflected nothing of the glory of God but only the banality of the speakers. After absorbing themselves in that which God had done for them as recounted in his Word, the students were ready to think of nothing less when telling what God had done in their lives during the previous week. Usually one of the students led the testimony time. Miss Mears always chose a sensitive and capable leader to do this, because a fine meeting could be ruined if the testimonies ran afoul.

Sometimes, when the testimonies did become self-centered and trivial, Teacher would command the situation to bring it back to a more Christ-centered emphasis. She was not beyond dressing down the troops in a way that her students could understand:

This has been the most ridiculous testimony time I think I have ever heard! All we have been talking about is silly little things that don't amount to a hill of beans! Have we lost sight of why we are here? There hasn't been one word about winning the nations for Christ. How about these great campuses in this area? Hasn't anything been done out at UCLA this week? Hasn't anyone witnessed to a student at USC? God weeps over these lost students, and we come here to talk about trifles. St. Paul dreamed about kingdoms brought to Christ. Knox cried, "Give me Scotland or I die." Luther wept over Germany.

Then the tide was changed as the young people were made to see what God could do through them. After all, Christ's omnipotence was the key. Nothing of importance had happened in their lives during the week because they didn't honestly believe that God could do it. How did this kind of talk affect the visitors? As Teacher would be dealing with the Christian students, many an unconverted newcomer sat up and took notice, often accepting the Lord right then and there. The visitors knew that this woman meant business and that Christ was real to her, and they loved it. They were sick of trivialities in their empty lives, and they wanted something dynamic and vital.

Her older students often squirmed under this kind of treatment as they were made to feel that the testimonies had failed because they weren't in fellowship with Christ. The fact was that this was true, but they hated to admit it. Teacher, however, knew how to crack the whip over those leaders who supposedly held the reins of the class:

"Where are the leaders of this department? Don't they have anything to say tonight? This class will never go beyond the leadership. Don't expect anyone else to have anything to testify if you don't. You are the key."

The following week testimony time would be greatly improved.

At the close of the Wednesday night meeting the class would have refreshments. The object of this refreshment time was to continue the fellowship. Everything was calculated on that one word: fellowship, fellowship either around the Word, prayer, testimonies or punch and cookies. An hour after prayer meeting ended, most of the students were still hanging around talking. Teacher was usually off to the side leading someone to Christ. At times a little room in the back of the hall would be filled with students seeking the Lord. A group always gathered around the piano singing hymns, and some of the officers of the class might be planning the next social or deputation project. Patient Tom Craig, the Scottish custodian, would leave the college chapel to the end when locking up the church for the night, waiting until Miss Mears had finished counseling the last student. Sometimes he would have to encourage the students to leave by turning off the lights, but conversations would continue in the dark. Miss Mears was usually the last to leave; she always had someone else to talk to. Few realized that she had been running at full steam all day and was completely exhausted; but this did not matter to her. These were her sons and daughters. She loved them, and through them she intended to change the world.

After another hour of fellowship around coffee cups and apple pie at Coffee Dan's or some other restaurant on Hollywood Boulevard, one of the college students would finally drive Teacher home. She would be talking a mile a minute about someone she had prayed with who had accepted Christ or some young fellow who had decided to go into the ministry. Wednesday nights were thrilling experiences, not so much because of Henrietta Mears, but because her students were brought face to face with Jesus Christ.

There were three main meetings per week for the college class. Sunday morning, the most formal meeting, was set apart for the teaching of the Word. Wednesday night aimed at enriching the devotional life. But the Sunday evening meeting was entirely different from these other two. Miss Mears believed in self-expression; she knew that her active and loquacious collegians had to have a meeting where they could say what they wanted and where they could give vent to their spiritual energies. Consequently, Sunday evenings were reserved for forums, panels, musicals, and testimonials. Some of the most interesting Sunday evening College Hour programs were given over to the department deputation teams where the students who had been witnessing at the jails, camps, colleges and hospitals could report on what had been happening. Teacher encouraged anything that allowed the students to interact with what they were doing and learning. Some of these College Hour programs were utterly amazing.

Once, after Miss Mears had returned from a trip to the Far East, brimming over with enthusiasm for missionary work in Japan and Formosa, the students organized a program around the Oriental motif. They removed all the chairs and commandeered three hundred or more cushions which they placed around the college hall. Chinese lanterns were hung everywhere, and travel posters were taped on the walls. The girls of the social committee dressed up in kimonos, and served tea and Chinese cookies. Soft Chinese music was played in the background. The grand surprise climax came when the lights suddenly went out and a spotlight picked up Teacher, sitting in a rickshaw, dressed in a fancy kimono and waving a paper fan. Two of the college men were dressed as coolies; and as the spot picked her up, the coolies pulled this beloved "dragon lady" through the back doors right down the middle of the room to the front. Someone was banging on a gong, and there was in general the most delightful confusion. (Where did they get the rickshaw? The students were constantly borrowing props from the movie studios.) It was all great fun, and it is to Teacher's ever-lasting credit that she knew how to enter into things. At first she thought the rickshaw idea was a little far out, but it didn't take her long to see that the young people wanted to impress the department with missions in the Far East. She played her part well: As she bounced down the room (the coolies almost spilled her over backwards) she put on the airs of an empress from old China, waving her fan ninety-to-nothing. Once the clamor had died down, she laid the fan aside and delivered a most challenging missionary message. That night her collegians beheld the needs of hapless Orientals as they had never viewed them before. A few months later, two doctors and two nurses were sent over from the department to help missionaries on Formosa. Many of these Sunday evening programs were on missionary themes.

For a number of years, there has been a summer deputation program for the students of the First Presbyterian Church of Hollywood. The church has sent deputation teams to a score of foreign lands to help missionaries and to work in international camps with other Christians. Under Miss Mears' direction, for several weeks before these teams left and for several weeks after they returned, the college department heard their reports and saw their slides on Sunday evenings.

Teacher thought that these student-centered programs were profitable for several reasons: It always made a deep impression on the young people as they heard missionary challenges from speakers their own age whom they knew. These student programs also helped them to organize their thoughts on vital subjects. This self-expression involved the students dynamically in their group goals, all of which helped Christianity to become more practical. But most important, as they spoke before their friends, they were committing themselves before the Lord. They soon learned that they could not speak on missions publicly unless they were willing to do something about them personally. Many students said that when they were asked to talk on prayer, witnessing, or Bible study, that they had to come to a fresh realization of the importance of these subjects in their own lives before they could share them with others.

The collegians put on one missionary program where all those who were interested in some specific overseas field took part, but in the language of the country that was the individual student's concern. Only the announcements and final message were in English. The Scripture readings were in both Spanish and Russian, testimonies were in Japanese and German, the music was sung in an African dialect, and someone read a poem in Korean. This multilingual program was a puzzle to most of the audience, but again, those participating in it were committing themselves to life's callings and that before the people who knew them best, their college friends.

At special seasons of the year, especially on Christmas and Easter, there were the most delightful programs.

Often these were musicals. In a department as alive as this one there was an abundance of talent. (There were two pianos and a Hammond organ plus a stage to work with. On several occasions the students assembled a small orchestra.) These Sunday evening programs were thus opportunities for the creative people in the department to go to work. Sometimes they had literature evenings, when Christian poems and prose works were read to the accompaniment of a harp. There was a group of students interested in drama, and many times they offered plays on biblical themes. One of these dramas dealt with Paul in Athens. Of course, it was all in costume. Four of the fellows organized a quartet: The high tenor was student body president at Occidental College. The pianist was outstanding. The lead tenor finally married her and today they are pastoring a large church in Chicago. This quartet was in constant demand not only in the department but up and down the West Coast. For several months it appeared on television.

The young man who organized the quartet also led a choir. This was not the regular college choir which was a part of the music program of the church. It performed only in the department. It lasted for over a year and sang nearly every Sunday morning and often on Sunday evenings. By anyone's standards it was good. It could do anything from Negro spirituals to classical anthems. Many musically inclined students found in this choir a further attraction to come to the department. A few years later there was another such choir which had its own radio program for several months.

On Sunday evenings the class frequently had a whole program devoted to a single campus, everyone participating on that program being from the same school. Of course the rivalry between schools was much fun as all the students from one campus tried to get the most people out. This was another technique to attract students from the universities. Teacher encouraged anything along this line.

It can be easily seen how a College Hour chairman (as the director of Sunday evenings was called), working with such a variety of demanding programs week after week, could quickly wear himself out. Anyone who has ever organized only one such program will marvel how this pace could be kept up Sunday after Sunday. The trick lay in getting others to do the work. At the beginning of the year when the new officers were taking over, all those who thought they might have an idea for a Sunday evening program were invited to a brainstorming session. The entire executive staff was also requested to come. There would be from fifty to a hundred people at this meeting. Everyone was asked to contribute as many ideas as he could without too much discussion of details. All the suggestions were carefully recorded by the program chairman's secretary with a note on who showed the initial interest. On the basis of these raw ideas the chairman then appointed subchairmen, who would be responsible for one or more specific meetings. It was up to them to set up their own committees and to see that all that was necessary for a good program was done. People who already held down important posts in the department were expected to have one or two nights per year when their committee would take over. As a result there would be individual programs put on by the deputation teams, the membership committee, the music committee, the pre-seminarians, etc. In this way the program chairman was assisted by nearly the entire cabinet, but he still had to be a very strong leader with a great deal of time to spend on his job. His office was second only to the president's in importance. Miss Mears was always willing to discuss his problems with him and to offer suggestions, but she never made the mistake of taking over his responsibilities. Her task was to make sure that the program chairman did his job. Miss Mears built into her students a sense of their own responsibility by making them do the work themselves. When Dr. Louis Evans, Sr. was the pastor, there was a youth night once a month on Sunday evenings. This meant that the entire Sunday evening service was run by, and geared for, the youth— all, that is, except the sermon, which Dr. Evans himself preached. The college department, along with the high school students, organized these youth nights, which were very successful. It was thrilling to see a thousand or so young people gathered for a Sunday evening church service, listening attentively to Dr. Evans' dynamic challenges.

In all these programs Miss Mears charged her students to maintain the highest degree of excellence possible. She was incapable of lowering her own standards when she knew that she or those working with her had not done their best. For many of those who did not understand this attitude at first her high norms could be a mind-stretching experience. But she expected her young people to reach as high and as far as they were able.

It was sometimes hard for the youth to resolve the differences between Teacher's high standards and their own need to be trained up to them. What were they to do when they had to put on a Sunday morning program of excellent quality and yet most of them were green at the job? Teacher was patient as long as they did their best. But when her leaders slipped up and did not do their best when they knew better, Teacher knew how to reprimand them.

In all of her own leadership Teacher remained impartial and objective, and it was this quality of objectivity that saved her from many errors, for she had an intense love for her collegians. They were her family, the sons and daughters she had never been permitted to bear physically; and all the emotion and ambition that are usually reserved for one's own children were lavished on them. But Teacher's love for her students as sons and daughters was heightened by her sense of world mission. They were important to her not only personally but potentially—for the cause of Christ among the nations.

Add to this the undoubted fact that Henrietta Mears was a very intense and energetic person with enormous reserves of mental and emotional strength, and you will see how all this could have created a fatal obstacle in her ministry if she had not preserved the objectivity and businesslike approach, the lawyer's mind, which was the other side of her personality. She did not fall into the trap where parents so often miscalculate the possibility of their children doing wrong. Miss Mears knew what weaknesses her children were capable of, but she also knew what noble purposes could be theirs; she was quick to discourage the former and to encourage the latter. She combined in rare fashion demanding standards with a warmhearted acceptance, and to the wonder of all who knew her, the two did not exclude each other. And in all this, her students grew in their love for her and for her Christ.

7

Calling Leaders

Calling Leaders

Our duty is to understand youth, but more, to help them understand themselves that they may release their varied abilities in the service of Christ and his Kingdom. We must help them to discover a life work, not work for life.

—Henrietta Mears

It was a hot summer day—beach weather to a Southern Californian. The rickety cattle truck clattered down Sunset Boulevard past the sumptuous homes of some of Hollywood's brightest stars. Dressed in their beach togs with gaily colored towels flapping over the wooden sides, the collegians of the First Presbyterian Church of Hollywood were headed for the surf. Clanks and squeaks of the old truck kept time to their vigorous songs. And bouncing back and forth in the middle of the happy gang, singing and laughing, sat Henrietta Mears.

Next to her was a collegian with a contagious love for people. Everywhere Jimmy went his warmth and joy for life glowed with a heavenly iridescence, made all the more captivating by a congenital abnormality in his physical structure. As the rest joked and sang, Miss Mears said to this young man, "Jimmy, have you ever thought about going to seminary?" This idea had never appeared on his spiritual horizon, but Teacher loved to extend people's horizons. Years later, while pastoring a church in California, Jimmy wrote to her: "I was so impressed that you gave so unstintingly of your time and of your Christian spirit. Here you were riding in the cattle truck with us, singing, sharing words of wisdom along the way, and asking the question which opened my eyes to greater service, 'Have you ever thought about going to seminary?'"

Miss Mears never told a student that God was calling him into the ministry. She reverently left that sacred responsibility within the province of the Holy Spirit. But she knew that one of her most important tasks in Hollywood was to create an atmosphere which God could use to speak to young people about church-related professions.

Two years before her death, Dr. Harold John Ockenga, pastor of the Park Street Church in Boston and first president of Fuller Seminary in Pasadena, wrote to Dr. Mears:

> What a work you have done! There is no young people's or Sunday School work in this nation equal to yours. When I think of the tens of thousands of people who have studied the Bible under your leadership, of the thousands of young people who have faced the claims of Christ and made a commitment to him, of the hundreds of young men who have gone into the ministry and other young people into Christian service, I cannot but stand back in amazement. Your vision, your faith and your courage have been unequalled, and only heaven can measure the fruit of your labors . . . As you know, it was one of my fondest hopes to have you as a professor of Christian education in Fuller Theological Seminary. Your contribution to ministers would have been the acme of your educational career.

To challenge young men to enter the ministry was perhaps the greatest of Miss Mears' gifts. In the course of her career in Hollywood over four hundred collegians heard God's call and turned their energies to pulpits in America or to missionary stations scattered around the world. One of her greatest delights was traveling the globe to visit missionaries who had been her pupils.

It is one thing to be a seminary professor and to instruct young men and women who have already committed themselves to the ministry; it is quite another to inspire university students who are trying to choose a life's calling. Miss Mears definitely had this latter gift.

What she did in Hollywood was all the more remarkable from two other considerations: First, Hollywood, California, was not the average church leader's choice for a theological spawning ground. Henrietta Mears came to the movie capital when it was just entering into its hectic, carefree and usually immoral apogee of fame. Sound movies were coming into their own and cowboys were galloping from Hollywood studios onto theater screens around the world, while heroes and starlets were setting the sex patterns for youth in nearly every nation on earth. The celluloid capital was not exactly the backside of a desert where a thoughtful Moses could have plenty of time to meditate on the fate of his people and to hear the call of God to deliver them. Could a lily grow in a quagmire? "Could anything good come out of Nazareth?" Could Hollywood produce anything spiritual? Henrietta Mears thought so.

It seems that God delights in taking the most contrary situation and making it redound to his glory. Certainly from the first-century Christian's viewpoint, Saul, the persecutor, was not a likely choice for their most prominent missionary! Yet these surprise tactics, so frequently employed by the Creator, produce some of the most remarkable results. Undoubtedly he delights in shocking people into realizing what he is capable of doing. In looking back on her long and successful career in Hollywood, Dr. Mears frequently told Sunday School workers from other cities:

If God can do it in Hollywood, he can do it in your city. You may think that this has been easy for us out here and that you have an impossible situation. But I will tell you honestly that I would have chosen any place on the face of this earth to go rather than Hollywood if it had not been for God's definite leading. What you see accomplished here is only a fraction of what can be done in your city, if you will just believe in a God who can do the impossible.

But perhaps God had another motive behind this exceptional call to Henrietta Mears. Hollywood is a superficial town. It is based on illusion: the screen technique that makes cars fly and mice talk, the story plot that insists everything end happily, the star who must be bigger than life to survive in a cutthroat industry. Legion are the teenagers who flock every year to this fairy castle to be discovered, to be catapulted into the heavens and there to sparkle for the admiration of a doting public. For the first few months of their pilgrimage they pay their obeisance in the offices of agents to whom they commit their eternal destinies, body and soul. Weeks of rejection, failure, and faltering bank accounts cast a deepening shadow of despair, until the last flickering hope fades into the oblivion of lonely desolation and ruin. The Gentle Physician laid down the dictum: *They that be*

whole need not a physician, but they that are sick . . . I am
not come to call the righteous but sinners to repentance
(Matt. 9:12,13). And it would be difficult to find another
community where the falsity of fame is so thoroughly appreciated as in Hollywood, where people have spent all
their substance on the fake physicians of the spirit only to
go bankrupt without cure. Those who have gone through
this tragic experience and have later found healing in the
touch of the Sinner's Friend know and deeply love Jesus of
Nazareth.

This contrast—the despair of the world and the salvation of Christ—produced through the years in thousands
of young hearts an exuberance to live for the glory of
God. The simple appeal they so often heard from Dr.
Mears' lips was not without effect: "Young people, I
want you to think about what you are going to do with
your lives. What are you living for? When you come to
the last days God allows you on this earth, will you be
satisfied? Remember, 'Only one life, 'twill soon be past;
only what's done for Christ will last!'" They thought,
they prayed, and they went out to preach Christ's message
of abundant life.

The second marvel was that Henrietta Mears' ministry
came at a time when skepticism and atheism were at a
peak in our country. In the thirties, forties and fifties in
Southern California, it was very difficult indeed to find
a professor who would admit to the authority of the
Scripture, let alone accept the deity of Christ. Most of
the colleges in the area have for years been antagonistic
to religious conservatism. One instructor on a state campus
began his introductory course in philosophy before some
five hundred lower classmen with this profound insight:
"There is no God! That is the very foundation of this
course. Now that we have gotten that clear, we can begin

our study of philosophy." On a nearby denominational campus the professor of Bible was a noted liberal, who through the course of her many years instructed thousands of uninformed freshmen that the miracle stories of the Old Testament were myths which could no longer be believed. Taking this approach, she wove a web of textual criticism in which many a naive student became entangled and lost his faith.

Miss Mears refused to raise a cudgel against such people. Indeed, if she ever met them, and she frequently did, she treated them with warmth and love. But in her teaching, especially in the college department, she never compromised her own conservative beliefs; nor did she fail her responsibility to give Biblical answers to these attackers. She frequently spoke on the authority of the Scriptures, the existence of God, the deity of Christ, the physical resurrection and the virgin birth, and she would accept no adjustment in these doctrines. Not everyone who heard her agreed. But none of the liberals could outlive her! Christ was not a doctrine to be disputed, he was a Person to be obeyed and enjoyed. Her life radiated his presence.

One evening a young man from the University of Southern California, who had just received his Ph.D. in mathematics, came to the college department. One of the students was talking about the reality of Christ and said, "There may be someone here tonight who has thought that if he could just reach the apex of academic pursuit, he would be happy, but he's not. Only Christ can give real life." He did not know the young mathematician in his audience, but an hour later the Ph.D. was on his knees confessing Christ. This incident pointed up Henrietta Mears' ability to deal with intellectualism. She outflanked it. She chose her own field of battle—spiritual reality. She was perfectly willing to let the liberals talk themselves blue with their arguments against the Scriptures, but when the right moment came, she introduced them to a Person who had the answers, and their doubts were put to rout.

But once a person met Christ, there was nothing Miss Mears wouldn't do to establish him in the verities of the faith. In this task she was assisted by some of the most able men and women of God in the land. During her early years at Hollywood Presbyterian Church, she frequently called upon her good friend, Dr. Harry Rimmer, to speak to the collegians about such current problems as evolution and the Bible, the miracles of Jesus, prophecy, and Old Testament chronology. Later another famous preacher, Dr. J. Edwin Orr, helped greatly to establish her "preacher boys" in doctrine. His brilliant lectures on the existence of God, justification, sanctification, and a host of other relevant topics, for years helped many a confused collegian to crystallize his thoughts. A man of astounding learning and practical insight was Dr. Wilbur M. Smith, who time and again grounded the students in the faith. His emphasis on the Resurrection and the deity of Christ was a major asset to the over-all curriculum of the college department. Dr. Smith was professor of English Bible at Fuller Theological Seminary. When this school was founded after the Second World War, Miss Mears made use of all its professorial talents for the sake of her young theologues.

For many years Dr. William Evans—the father of the former pastor of the First Presbyterian Church of Hollywood, Dr. Louis H. Evans—was living in semi-retirement in Los Angeles. This noted Bible scholar contributed many hours a week to Miss Mears' young people, and for several years the high school and college department

147

deputation teams met in his home on Friday nights to listen to his discussions on the Bible and how to preach it. Dr. William Evans had the complete Bible memorized in the King James Version and the New Testament also in the American Standard Version. The young people would delight in giving him passages from either version to quote from memory. This sort of dedication to the Word of God inspired many of the youth to begin their own memory programs. There was one contest in the college department to see who could memorize the fifteenth chapter of I Corinthians first. The following Sunday "Dr. William" preached on this passage and began his sermon by quoting from memory the entire fifty-eight verses. He had written a book on how to memorize the Scriptures, and many of the young people studied it avidly. It is not always that one finds college people eager to memorize whole chapters of the Bible. Usually they think that memory programs are for the younger students. This myth was shattered in the First Presbyterian Church of Hollywood as even the older folk were busy storing up the Word of God in their minds as well as their hearts.

Dr. William Evans was a great asset to Dr. Mears' ministry. Both of them thought alike in many fields. When he was well past eighty and still preaching vigorously, one of the collegians went over to his house and asked him, "Well, Dr. Evans, how many hours have you spent studying the Bible today?"

His reply was magnificent: "This has been a rather busy day, and I haven't done as much as I would have liked. I suppose I have only put in five hours today."

Dr. Evans wrote over fifty books on the Bible, one of which was *How to Prepare Sermons and Gospel Talks*. Many of Miss Mears' seminarians cut their first homiletical teeth on this work. As students met at his house for deputation training, he would tell them how to preach at the jails and in the missions, how to use illustrations, how to give testimonies, and the like. His instruction even went into the subject of how to put authority into one's voice.

One Sunday morning when Dr. William was substituting for his son, he chose the subject of the virgin birth. All were electrified by his brilliant dissertation. As he came to the climax, he picked up his Bible and tore out the pages which narrated the birth of the Lord. The tattered pages floated down from the John Knox pulpit as he said, "If we can't believe in the virgin birth, let's tear it out of the Bible!" The audience then sat in amazement as he drove his point home by tearing out the resurrection chapters, then the miracle narratives, then anything of a supernatural character. Few if any had ever before seen a preacher rip the Bible apart in the pulpit. The floor was littered with mutilated scraps of paper. Then in his dramatic way he held up the only remaining portion and said, "And this is all we have left, the Sermon on the Mount; and that has no authority for us if a divine Christ didn't preach it." A few more words and he told the audience to bow for the benediction.

But a man in the vast and sedate congregation stood and cried, "No, no! Go on! We want more!" Several other people joined in, so Dr. Evans continued for another fifty minutes. This type of preaching was not lost on the impressionable minds of the youth. And whenever Dr. William Evans preached the front rows were filled with the oncoming generation.

Dr. William Evans died on a Sunday morning at almost the very moment when the church service began. His son ascended the pulpit and announced that he had just returned from bidding his father farewell. Dr. Louis Evans had told his dying father that he just couldn't preach that morning; but Dr. William's final words were, "Son, don't break your stride!" Dr. Louis Evans' sermon that followed was not only in his words but in his courage and faith.

And in the college department, Dr. Mears announced that their beloved mentor had stepped into eternity a few moments before. Then she said, "Fallen, fallen is one of the mighty men of Israel!" And her lesson was on Elijah's ride to heaven in the fiery chariot. She spoke at length of the mantle the prophet threw to his assistant Elisha, and she said, "I pray that Dr. Evans' mantle will fall upon some of you young men here today." Future theologues lived and worked in an atmosphere of giants. They always had before them the very finest men of God for their examples.

There are some great men and women who have a tragic fear of other great people. Anyone who might threaten their own abilities or position is kept a safe distance. Miss Mears never allowed this pettiness to touch her. She reveled in talented people, even if their abilities went beyond her own. She delighted when some young person would discover things she had not seen or could take one of her programs farther than what she had envisioned herself.

When outstanding preachers were in town, she encouraged her collegians to hear them, and she often invited visiting churchmen to take over her pulpit in the college department. Many times she welcomed them out to her home to spend a few days. She told her students that as a girl her family table was always open to guest preachers and missionaries and that this custom had made a deep impression on her. She created the same environment for her young people. It was not uncommon for some of them to be invited to her home to meet some Christian leader, perhaps to have dinner with him, and then to sit in her beautiful living room to talk about spiritual things.

In all of this Miss Mears set the stage for God's call. The Christian ministry was made exciting, adventurous, worthy, dignified, challenging and satisfying. She never allowed it to be viewed as the last resort for those who had failed in other professions. Just the opposite was true. Her youth looked at their leaders and saw virile, intelligent, purposeful men who were profoundly conscious of a great God. Teacher did all she could to make the pulpit attractive to the most active and ambitious young Christian.

Miss Mears greatly admired her good friend, Billy Graham, and encouraged her college department to stand behind his various crusades in the Los Angeles area. When Dr. Graham came to the Hollywood Bowl, all anticipated a repetition of his famous tent crusade held a few years before in the center of Los Angeles; but the Bowl meetings were not up to expectations. Many of the young people were disappointed that the crowds were not larger, and they began to pray about what could be done. The church had a membership of over seven thousand, and some began to think how inspiring it would be if, for one night, the entire congregation would come out to one of Dr. Graham's meetings. The idea was presented to Miss Mears and Dr. Evans, who quickly approved. Headed by collegians, a committee set a target date. They cut up the pages of the church directory and from the college department and other groups recruited volunteers who would phone every name on one side of a page. Then they selected people to go around to the various Sunday School classes to make announcements. Posters were hung up all over the church, and the leaders were instructed to push the special night as hard as they could. All the while Teacher and her collegians were praying furiously. Large banners were made so the members would be able to find the section in the Bowl roped off for them. Monday was chosen for the strategic night, because this was ordinarily the least attended session.

The students' hearts nearly leaped out of their chests as Dr. Graham read off the names of the various churches at the meeting that night. When he said, "The First Presbyterian Church of Hollywood," five thousand people stood. And at the invitation, scores of them went forward to profess Christ. Miss Mears' students were flushed with success. They immediately got hold of the entire Los Angeles telephone directory, tearing out the pages and cutting them in half. Then, with Dr. Graham's approval, they passed them out on various evenings to volunteers, along with instruction sheets, the idea being that each person was to phone and invite to the services every person on his list. This did not work as well as the previous plan, probably because the students didn't stop to think through details, but some people did respond. Dr. Graham was so grateful for the enthusiasm of Miss Mears' collegians that he brought his entire team to the department for the next Sunday morning and took over her class, a very exceptional thing for him to do, as his rule was not to preach in any one church lest he be obligated to do the same for all the churches. The students were delighted.

During the Billy Graham Crusade in the Hollywood Bowl, there were some remarkable conversions among the youth of the church.

There were two scalawags in the college department who were not Christians, although they had been raised in the church. They were capable of any mischief, and the session had seriously considered banning them from all church meetings. Hiding behind the railing of a balcony across from the church, they would take great delight in shooting beans at the members on Sunday mornings. One day they went to sneer at one of Dr. Graham's services in the Hollywood Bowl. But when the invitation was given, the boys looked at each other and made a beeline for the altar rail. Today one is serving the Lord on the mission field; the other is a Presbyterian minister.

Whether during special crusades, or in the usual course of her ministry, Miss Mears witnessed thousands of such transformations.

One young man was invited to the annual New Year's conference at Forest Home. He had been raised in a moral atmosphere and had no great consciousness of guilt, although he was looking for direction in his life. Everybody was having fun. On the last day of the week-end camp, Jack slept in and was late for breakfast, so he went to the coffee shop for a bite just as the final service was beginning in the auditorium. He was with other friends, some of whom, like himself, were not too interested in religion. Suddenly the coffee shop door flew open and Henrietta Mears boomed out, "All right, everyone up to the fagot service! Come on, Jack, you can have breakfast later on. Everyone come along, now. We're all going to the fagot service!"

As Jack sat in the testimony service listening to others relate what had happened in their lives, he felt a compulsion to say something. When his turn came, he said, "I don't know what this is all about, but I feel like all of you are on a boat leaving, and here I am on the shore watching you wave good-by. I would like to be on the boat with you. I want what I see and hear this morning." Miss Mears quoted to him Christ's invitation, *Behold, I*

153

stand at the door and knock: if any man hear my voice, and open the door, I will come in to him, and will sup with him, and he with me (Rev. 3.20). She explained what these words meant, and the young man accepted the Saviour right then and there. As he returned to his seat he closed his eyes and prayed for the first time in his life—not for himself but for his friend sitting next to him, that he too might open his heart to Christ. When Jack looked up, he saw his friend standing in the testimony line, and he wept as he heard him confess his faith. Jack Franck went on to become one of Miss Mears' most faithful staff assistants at the Hollywood Church and later on took over the leadership of Forest Home, being instrumental in leading hundreds of other people to Christ.

Legion are the individuals who found Christ under Miss Mears' ministry and entered into the highly charged atmosphere of dedication and service that she created in Hollywood. Today they preach from hundreds of pulpits around the world. They serve in schools, speak over the radio, lead choirs, direct Sunday Schools and work on dozens of campuses. Their footfalls are heard in African jungles, on high mountain ranges in Formosa, in the sweltering cities of India and in many other countries. And what is more important, they are reproducing their kind wherever they go, for they learned from Henrietta Mears that the true disciple trains other disciples to take his place. So it can be said that the combined ministries of her spiritual children extend far beyond what she did in Hollywood. And this was her greatest dream: that her work in Hollywood might be but a spark to ignite brightly burning fires in every nation of earth that in coming generations multitudes might hear the Galilean's call and be saved.

8

Training Leaders

Training Leaders

An efficient leader may, through his knowledge of his job and the magnetism of his personality, greatly increase the efficiency of others.

—HENRIETTA MEARS

Nearly every pastor, missionary and Sunday School superintendent knows the importance of training leaders. Paul instructed Timothy: *The things that thou hast heard of me . . . the same commit thou to faithful men, who shall be able to teach others also* (II Tim. 2:2). The facts are all too obvious: None of us is indispensable; there comes the time for every man—no matter how grand his work has been—to lay his staff down and to watch as others take it up. And a man's greatest talents are not in how much he has been able to do alone, but in how effective he has been in getting others to work with him. A good leader leads men; a great leader trains other leaders.

As Henrietta Mears sought out leaders and trained them, her energies, ambitions and abilities achieved their maximum development. Once at Forest Home, as a purposeful looking football player walked by, Miss Mears said, "What a wonderful leader John would make!" This was her theme; she repeated it at conferences, meetings, Bible classes and in a thousand conversations: leadership.

Some think that Miss Mears was only interested in supplying leadership for the full-time church occupations. It would be wrong to say that this was not her first concern; but her vision encompassed every area of life. She was also desirous to see her young collegians step into the business world, teaching, medicine, indeed, into all occupations, as Christian leaders. Her nephew was one of the developers of color TV; a brother was the president of several banks at an early age; other of her close relatives were outstanding in the professions, industry and commerce. These served in her mind as a norm for the ambitious Christian youth. Sometimes her standards left her students gasping—as one of them said, "We can't all be Luthers in religion, Faradays in science, or Gladstones in politics. I feel left out of Miss Mears' vision!"

And Miss Mears herself confided in private:

I know that when I tell my young people the marvelous things God has done through the lives of others, it encourages them to strive to achieve higher goals. But it doesn't necessarily follow that he will do the same through them. But he has done it for some, and I know that the principles I lay down for them are valid. Besides, I want them to aspire to the very highest attainments possible for men and women whose lives are possessed by the Spirit of God.

Miss Mears stressed that "Leadership begins with Christ. No matter how brilliant a youth may be, he must experience the regenerating power of the resurrected Christ before his real potential can be liberated." And it was amazing to see timid students, who had not really found much to do in life, join the college department and burst into activity and accomplishment once they came face to face with the Lord.

Absolute surrender to the influence of the Holy Spirit was a cardinal factor in Miss Mears' own life. When she was in college, soon after the death of her saintly mother, her minister, Dr. Riley had said to her, "Henrietta, I am praying that your mother's mantle will fall upon you." Many years later Miss Mears related how she felt when Dr. Riley held out to her such a high expectation:

I felt absolutely powerless from the thought that I could possibly live up to what my mother had been and had done, and I prayed that if God had anything for me to do that he would supply the power. I read my Bible for every reference to the Holy Spirit and his power. The greatest realization came to me when I saw that there was nothing I had to do to receive his power but to submit to Christ, to allow him to control me. I had been trying to do everything myself; now I let Christ take me completely. I said to Christ that if he wanted anything from me that he would have to do it himself. My life was changed from that moment on.

It was through this submission to God's Spirit that vision began to grow in her mind, and she passed on this key to successful leadership to thousands of young people: "Allow God to tell you what you are to do. But you say, 'Miss Mears, I don't know what God wants me to do. I've been praying about it for months, and I just don't know!' Well, is there the faintest glimmer of light? It may be ever so small. What is it? Follow it! And as you do, God will reveal the rest." This was the encouragement that many students needed. They had some glimmer of light, but it had seemed to them too faint, perhaps too ridiculous. Miss Mears knew that a youth will be listless, aimless and bored unless he has something for which to strive. Once there is a goal, all his energies will leap into the game.

So in her inspiring of leaders, it was these two factors that went hand in hand: the Christian's relationship to God, and his goal. The contact with Christ produced the goal which in turn produced a greater desire to know Christ. It was not by accident that the motto of her college department was: "To know Christ and to Make Him Known."

Moreover, Miss Mears had a wonderful appreciation of the need to be specific with God's plans. When she came to Hollywood, she wrote down on a piece of paper all the things she wanted to accomplish as Director of Christian Education at the First Presbyterian Church. "I wrote them down, and through the years every one of them has been accomplished, and many more. I didn't trust my memory, nor did I merely have vague ideas. I wrote down specifics." This, too, was always an elemental part in her training of a leader. Time and again in the college department cabinet meetings she would have her students take pieces of paper and write down what they wanted to accomplish as a department. She encouraged them to be as specific as possible, to the most necessary detail.

After setting down goals before her, she then wrote opposite them how she was going to reach them. Again these means and methods had to be committed to paper. Her style was brief and practical but sufficient.

> Don't bother with elaborate plans. The simpler they are the better. Often we hide behind fancy ideas and plans because we secretly believe they are

going to fail and thus relieve us of our responsibility. Be practical. Don't try something you know from the beginning is not going to work. Think a thing through and choose the best way of doing it. And don't underestimate what you yourself have to do.

Time and again she would have to call her students to their senses as they would plan some big event—a party, a meeting, a camp—when they had not allowed themselves enough time to do it, or they had not enlisted enough personnel for the job. "Always make sure you have sufficient troops to win the battle," she would say.

In all of this she carefully saw to it that a leader was not allowed to fail, or at least, to remain in failure. The deputation teams would sometimes come back almost in tears. They had gone out to some campus or mission, and the program had fallen apart, the message had been awful, and the whole performance a flop. All the discouraged team could see was a huge ogre called FAILURE. Miss Mears would sit them down and say, "All right now, fellows, why did you fail?" Then the reasons came to light: the program had not been thought through far enough in advance, Bob had not been prepared to preach, Louie hadn't figured out what songs they were going to sing, and Sam hadn't had time to practice them on the piano, Gary's testimony was not to the mark, and so on. As all this was being discussed a metamorphosis took place. Now that the causes for failure were understood, and ways for overcoming them in view, the team could hardly be kept from racing out and holding another meeting. Miss Mears often used the example of how the Lord always rescued Peter from his many failures. She pointed out how Jesus never left Peter in discouragement but helped him to see his way out.

161

In this there was a delicate balance between expecting from a person herculean tasks but not asking him to do something he was bound to bungle.

You would never ask me to sing the soprano solo on Sunday morning. It would be criminal. That is not my talent. My job as a trainer of leaders is to spot the potential of a person: What are his talents? What is his potential? It doesn't matter if he is doing anything now or not. I must see where he is capable of going. Then I encourage him along that line.

Miss Mears believed that God called people according to their talents. Many a young musician told Miss Mears that he felt called into the ministry. Without discouraging this possible leading, she gently pointed out that God had already given him a wonderful talent. Couldn't that be God's call?

In the college department hundreds of young fellows felt called into the ministry, and they invariably talked it over with Teacher. Her response was like a bucket of cold water: "How do you know God wants you in the ministry, Bill?"

"Well, I just feel he does."

"But is there anything specific?"

"Well, no, I just think he wants me to be a minister."

"But is there anything else you could do?"

"Sure, there are plenty of other things I could do. But I can't! I just have to be a minister!"

That was the note she was listening for. "Woe is me if I preach not the gospel!" Miss Mears would never encourage a fellow to make the pulpit his career if he felt that there was something else he would be just as content in doing. It was this ultimate abandon—so necessary to the preacher. Anything less was not enough.

The call might be the pulpit, but the training began with straightening up chairs and passing out hymn books. If a student was willing to do the menial tasks, he could be entrusted with the bigger ones. There was a fellow in the class who had been employed in one of the large department-store chains. He had worked himself up to quite a high position before he was converted. In the college department Bob would walk through a room and pick up and examine any old scrap of paper on the floor. When asked about it, he said, "I learned in Penney's that no detail is too insignificant not to be bothered about. A very important piece of paper may have fallen that could cost the store hundreds of dollars." Miss Mears always admired Bob, because, although he held down high positions in her group and later on in several missionary organizations, he never felt above being concerned with the most insignificant detail.

The college department cabinet (comprising all the officers of the class) was always quite a bureaucracy. There were sometimes cabinets with as many as seventy-five active members, plus many others who helped on occasion. For many onlookers this seemed wholly unnecessary, and several presidents swung into their new office with reform in their blood: cutting the cabinet down to manageable size. Miss Mears always vetoed this idea. First, as the new presidents were soon to learn, a few people could not run a large department. There was just too much to do. But of greater importance, more students on the cabinet meant more people involved in the activities, and therefore, more leaders being trained.

There was another reason for large cabinets: college people want to be "in" on everything that is happening in a group. If they feel that they are being excluded or that their talents are not needed, they will soon flag in interest and drop away. "Use them or lose them." Therefore, Miss Mears had to create jobs for new people—even when none were open—to keep everybody busy.

One day Miss Mears received a letter from out of state written by an anxious parent saying that her son would be visiting her college department. Al hadn't been interested in their home church, but now that he would be attending college in Southern California, it was hoped that Miss Mears could do something with him. Teacher was on the alert. When Al walked into the department for the first time, Miss Mears grabbed him and asked him to usher since they were shorthanded. That was rather a bold treatment for a visitor, but Teacher knew that he might never come back if he weren't put to work immediately. After the hour, Miss Mears told him what a wonderful job he had done, and asked if he wouldn't usher again next Sunday morning. Soon Teacher moved him up to the position of chief usher: Al had to line up all the ushers for every meeting, and of course be there himself. Next semester Al was elected a director of the department and became one of the most outstanding program chairmen the department ever had. He spent all of his college career in the department and today is an active elder in his church. He told Miss Mears many years later that she was the only one who had ever inspired him in religion. One of the reasons for this was that Teacher made him feel important and needed. She put him to work.

Often Teacher would take a non-Christian in this fashion and give him a responsibility. The fellow was placed at the very center of the activities and thus given full exposure to the gospel. Of course, she would never entrust a major responsibility to a student until he made a profession of faith. But her group was spiritually strong, and Teacher was confident of their own abilities to insure a biblical emphasis. So she often encouraged a student who had not yet made a decision for Christ to get active in some less essential job. She believed that working in a group meant involvement in its thinking. Once or twice this did lead to problems, but for the most part it had the desired effects. This, again, was an example of Teacher's bold and imaginative attitude toward leadership training.

The organization of the college department would have been a credit to a good-sized business firm. There was nothing loose or sporadic about it. As much authority as possible was placed in the hands of the students and they were expected to run things efficiently. The inner directorship was made up of all the top elected officers: the president, one or two men's vice-presidents, a women's vice-president, the College Hour (Sunday evening program) chairman, the social chairman and the personnel, new members, evangelism, and deputation chairmen. There were often other areas included on this board of directors, so that it sometimes numbered as many as fifteen. These directors met once a month officially, but usually every week unofficially. Their responsibilities covered every area of the department.

Next came the general cabinet whose members were appointed by the directors. This larger body was made up of the committee chairmen and their workers. Thus under the director of socials there were committee chairmen for the Christmas banquet, the Easter breakfast, each of the bi-monthly socials, the recreation nights, the summer beach parties, swims, and so on. And each chairman would in turn have his own staff.

The area of personnel was always an interesting one.

The entire membership of the department—as many as six to eight hundred names—was broken down so that under one personnel director there would be four or five captains, representing the major geographical areas of the members. Under each captain there could be as many as fifteen or twenty lieutenants, under whom came the various individuals living in his area. So on this one committee alone there were sometimes as many as sixty to a hundred people working. And they worked indeed. They had to keep tabs on every member of the department. If someone had not been in the group for two weeks, a phone call was made. If one had been absent for a longer period, he was called on in person. For special occasions every member of the group was given an invitation by phone. This committee had to keep the rolls up to date and report any changes of address or status. The director was kept busy meeting now with one captain and his team, now with another. All this labor had an enormous effect on individuals who would have otherwise felt lost in such a large group, and many students came back to the department time and again because someone knew they existed and was willing to give them a phone call to say hello.

The deputation teams were one of the most exciting areas of activity. Again, the director of deputations had assistants under him, each one in charge of a specific responsibility. There was a captain for the jail work, another for the city missions, a third for the delinquent boys' camps, another for hospitals, one for each campus in the area, and the like. And under each one of these captains were the individual teams. All the deputation teams met together on Friday nights for training. It was not uncommon to find fifty or more students on the second floor of the church gathered for three hours of study and preparation.

These training sessions were broken down into periods. First, there was a Bible study; then, lessons on how to do personal work. After this the teams met separately to talk over their specific responsibilities. Sometimes leaders of the church were brought in to these smaller meetings to advise. Then all the teams were brought back together for prayer. By this time the students had been thoroughly instructed and inspired as to what had to be done the following week: one team was going to a little town to hold street meetings; another would be speaking twice in the jails to hundreds of young people; a third was lined up to play two or three games of football in the boys' camps and then to hold services for them; yet another team was to visit fraternity row at the University of Southern California for evangelistic meetings. With all of this before them, the students felt the need of prayer. They would get down on their knees and for a half-hour to an hour would seek the Lord's guidance, asking him to direct their steps.

How many lives were transformed! There was one girl who had been invited to sit in for the evening activities even though she was not a team member. She was so thoroughly impressed with what was going on that when prayer time came she burst into tears and for the first time in her life prayed. All the horrid sins of her past came out. On and on she went, confessing, weeping, and asking for the Lord's forgiveness. There was hardly a dry eye in the room. She rose to her feet a transformed person and became one of the most active deputies.

These deputation engagements were tremendous! Once the young people rented an old truck and loaded it, plus several cars, with students and drove up to the town of

Fillmore. One of the gas station owners was a Christian, and he let them park the truck on his property. They took the sides off and transformed it into a stage complete with piano. As the people walked by, the student chorus sang and gave testimonies, while the rest of them passed out tracts and witnessed. That night, as had been prearranged, they gathered in the city's auditorium. It was filled with people who had been personally invited that afternoon, and the collegians again sang for them, gave testimonies, and one of the members preached an evangelistic sermon. Many found Christ. For that one adventure there were fifty collegians on the team.

Miss Mears' collegians went many times to the college campuses, to fraternities and sororities. Once, at the University of Southern California they organized a whole week of meetings with Dr. Wilbur Smith to speak. He chose as his topic the deity of Christ. They secured the use of the philosophy building's main hall, which seated about two hundred. They plastered the campus with posters, nearly three hundred and fifty, and put invitations in every mailbox. Announcements were made in the fraternities. Someone got hold of two late model Buick convertibles and loaded them up with students. One fellow rigged up loudspeakers on the cars, and they went up and down fraternity row at noontime playing "Onward Christian Soldiers" and blaring the news about the meetings. Around the clock prayer meetings were organized on campus for several weeks in advance. When Dr. Smith finally began his lectures, the auditorium was filled. Some of the philosophy classes dismissed for the week to attend. Dr. Smith covered the virgin birth, the miracles, the atonement, the Resurrection and the person of Christ. On the last day he wove his own testimony into his talk and gave an invitation to which several non-Christian students responded.

It is little wonder that these deputation teams produced many young ministers and lay leaders. Three of the deputation directors were Richard C. Halverson, who went on to become the minister of the Fourth Presbyterian Church in Washington, D.C., and an executive in several important organizations such as World Vision and International Christian Leadership; Louis H. Evans, Jr., who organized and built from the ground up the Bel Air Presbyterian Church near the campus of the University of California at Los Angeles, and is now at the La Jolla Presbyterian Church; and Bill Bright, the founder and president of Campus Crusade for Christ, one of the most vigorously evangelistic student movements of our time.

It was natural for Dr. Mears to be interested in the arts, and for many years a "Creative Club" met in her home. This artistic assemblage was composed of the aspiring musicians and poets in the department who wanted to express themselves, but because of the nature of their accomplishments could not be fitted into the regular program. Teacher brought them out to her home for a lovely evening and listened as each one shared what he had to offer: poems, short stories, musical compositions, architectural models, paintings, and animations. Some of these people went on to become choir directors, authors of Sunday School material, radio ministers, and the like.

The First Presbyterian Church of Hollywood is blessed with two of the country's most outstanding choir directors, Dr. Charles Hirt and his wife, Lucy. These capable, dedicated folk worked indefatigably with the youth, with the result that there are few of them who do not have a broad appreciation for all kinds of church music. Several times a year Dr. Hirt used to give training courses especially for collegians which covered everything from song leading to church musicology. He stressed the importance of knowing exactly what they wanted to accomplish in a given situation with the hymns. They learned the difference between a gospel chorus and a hymn, between the solo chosen for a worship service and one designed for a college department singspiration. They also learned how to analyze the thoughts of what they sang and to phrase the music with the meaning. Dr. Hirt explained the words of a new anthem with such clarity that many members of his choirs were first introduced to the gospel through him. This training was integrated into the activities of the college department, and not the least of its benefits was that budding ministers gained a deep appreciation for good church music. Miss Mears and Charles and Lucy Hirt were close friends, and often they could be found in Teacher's office praying over the various programs of the church, that they would honor the Lord.

Another important leadership training project was the Timothean Club. As its name implies, this was made up of those who were interested in church occupations, primarily the ministry and missions, but including Christian education and even church administration. This group was always large. It met once a month, usually with one of the ministers, with a variety of people to talk to the students, including visiting denominational leaders. The ministers were generous with their time and took a great interest in their young people. They would share their experiences with them and would freely answer their questions. There was no subject of administration they did not cover, and for several years a few of the youth at a time were permitted to observe the session and other business meetings of the church. The preachers took the pre-seminarians to their libraries and explained step by step how they prepared sermons. At times, especially on Sunday nights, they would have young men help them out in the church service. And on occasion some would go with the ministers to call on the sick or bereaved. This early training meant more to many of the youth than seminary later on, because they were involved in a live situation during younger, more formative years.

As five or six seminarians returned every year for the summer months, Miss Mears worked out an extensive training program for them. They were integrated into the church staff and had definite responsibilities to fulfill. But they were also expected to put in a number of hours every day studying. And the younger men were required to attend training sessions led by some of the older seminarians, including theology and Bible study along with Sunday School organization, evangelism and camping. Of course, they all worked in the Sunday School— teaching, organizing summer activities, participating in special seminars, working at conferences, and so forth. The Christian Education office was usually quite a madhouse during the summer as these fellows went about their work; but it was an enviable position, and pastors from other churches asked Miss Mears if their seminarians could spend a summer under her guidance.

Most of Teacher's seminarians possessed little of this world's riches. Their tuition, books and transportation expenses quickly depleted what meager funds they managed to earn, and working during the summer at the church did not afford them more than a bare subsistence income. When it was time to return from college for the summer work, one young man lacked a quarter to purchase his coach train ticket at ministerial rates until he remembered his locker key, which he turned in for his deposit—25 cents. A sigh of relief passed his lips. During the depression years, when Miss Mears' work in Hollywood was rapidly expanding, her young theologues learned their most vital lessons about complete dependence on God; and many a time they prayed "Give us this day our daily bread" with more than a passing interest.

Miss Mears always bought her budding ministers their "preacher's suit" and winter overcoat, if needed. Thus she knew they would be well groomed in a dark suit, whether in the pulpit, at a reception, or perchance a wedding. Miss Baldwin had their shirt measurements and would never miss the semi-annual Dollar Days at the National Shirt Shops.

On one occasion, Miss Mears and Miss Baldwin decked out one of the fellows with special care, for in a few days he was to be ordained. As the solemn event arrived, Homer was checked over carefully to see if he was presentable. How proud the ladies were as he stood before the congregation to pledge his fidelity to God and his service. But horrors! As the young preacher knelt for the prayer of dedication, two large holes in the bottoms of his shoes yawned at the amused front row of worshipers. Misses Mears and Baldwin had forgotten to shod his feet with something more than the preparation of the gospel. After the service, one of the men handed Miss Mears ten dollars and said, "Buy Homer a new pair of shoes."

While attending UCLA shortly after his conversion, Homer Goddard presented Miss Mears with forty dollars. Teacher, knowing the penurious state of his income, registered such surprise that he must have thought he was being accused of having robbed a bank.

"Homer, where did you get all this money?" she exclaimed.

"I saved it, Teacher," he said shyly. "I want you to

choose some boys to send to camp, because it meant so much to me when I was sent to Mount Hermon last summer. You just have to take this money, Teacher. It is my lunch money that I saved."

Another young man, Dave Cowie, had been aided in similar fashion by Teacher's generosity. One day, he phoned Miss Mears and jubilantly announced, "Teacher! I have just paid my debt! I have just bought Dick Halverson his first 'preacher's suit.'" Miss Mears always encouraged these young men to think of her gifts as a loan that they would in turn pass on to others.

Miss Mears was solicitous also about the nutritional needs of her boys. However, when a fellow had few resources, this posed a problem. She advised one student to eat his lunch at the Tick-Tock on Cahuenga at Hollywood Boulevard, because this famous restaurant at noontime provided full dinners at luncheon rates, with unlimited quantities of rolls. Teacher believed that this one good meal would see her needy charge through the day regardless of how skimpy his breakfast and supper might be, and she checked on him regularly to see that he was following her advice.

Another aspect of college department training was the prayer fellowship for the leaders, which they enjoyed on Saturday mornings. To be a director in the department demanded certain obligations: one had to be present at the Sunday morning Bible hour, attend a majority of the other meetings, and be present at the Saturday morning prayer meetings at Teacher's home.

These Saturday prayer meetings were not executive planning sessions, nor were they gab-fests. For years, right at six A.M., Teacher would already be on her knees as students trooped in to join her, or she would have her well-marked copy of Oswald Chambers' devotional book,

My Utmost for His Highest, turned to the page for the day. After reading the Word, and with very little discussion, Teacher would ask for specific requests. She would then make a few brief remarks on the greatness of God and his willingness to answer believing prayers, and down on their knees the group would go. There was no pattern to the praying, some speaking out several times in the morning. They asked the Holy Spirit to be their Leader. Teacher encouraged the students to be specific. "Don't waste words on the Lord. Tell him definitely what's on your mind." As they prayed on, the late-comers would straggle in and kneel, and before they rose there would be twenty or more students earnestly talking over with the Lord the activities of the department.

Teacher generally closed the prayer time. To hear her pray in this intimate fellowship was an unforgettable experience. She climbed right up to the bastions of heaven and threw the doors open to get a good view of God. Her prayers were filled with faith. She would "claim" things from the Lord:

Now, Father, thou hast promised that if we ask anything in thy Name and according to thy will, we can expect it. First of all, we want to see thy glory. We long to know the power of the resurrected Christ. We are tired of living humdrum, routine, empty Christian lives. Fill us with abundant life right now! We don't dare trust ourselves. As the deputation team goes up to Fillmore this afternoon, go before them! Speak through them! Give them the abundance of the power of thy Holy Spirit. And we ask for the class tomorrow morning, for these three hundred students that will be there to hear the Word. Give me wisdom to proclaim thy truth as it ought to be proclaimed. Now Father, we believe thy promises! We claim the victory which thou has said thou wilt give to us, that Christ may receive all the glory!

No account of Teacher's prayers can be committed to paper. She created a mood with her voice, her utter sincerity and her closeness with God. There was never any problem hearing her when she prayed. She was not a timid woman, even with God, and sometimes people got the distinct impression that she was ordering the Lord to do things. She was not the type to be sentimental or weepy when she prayed, but at times she could be broken before the glory of God. But usually she was like Elijah commanding the fire down from heaven. She was never formal with God. She just spoke to him as a person speaks to a friend, without worrying about grammar or niceties. The most prominent characteristic of her praying was her complete enthrallment with the Person of Christ. She knew him and he knew her; they were on speaking terms with each other and excercised this relationship freely.

Miss Mears would say, "My friends often wonder if I can hear the Lord speaking to me. Well, I suppose it must be the Lord, because I keep answering him back."

When the Word of God was being read, Teacher was all concentration. She would lean back in her red leather armchair, her head resting on her hands, her eyes closed and her brow furrowed. Any phrase that especially moved her was met with "Isn't that tremendous!" or "Now, that's what we need to learn!" or merely with her own peculiar grunt, which all present took to mean "Amen!"

These Saturday morning prayer meetings fed both spirits and bodies, but the spiritual food was usually more orthodox than the physical. Teacher loved outlandish combinations of food. The young people could hardly believe their eyes the first time they attended one of these meetings when after two hours of praying, they rose to their feet, hungry, to find spread before them—at eight o'clock in the morning!—grapefruit juice and strawberry shortcake. That was it, no more, no less! But in her later years Teacher mellowed to orange juice and rolls dripping with orange topping, which she would sop up to the last delicious drop with the remaining crumbs on her plate. (To watch her eat was a study in abundant living!) In her, refinement and breeding were tempered by gusto and speed. She was always a lady, but never prissy. The students loved it! As they sat around her beautiful glass top breakfast table and ate her delectables— the rolls going around for the fourth time—they talked and laughed about everything. King Solomon in his gold-studded banquet halls could not have had more fun.

After breakfast, most of the students would have to leave, but some would hang around, perhaps until afternoon. Teacher accomplished much in the lives of individuals on Saturday mornings. She would sit for hours counseling. When she was talking to a student, it was always understood that they were not to be interrupted. How many hours she spent with the individual members of the cabinet, listening to their problems and dreams! She was always available.

Miss Mears believed in mass evangelism, but she knew that leaders can be trained only one by one. She said, "If you want to fill a dozen milk bottles, you must not stand back and spray at them with a hose. You may get them wet, but you won't fill them. You must take them one by one."

She also believed that the leaders of a group must be separated from the other members. Sunday mornings she

Dr. Mears and Miss Baldwin took many adventurous trips together. Here they are visiting villagers in the West Indies.

This photo was taken during Miss Mears' and Miss Baldwin's first tour around the world in 1935. Miss Baldwin is on the far right.

A donkey ride at the Pyramids in Egypt.

Dr. Mears took several trips around the world in the course of her career at the First Presbyterian Church of Hollywood. Her adventures in far-off lands excited the imaginations of her youth and gave them better perspective of other peoples. Here she and Miss Baldwin go camel-riding in Egypt.

This is the first photograph taken of young seminarians who grew up in Dr. Mears' college department. L. to R., front row: Bob Ferguson, Homer Goddard, Kenneth Cook, Henrietta Mears, Dr. Stuart P. MacLennan, Cyrus Nelson, Bill Dunlap, and Kenneth Nelson; back row: Don Cole, Dick Halverson, Ed Rogers, Paul Fisk, Charles Miller, David Cowie and Jack Barnhart.

Dr. Mears always took interest in milestone events of her young people. Here she is shown with Kathy and Dale Bruner now missionary teachers in the Philippines.

Eating with gusto at a watermelon feed put on by her collegians.

Charlotte ("Mother") Atwater, shown at Dr. Mears' immediate right at a birthday party in Mother Atwater's honor, was a close friend of Dr. Mears, praying for her and personally winning many collegians to Christ. Mother Atwater would rise at five every Sunday morning and pray for several hours for God's blessing in the group.

Miss Baldwin, with an assistant, signs up members of the college department for a conference.

Dr. Mears founded a fellowship for college-career girls to introduce young women to Christ and Christian service.

Dr. Mears did much to revive interest in Sunday School work, inspiring leaders across the country at rallies—such as this one at the Moody Church—sponsored by the National Sunday School Association.

Dr. Mears was assisted by Miss Ethel May Baldwin. The two ladies worked together at the First Presbyterian Church of Hollywood for more than thirty years.

On Thanksgiving Day, 1936, Miss Baldwin, Miss Elling-husen, D. Stanley Engle, and Miss Mears held a prayer meeting in the first Gospel Light store, two blocks from the famous corner of Hollywood and Vine.

As her Sunday School grew rapidly, Dr. Mears frequently had to improvise for class space. During her career in Hollywood three new educational buildings were completed.

During early camping days Dr. Mears had to ride in on a donkey. Food was also packed in on animals. This was taken in September, 1929.

"Mount Hermon or Bust" was the slogan for these early campers, before Forest Home was acquired. Eight hundred miles round trip, Mount Hermon was too far away from Hollywood to serve as the camp site for Dr. Mears' youth.

Dr. Mears addresses a youth conference at Forest Home.

Dr. Mears was always available for counseling; she personally led thousands to Christ.

Dr. Mears always brought in outstanding Christian leaders for her conferences at Forest Home. Here she is shown with Dr. J. B. Phillips, famous translator of the New Testament. Starting with the back row from L. to R., are: Bill Bright, Dr. Bob Smith, Dr. Mears, Dr. J. B. Phillips, Dale Bruner; front row: Cy Nelson, Bill Dunlap.

Decisions made during a conference at Forest Home were recorded in a Book of Remembrance, over which Dr. Mears usually presided. She believed that writing one's name down after public affirmation of a decision helped crystalize it in the mind.

The Gospel Light Leadership Training Conference at Forest Home, June, 1949: In the first row, center, are Dr. Mears, and to her left, Esther Ellinghusen, Cyrus Nelson, Mrs. Nelson, and, second from Dr. Mears' right, Dr. Wilbur Smith.

With Dr. Mears, from L. to R.: Dr. Charles E. Fuller, of the Old Fashioned Revival Hour, a close friend of Dr. Mears; and the Honorable Arthur D. Langlie, Governor of the State of Washington, at a Forest Home banquet in Hollywood.

Dr. Mears, Donn Moomaw and Billy Graham at a Forest Home banquet.

A film was made of Forest Home entitled "Decision" in which several Hollywood personalities took part. At the premiere were, front row, L. to R.: Connie Haines, Eva Pearson, Colleen Townsend, Lois Chartrand, Dr. Mears. Back row: Bob Mitchell, Charles Turner, Bill Beal, Louis Evans, Jr., L. David Cowie, and Murray Bernard.

Dr. Louis H. Evans, Sr., who succeeded Dr. MacLennan as pastor of the First Presbyterian Church of Hollywood, is shown with his father, Dr. William Evans, noted Bible teacher, and Dr. Mears at Forest Home.

The massed choirs of the First Presbyterian Church of Hollywood. Dr. Charles C. Hirt with his wife, Lucy, worked expertly with the youth of the church, providing them with a deep understanding of fine sacred music.

From L. to R.: Dr. Louis H. Evans, Sr., Dr. Mears, Dede Harvey (then a member of the college department), and Dr. Richard C. Halverson, then assistant pastor.

L. to R.: Dr. Richard C. Halverson, Dr. Mears, Dr. and Mrs. Raymond I. Lindquist. Dr. Lindquist succeeded Dr. Evans as pastor of the church and was the pastor at the time of Dr. Mears' death.

Dr. Mears heartily enjoyed laughing at herself as a teacher in her Sunday School, George Henriksen, characterizes Dr. Mears for a teachers' banquet at the church.

Dr. Mears and, to the far right, her sister Margaret, just returned from a trip around the world in 1947; Miss Margaret was her sister's constant companion in her ministry.

Dr. Mears was always a gracious hostess, frequently opening her home for parties, weddings, Bible studies and prayer meetings.

A "sermon" on the book of numbers (the telephone book): a verse-by-verse exposition of "Old Mother Hubbard!"

reserved for the class as a whole; in the Sunday School hour, the average member would not find a speed beyond his own steady pace. But on Saturday mornings with the leaders isolated, she would let them run ahead at a faster spiritual clip. The driving momentum of the class as a whole was generated from the impetus of the Saturday prayer fellowships. After praying and breakfasting together, the young people would sit around for additional hours of informal discussion of activities, seeking new ways to venture out. One of Teacher's favorite stories was that of Jesus and the frustrated disciples, where the Master told them to "launch out into the deep" for a more successful catch of fish. Teacher loved to exhort youth to plunge into the deep and adventurous waters of faith to prove the promises of God.

But here a brilliant facet of her leadership training technique was revealed: although she would pull no punches in encouraging a person to step out into new vistas of service, she refrained from defining those possibilities and from confirming any choice as the absolute will of God. She left decisions and responsibilities for them up to the individual. After the 1947 revival (described in a later chapter) two of the young leaders were challenged to visit a conference near San Francisco. Some university students in that area had organized into a fellowship called Students Concerned. They were not Christians for the most part, but were seeking reality and an answer to the problems of the world. The two young men felt they should accept an invitation from these unconverted students in order to share with them what was happening in Los Angeles. It was an open door of import that could not be lightly ignored. But to go meant for the two students a disruption in their studies and in other personal affairs. They came one Saturday, and after the regular prayer meeting, they asked Teacher what they should do.

Her only reply was, "Well, fellows, let's pray about it." So they prayed. Afterwards, they again asked her what they should do. Teacher read a few verses from the Bible and again suggested they pray, which they did. But again the fellows asked her for a decision. She said that they should pray until they were absolutely convinced one way or another. They continued to ask her to decide for them, and she continued to tell them to pray, never suggesting what she thought they should do. This procedure went on into the late afternoon, until finally the young men came to a resolute decision to go to the conference. It was their choice. She had helped them make it only in so far as she had encouraged them to seek the Lord's will for themselves.

One can imagine the restraint Teacher had to exercise, being a person of decided opinions and a professional counselor. But Miss Mears was more interested in the training of leaders than the successful accomplishment of a particular program. One of her pithy maxims was: "Many are called but few are choice." It was her desire to train young men and women to be choice before the Lord.

9

Go Climb a Mountain

Go Climb a Mountain

The other day a young business executive came to my cabin at Forest Home and said, "I don't know what it is, Miss Mears, but since I have come here, I have felt a great need in my heart." Within a few moments he found Christ as his personal Saviour. That's why we established Forest Home—that men and women might have a place from the noise and tension of the city to meet God.

—HENRIETTA MEARS

It is sometimes difficult to relate very personal and spiritual experiences that one possesses in his private storehouse of memories when these incidents have not been shared by his audience. But the many stories of happenings among the youth of the First Presbyterian Church of Hollywood, as they grew up under the mentorship of Henrietta Mears, are associated in their minds with high points of decision. Teacher wanted her young people to build up happy memories, so that their thoughts of God would be woven into the tapestries of their lives with threads of laughter, camaraderie, worship and fun. She believed it was important that a young person's camping adventures should be filled with every wholesome pursuit, so that in future years, reminiscences of camp would excite recollections of fun and friends along with God and his high calling.

The early years of camping were filled with adventure and the unexpected. In 1929 a group of 125 collegians trudged up a four mile trail to Switzers' camp, Miss Mears hiking right along with the rest of them—that was the first, and only, time she ever hiked to camp. After that she found a four footed animal—a mule—much more to her liking. The food supplies had to be transported by burro pack-train; but lest the butter melt during the long trip of the burros, one of the fellows always carried it on his back. As the moon would begin to peek over the top of the mountain, those hikers who had arrived ahead of the others would wend their way to the Stone Chapel on the point. As the beams of the flashlights revealed the hikers coming up the pathway across the canyon, those gathered on the wall of the Stone Chapel would sing their favorite choruses, listening for a reply from across the canyon. Refreshing physically and spiritually, Switzers' Chapel left rock-etched memories in the spirits of all who were fortunate enough to spend time in that place. The first part of the camp to be seen and the last to be forgotten, this unique Stone Chapel stood out as boldly in memory as it did in actuality. Perched impertinently on the lip of a ragged gorge, yet built into the solid rock of a mountain side, the Chapel itself was a monument and a parable of Christian life, daring the pit, yet held fast and strong. The first roots of the great conference work to be undertaken by Henrietta Mears were planted. One boy accepted Christ as his Saviour, one pledged her life to Christ, and one heard the call to leave work and start his school training for the ministry.

In 1930 four delegates were sent to a Mount Hermon Young People's Conference that Miss Mears had heard about. This conference ground is located in northern California over four hundred miles away. The very distance lent enchantment. These Christian "spies" brought back such glowing reports of the promised conferences that the next year eighty young collegians made the long trip, and after that no less than one hundred seventy-five found their way to that alluring spot. Mount Hermon became a place of reflection and retrospection, repentance and renewal. Our repentance and his renewal! Although Mount Hermon had long been established and well equipped, its great distance from Los Angeles precluded it from serving any but the college students.

Other camp sites were tried in an attempt to find a place that would be suitable for the increasing numbers of Miss Mears' youth. The obstacles she had to surmount were enormous, but her tenacity and determination readily overcame them. She heard about Camp Bethel near San Dimas, off Foothill Boulevard, close to Pomona. It was accessible to Los Angeles, and yet it was far enough away to discourage parents from dropping in to see their children at camp and leaving behind a bunch of homesick ones, and far enough away to discourage her collegians from running up for a meeting, instead of attending the entire conference. Yes, it had possibilities of being able to get the various age groups off by themselves and to do a constructive piece of work.

And then there was Bill Stahl. He was one of her boys who was studying to be a doctor, and during the summer months he worked for a doctor in nearby Pomona. "Why, of course, Bill can be our camp doctor," thought Miss Mears. Little did she know that the nocturnal habits of a moth would result in one crawling into the ear of a little girl, and that it would be necessary to awaken Bill about 2:00 A.M. one morning to get the flapping wings stopped and the bug out of the child's ear.

There was another matter she had considered. There wasn't much doubt but that David and Clyde would have to attend at least one summer session at the University of Southern California. "They can be at camp during the afternoon for the recreation time, and at night for the evening meetings," Miss Mears was thinking. "And then they can leave early in the morning for their classes. They can study on the way in. One can drive and one can read the material so they both can study. It is certainly fortunate that they will need the same courses!"

Yes, the distance was fine. But the facilities were another matter entirely! The main auditorium substituted as a chicken coop when not being used by humans. This camp site afforded a lovely large dust bowl, but only an enlarged bathtub swimming pool, a situation most unbearable when planning a conference for young people! With next to no facilities to work with, Miss Margaret Mears usually managed the kitchen. All the supplies had to be hauled in by car, and new supplies were purchased in La Verne during the week. To save the upholstery of the car from getting dirty or being torn, the hauling problem was solved by removing the back seat. Henrietta served as organizer, purchasing agent, disciplinarian and speaker. She had a remarkable ability to meet unexpected situations and offer solutions—an ability without which she could never have coped with the many problems that arose.

There was a young fellow with whom Miss Mears' boys had become acquainted. They would tell her about all the wonderful scientific experiments Bud Moon was using along with his Bible, and urged her to invite him to speak. He delighted everyone by shining his "magic light" around the walls of the chicken-coop auditorium. Multi-colored jewels would glisten and spring into sight as the light reached farther and farther into the corners. And he also had a new machine called a wire recorder with which he could record his voice. Then he would play back and let them hear what he had recorded; but after he erased the words, not a sound came from the wire. He referred to Matthew 12:36,37 where it tells that we shall give account of every idle word spoken, and to Luke 19:40 where Jesus said that if the people had held their peace and not shouted their hosannas that truly the very stones would have cried out. Everyone envisioned every stone holding some idle word they had said, and were so relieved when Bud explained that God would wipe out all of them when they accepted his Son, Jesus Christ, as their Saviour. All of his scientific displays were calculated to illustrate some biblical theme. Although at times even Miss Mears was fearful this youthful, imaginative scientist would send the entire camp sky high in an explosion, she delighted in his attempts to bring to her youth "sermons from science." Years later, when this scientist became known as Dr. Irwin A. Moon, director of Moody Institute of Science, Miss Mears phoned him, and said, "Now Dr. Moon for old times' sake and the many moments I have sat on the edge of being blown to bits, I want you to do this for me." He laughed heartily, knowing she had never been in safer hands, and accepted. When Miss Mears was once at the Mayo Clinic in Rochester, she chose Dr. Moon to take her place at an important missionary luncheon to bring a word picture of the world as he had seen it since those early days at Camp Bethel.

No matter what the physical condition of the camp site, the Lord was there, and the Holy Spirit wooed and won those who were to make decisions for Christ. At Camp

Bethel, Miss Mears knew that the spiritual foundation had to be sure, for most certainly the cabins up on stilts seemed most insecure. The rains came and the floods descended, literally, during the winter conference of 1936. Miss Mears and Mother Atwater could hear the rush of the water around the flimsy cabins, but had no idea how serious the flood was, and how close it came to them. They prayed all night. They had already hung blankets along the canvas sides of the cabin, and had kept the gas stove going day and night, so that they could bring the girls in to dry them out. During this memorable occasion, the dining room, which served as auditorium as well, was marooned on an island with water everywhere one looked. To get to this one dry place which was large enough to handle the group, Miss Mears had the ingenious plan to place the cars side by side so the campers could walk from one to the other without putting a foot on land—covered with more than twelve inches of water. The only problem was that there weren't quite enough cars to cover the wet area. So some of the fellows gallantly carried the girls across these last mudholes. Everything was moving along nicely until one hapless fellow stepped into a hole deceivingly covered with water, and both girl and boy went down into the deep. Dripping a miserable chocolate-colored liquid, he sputteringly tried to explain, "Honest, Miss Mears, I didn't mean to do it!" Under such circumstances how does one wash long blonde locks to get this muddy solution off a beautiful young girl without her catching pneumonia?

Miss Mears had a redemptive attitude toward discipline. Only in a most extreme case would she ever ask a parent to come and take his son home from camp; always, she would try to rehabilitate a delinquent by keeping him in the group. Her guiding principle was: "An incorrigible is not necessarily impossible." This philosophy did not mean, however, that Miss Mears precluded punishment.

Less than a mile away from Camp Bethel was a beautiful little park, which was used for picnics and ball games. But for individual use, this park lay outside the bounds of the camp. At the beginning of each conference, Miss Mears would warn one and all, "If you should decide that you just have to go to that little park down the road, just pack your suitcases, and keep on going toward home." The boys went to the park, once! As they returned, Miss Mears was waiting for them. It had flashed through her mind that many years before, in Minneapolis, a church worker had told two boys who were making a race track of the church balcony to get out and stay out. And they had done that very thing. What to do in this situation? One must remember that Hollywood youth had had but a scanty spiritual heritage, and at times discipline was not their most outstanding attribute. Miss Mears had no tradition on which to build, for camping was virtually unknown at the church. She had to set her own norms of discipline, which she usually had to bring into focus on the spot as some issue emerged. This was the moment!

The lads were brought into her cabin. She asked them if they had understood when she told them the park was out of bounds, to which they answered affirmatively. Then she carefully explained that it was not against her that they had sinned, but against the Lord, and that it was not to her that they owed an apology, but to him. This spiritual application of a disciplinary problem had its effect. The boys knelt with her and weepingly sought God's forgiveness. Their hearts were filled with joy as they realized that he forgave them, and his love was so real to them that they became a spark that ignited the faith of many others.

187

Miss Mears met every situation with a fresh and creative spontaneity. There is a difference between defending one's actions by appealing to a set of changeless rules, and finding one's guidance from the moment-by-moment leading of the Holy Spirit. No one questions the need for fixed laws if human relationships are to have any consistency; but when dealing with youth, the dynamics of their growing personalities can be stifled by an indiscriminate application of an inflexible code. *The letter killeth, but the spirit giveth life* (II Cor. 3:6) was the creative principle of Miss Mears' discipline. She leaned on the Spirit of God, not upon a static legalism. Often there was but a delicate thread showing where the one ended and the other began, but her own sensitivity to God, and to people, kept that thread from breaking.

One day some of her youth were involved in a misdemeanor. One of the fellows, as he was preparing to go to Miss Mears' cabin, was warned by his brother, "Watch out, Bill. Don't let Miss Mears pray with you, for if you do, you'll be a goner!" Bill and his friend came to Teacher, and the door was closed.

"Boys, we are going to pray about what you did this afternoon," she said. Bill was filled with great satisfaction for hadn't he been warned exactly what to look out for? As they knelt, he physically held up his fists in front of his face, ready to defend himself against Teacher's prayer. He had resolved that when Miss Mears began to pray, he was going to run out, leave the camp, and never come back to the Sunday School. A minute passed in silence, then five, ten—Teacher remained absolutely silent. The anxiety in Bill's heart grew as he sought to understand what she was trying to do.

Then Don, the other culprit, broke the tension as he blurted out, "Lord, if there is anything in my life that

188

is keeping the Holy Spirit from blessing this conference, show it to me!" Bill was thunderstruck. His own friend—his companion in guilt—had been the first to pray. Miss Mears remained silent. Bill was overcome with shame. For the first time in his life, he realized that he had the ability of free choice: he could say "no" to God if he wanted, and no one, not even Teacher, would question his decision.

"What about my life," he thought. "God wants me and I am holding back." His fists shook as he fought to control his tears. Finally, he cried out, "God, here is my life. If you want me to be a garbage collector for the honor and glory of Jesus Christ, I'll be one!"

Years later, Bill Dunlap stood before his congregation and retold this incident. "My life was changed from that moment on. My father was the founder and president of forty-two department stores. I was slated to be his heir. And if Miss Mears had prayed one word that afternoon, I would have left the camp and today would be in the business world. But she kept still and allowed God to speak to us; and I learned then that I was not responsible to her, but to Christ. And that is why I am in the ministry."

A few years ago, the fad among teenagers was to see how many human bodies could be stuffed into a telephone booth, but some of Miss Mears' first teenage campers had another technique. A great deal of noise was coming from one cabin of boys, who had no respect for the tradition of sleep. Otherwise the camp had settled down. Realizing they would never stop unless she got up and spoke to them, Miss Mears rolled out of bed, put on her red leather jacket over her pink nightgown, and marched through the darkness to the boys' cabin. Suddenly into the midst of their hilarity came Miss Mears' penetrating voice, "Boys!" Someone inside whispered, "It's Miss Mears, you guys, everyone be quiet!" As if all didn't know that already! "If I hear another sound out of this cabin, you will all go home first thing in the morning. You need to rest. We all need our rest. Now, I want absolute silence!" And she waited. Not knowing whether or not she was actually still outside their door, they remained silent. That is, as silent as possible when unscrambling a mass of mattresses and boys. She thought she heard a shuffling noise, but not a voice was raised. Then, satisfied that all would be well, Miss Mears slowly walked back to her cabin. One of her future seminarians finally revealed to her what had been going on in the cabin when they had heard her say, "Boys!" There was a mattress and a boy, a mattress and a boy, right on up to the ceiling. When she told them that she didn't want to hear another word out of any of them, they were almost suffocating, but they knew she had meant every word she had said, and no one wanted to go home in the morning. One by one they came off the top layer, dragging their mattress with them. That was the shuffling noise she had heard, but otherwise there was silence. This incident was recalled many years later as the names of those fellows came into the conversation, and Teacher mentioned that some had gone into the ministry, or ventured out to the mission field, or were serving as lay leaders in churches. She took fond delight in speaking of her "missionary sandwich."

During the early years of camping, Miss Mears would bear almost the full responsibility for the spiritual tone. As conference time approached, she would wait on the Lord to know what trend he wanted the conference to take. One time the Lord spoke to her out of Romans 6:11: *Likewise reckon ye also yourselves to be dead indeed unto sin, but alive unto God through Jesus Christ our*

Lord. And all became alive unto God. Never one to be a spectator only, Miss Mears always participated in the decisions. Another time, for instance, the words of Philippians 2:13 leapt from the page, as she besought the Lord to show her what he wanted accomplished at the conference. *For it is God who is at work within you, giving you the will and the power to achieve his purpose* (Phillips). But even with this intensive preparation, each camp demanded of her decisions for which no amount of forethought could suffice.

One evening at camp, some of her more earnest college men told Miss Mears that they were determined to pray until God would reveal himself and they would see his glory. As Moses sought a new vision for a new task, so these young men besought God to reveal himself to them in all his glory. Never discouraging them for a moment, Miss Mears simply cautioned them, saying, "Suppose God answers you, as he did Moses, *I will do this thing also that thou hast spoken: for thou hast found grace in my sight, and I know thee by name* (Exod. 33:17)—are you ready to face the consequences? Make yourselves ready to do whatever God may ask you to do!" The young men left her. Taking one of the paths, they found themselves at a dried river bed. Dropping down on their knees, they besought God to hear them and reveal himself to them. Into the morning hours they prayed, wrestling with God, until he did come to them. God had said to Moses, when he besought him to show him his glory, *Thou canst not see my face: for there shall no man see me, and live . . . it shall come to pass, while my glory passeth by . . . that I will . . . cover thee with my hand . . . And I will take away mine hand, and thou shalt see my back parts: but my face shall not be seen* (Exodus 33:20,22,23). They knew God was in that place. The light of his presence was

191

manifest in each face as they came out from the inner circle to walk the common path again.

Many things combined to make it a night never to be forgotten. One could actually feel the complete darkness all around. The star-studded heavens shone in all their majesty against an immense field of black. The campfire at Camp Bethel blinked and cast shadows, as one after another moved forward to give his testimony and throw his stick into the flames. At the end of the line stood a great hulk of a young man. As his turn came and he stepped up to the fire, every eye was focused on him. He began to speak, slowly and softly, but powerfully, explaining that he was not convinced concerning the spiritual matters which everyone else seemed to be so definite and certain about. He just could not accept these things by faith, so casting his stick into the fire, he turned and walked out into utter darkness—to seek truth, as he said. Before we could recover, Miss Mears was on her feet, praying for Bob and endeavoring to give all some assurance of his state of mind. She had two facts that she clung to tenaciously where Bob was concerned. She knew him to be utterly and completely honest. And she had the Scripture she often repeated to Bob's dear mother to give her the security she needed: *Train up a child in the way he should go: and when he is old, he will not depart from it* (Prov. 22:6). She solidly placed her faith in what God had revealed through Solomon, and she prayed, and waited—for Bob to get older, at least. She knew he had a brilliant mind, that as a child he had memorized much Scripture, and that the Lord could recall it to his mind and reveal the meaning to him.

Out of sight, but never out of her heart or prayers, Bob went to study at the University of Oxford, England. He excelled in his courses and athletics, but Teacher knew he would do that. It was news of the bull sessions which interested her most. Word came that he always took the side of Scripture in any discussion. Bob was a great one for debate and would take either side to spark the occasion. But this time the fact was that he had taken the side of Scripture. God was working!

An avid mountain climber, Bob could not resist the pull of the Continent so near at hand across the English Channel. If he saved and scrimped, he could just make it before returning home for the summer. He could bicycle through Europe, lodging inexpensively at youth hostels. The Matterhorn in the Swiss Alps beckoned with its eternal snowy cap reaching 14,780 feet into the heavens. He arose early in the morning to go out and watch a group as they got ready for a climb. Safely tied to each other, the hikers pushed forward, and the fascination of it all drew him on. Lacking the finances to join the group—his honesty would not permit him to associate himself with them—he followed at a good distance. Having no thought of going on the climb, it was as though he were in a dream when he discovered he was past the point where one stands to be an onlooker. Now he was a participator, though the other hikers were nearly out of sight. It was impossible for him to turn around and go back, though he was scantily clad and was dangerously shod in sneakers. Up into the lucent mists he climbed, exulting in the handiwork of nature, but not daring to relax for a moment to enjoy it all. Like an angry giant whose domain was being transgressed, the mountain began to fight back, closing in on the lone figure, now inching along, with only fingers for spikes and nerves for ropes. Finally, he was in the trap, and the jealous giant pulled the string. Behind him lay an impossible descent; before him an impassable crevasse. For a few icy moments he looked down the giant's yawning mouth. There hung the rope on which he would have to swing out over that bottomless abyss to touch down on the other side. Surveying his chances, he knew his cold hands might not even hold the rope, even if his arch was sufficient to reach the opposite ledge. As he watched the sun reclining toward darkness, he began to realize that he was not alone, and that this chasm was there to test not his physical prowess, but his spiritual potential. "God, if you help me make this, I'll serve you until I die," he prayed, and with that he leaped out over the abyss. The giant growled with frustration as the youth fell into the dirt on the other side, sobbing with relief, gratitude—and faith.

But to remain immobile for long would mean to freeze to the spot, so on he trudged. He caught up with the group of hikers just as they were taking time out to rest. They were amazed, to say the least, to see him and to hear his story and insisted that he join their group for the return hike.

God works in mysterious ways his wandering sons to teach. Bob returned to California for the summer following this experience, and a girl persuaded him to go up to Forest Home for a day of the College Labor Day Weekend Conference. Once again it was the night to voice decisions made during the camp. As the meeting moved along, once again Bob was in the line. Sitting on the edge of her chair, Miss Mears, along with those who had witnessed the Camp Bethel "walk-out" wondered what Bob would do this time. Throwing his stick on the fire, Bob told how he had gone out from a similar campfire in search of truth, and he had found that the only way to discover truth was by faith, simply believing God, the very thing he could not understand before. Now he was back to start experiencing faith, as a little child, and to learn that even *if we believe not, yet he abideth faithful* (II Tim. 2:13).

Instead of returning to Oxford where he still had a scholarship, Bob wanted to attend Princeton Theological Seminary. He had not decided that God had called him to the ministry; he just wanted to learn more about the faith that was in him. He filled out his application so frankly and so honestly that Dr. John Mackay was perplexed as to why this fellow was interested in attending seminary. It was not until Miss Mears gave assurance that Bob would cause no dissension in the ranks that he was admitted.

With the lost beliefs of his childhood reforming into a mature confidence in God, the young seeker took up his studies with transformed dedication. On the mountain top he had seen the glory of his Creator, not in a flash of overpowering brilliance, but in the Almighty's ability to control circumstances and to humble a doubting heart. Completing seminary, he entered the Presbyterian ministry, becoming a chaplain in the Navy during the war. When Miss Mears took a year's leave of absence from the Hollywood Presbyterian Church on account of her eyes, it was to this man's direction that she committed her Sunday School. Bob Ferguson led the work on, inspiring his co-workers, instructing the teachers, and insuring continuity.

In the early thirties before two-toned paint jobs were the vogue for cars, Miss Mears had her two door Ford repainted canary yellow and Kelly green. The paint job on this brainstorm color combination had barely dried before the Carnation Milk Company came out with the same colors on its milk trucks, so Teacher's car was dubbed, "the Milk Wagon." When someone asked her why she had chosen that particular color combination, she replied, "My college boys like it." There was always a big parade one day during the Mount Hermon Young People's Conference. They drove eight miles to Santa Cruz and the beach. Since the fabulous radio pair, Amos 'n Andy, were all the rage, Miss Mears got the "brilliant" idea to portray Amos 'n Andy and their taxicab. The Ford was subsequently turned into a taxi. Dorothy Drew Choate, Dr. MacLennan's secretary, was Amos, and Ethel May Baldwin became Andy, the chauffeur. Not to be out-done, Miss Mears padded herself out, blacked up and was the passenger. With much blaring of horns the parade wound its way down to the beach and they had the nerve to go into a fabulous ice cream parlor for one of their delightfully extravagant chocolate sundaes!

The conferences continued at Camp Bethel, Mount Hermon and Camp Radford, but none of these sites was adequate for the active camping program that Miss Mears envisioned. In the summer of 1937, while holding a high school conference at Camp Radford, Miss Mears said to Cy Nelson, the dean, "The other day Bill Irwin phoned to tell me that I should drive up to see a privately owned resort in the San Bernardino Mountains called Forest Home. He thinks this might be something we could use. When we drive in to the bank this afternoon, let's find out where it is and go up." William Irwin was a good friend of Miss Mears'; his children were in the Sunday School. He knew how long she had been looking for a camp site, but all had been either too run down, or had no buildings and would cost too much to get started, or an exorbitant price was being asked. Finishing their business at the bank, they started out to locate Forest Home Resort, as it was known. From the answers to their questions it apparently had been *the* resort in that area for many years. As they approached the tree-shaded highway coming into Forest Home, they were impressed. The coffee shop, gas station and lovely cabins in the circle by the fish pond looked inviting; then Cy turned right, up past the dining room, the soda fountain, round house and the beautiful lodge. They were so overwhelmed at the grandeur of the setting, the magnificent stone work and expensive timbers, that Miss Mears excitedly said, "Don't even bother to stop, Cy, just turn to the left of that round house and go on back down the highway. I know we can't afford all of this," and she gave a sweep of her arm. "This is just ridiculous! The buildings alone are far too elaborate for our pocketbooks, and certainly we can't begin to pay for the land." And so back they went to the responsibilities of the High School Conference that awaited them at Camp Radford, dismissing Forest Home completely from their minds.

At home once more and settling into the work at the church, Miss Mears had not had time to telephone Bill Irwin before he called her. "Did you go to look at Forest Home, Henrietta?" he inquired.

"Oh, Bill, that is the most elegant place I ever saw, but I just knew we couldn't afford it, so we didn't even get out of the car. We just drove up past all those stone buildings and turned back onto the highway at the round house. What could we ever do to run such a big place even if we could afford to buy it, and we can't afford it!" But Bill Irwin had some interesting facts to reveal. It seems that the owner was very sick and quite old, and he had to go through an operation, and it was not at all certain he could survive the operation. His son did not want to chance the possibility of having to meet the inheritance tax on a place valued at $350,000.00 at the bank. It could wipe him out completely. Bill thought

197

that a reasonable offer could be reached. The "reasonable offer" was $50,000.00, and so an option was taken.

Surveying their situation after the excitement of the moment had died down, Miss Mears wondered how even this figure—low in comparison to the investment and value, but high in those times of deep depression—could be met. "But this is the moment for action and not speculation," she thought. "The option will close before I know it. I must get people up to see Forest Home." And so the news was scattered abroad to friends to "come and see" beautiful Forest Home in the San Bernardino Mountains which some day might be our Christian Conference Center. Interest was rampant! Miss Mears' enthusiasm was always catching. They rallied to the invitation in great numbers, and rejoiced in this beauty spot just a mile high and within easy driving distance of Los Angeles. So impressed were they that they began to come to Miss Mears and insist that she put their names down on certain cabins, just in case she decided to sell them to pay for the grounds. And so the day ended, and everyone went home.

Miss Mears was left alone to think. "If I do let these folks buy these cabins, what will I use for the children and young people? The money would not even pay the price being asked, let alone leave any over to use to build dormitories. I wouldn't be as well off as I would be if I were starting with only the ground. I'd have people occupying the places my young people should have, and a debt, and still no place to hold a conference. Besides winter is almost here, and no one is interested in Forest Home now. I guess we had better let the option go."

And so they let the option go! The responsibilities rolled on and on; the months came and went, and no one seemed to remember Forest Home.

But God, as it were, was standing on the highest peak overlooking Forest Home Valley. He beheld below him tens of thousands of children playing, singing and praying. He saw youth lifting their hands to him in dedication, resolved to go from the conference grounds to preach his gospel to the world. He heard glad choruses from innumerable hearts, ringing across the glens and down the canyons. He saw here an auditorium filled with hundreds of his faithful, and there a chapel where children were kneeling in prayer. And on the mountain top God said, "I want this place for my glory to dwell in," and he reached out to the sky and culled around him the thunderclouds. All day and into the night they gathered, billowing like the smoke from an immense furnace. A moment of hushed suspense fell over the earth as nature waited for the command. Then the God of Glory thundered, his voice shaking giant boulders from their beds and causing towering pines to bend to the ground in worship. Bolts of lightning crashed like heavenly spears from cloud to cloud, unlocking the suspended floods that now swept earthward like steeds racing to war. Down the torrents fell, forming a gigantic wall of water. Nothing so disastrous had ever been seen before. Rocks roared in the swelling tide, uprooting trees, crashing against cabins, cutting into mountainsides. From wall to wall of the valley the current leaped ahead, unbridled violence following in its wake. On Forest Home Resort property three cabins down by the stream were washed away, and one was left hanging over the bank. But the rest of the property was relatively unharmed; the surrounding countryside lay in ruins.

In the silence after the storm the shrill tones of the telephone bell were heard. Bill Irwin was asking to speak to Henrietta Mears. The son of the owner of the grounds had phoned and offered Forest Home Resort for $30,-000.00. What excitement followed!

Dave Cowie and Bob Munger encouraged her to buy, pledging that they would help her through the coming years. "Oh, I know you won't," she rejoined. "You fellows will go away to your pastorates; you'll get married; and I'll be left to run the camp! God always demands one person to be responsible, and I must know if this is his will." The following days were spent in seeking divine confirmation. It finally came as Miss Mears read the Lord's promise to Joshua: *Now therefore arise, go over this Jordan, thou, and all this people, unto the land which I do give to them . . . Every place that the sole of your foot shall tread upon, that have I given unto you* (Joshua 1:2,3). In these words, she found her answer and the assurance of the seal of God's approval. A non-profit corporation known as Forest Home, Incorporated, was formed, the members being Henrietta C. Mears, John Hormel, Dr. Stewart P. MacLennan, William Irwin, and L. David Cowie. The papers were signed; God had his conference center.

That I may know him, and the power of his resurrection, and the fellowship of his sufferings, being made conformable unto his death (Phil. 3:10)—this was the first message to ring out from the pulpit of Forest Home Christian Conference Center, preached by Dr. Cortland Meyers of Boston. That was the platform on which Forest Home's ministry was to be built—the crucified and resurrected Christ living his life through the believer. "To know Christ" became the prayer of hundreds of thousands of people, who, beginning with the opening conference, traveled to Forest Home in search of the meaning of life.

10

Camping with a Purpose

Camping with a Purpose

Forest Home is not a place but an experience. The center of camping is Christ.

HENRIETTA MEARS

Henrietta Mears commanded a definite "philosophy" of camping, and this philosophy was written down in the hearts and minds of those who worked with her. "Teacher never told me to stop doing something; her command was always 'Go!'" says Jack Franck, who for a decade was director of the Christian Conference Center at Forest Home. This constant thrusting forward, characterized by her enormous energy, created for some the impression that Miss Mears made most of her important decisions on the spot, leaving little time for analysis or planning; but just the opposite was true—careful planning was always the prelude to activity.

In Forest Home faculty meetings Miss Mears frequently asked, "Why are we doing this? What are we trying to accomplish with our program?" In this way she was fulfilling one of her teaching objectives—to get her assistants to think plans through for themselves.

This is not to say that Miss Mears approached every camping problem with her mind already made up. On the contrary, each situation was met with a fresh dependence on the Holy Spirit and the dictates of common sense. And from the lessons that came through her years of trial and error, observation and experience, evolved principles for a dynamic approach to camping, which have influenced conferences and youth leaders around the world. (An example is missionary Lillian Dickson, who after visiting Forest Home and seeing how Miss Mears did things, returned to Formosa with the determination to build a "Forest Home" for her young people there.)

Miss Mears saw, first of all, the advantage of taking people aside into the marvels and mysteries of God's creation and there allowing the Creator to speak to them about himself. Surrounded by the majesty of his handiwork, the majesty of God became real. "God must have time to talk to people," she insisted. "In the city a person may hear one or two sermons a week, but at camp he is face to face with God for seven days." Her starting point was thus to take advantage of the restful, quiet, inspiring seclusion of nature in order to introduce boys and girls, men and women, to Jesus Christ.

Believing that once a person came face to face with Christ, Christ would convince him of his need for salvation, Miss Mears stepped into each conference with expectancy and excitement, igniting those about her. "God is walking in this place," she would declare. "This is holy ground. Let us be still and listen to him." From this sprang her confidence that she should give God the opportunity to work in the lives of those present. She believed that God must have freedom to speak to individuals, and that every plan should be submitted to his leading.

This waiting upon God's direction related both to those who did not as yet know Christ as Saviour and to those who were already Christians but who had no definite goals to live for. Each conference, in other words, was a Damascus Road, where people came face to face with Jesus as Saviour and Lord, where they, as did Paul, asked the crucial question: "Lord, what wilt thou have me to do?" Miss Mears wanted people to have a personal encounter with Christ.

But with all her emphasis on the individual's relationship to a personal God, she never lost sight of the camp's relationship to the church. It may seem a paradox, but even though Forest Home was not envisioned as a denominational conference center, or one belonging to a single church, its purpose was to enhance the Christian's effectiveness in his church. Because of this, a deep loyalty was built up among ministers who through the years visited Forest Home. They saw their members returning as vital witnesses and more eager to work in their churches.

Thus these two emphases—the individual and God, and the individual in his church—pervaded every activity at Forest Home.

Since the life of the church should be enhanced by a conference, the day on which a conference began had to be carefully considered. Many Christian camps begin a week-long conference on Saturday or Wednesday. Miss Mears insisted that camps begin on Sunday afternoon. Her reasons were: First, the conferee had the benefit of attending his own Sunday School and church. Beginning camp on Sunday afternoon and ending on Saturday left no opportunity for a person to get out of the habit of going to church. With her eye on the total program of the church, Miss Mears did not want camps to run competition with the Sunday School or the worship service. Starting a conference on Sunday afternoon also allowed it to begin on a higher plane. The conferees had already been to Sunday School and to a worship service before the conference began. At the First Presbyterian Church of Hollywood on Sundays when the large conferences were beginning, Dr. Evans would direct his pulpit remarks to those who that afternoon were going "up the mountain," thus setting the spiritual tone for the coming week even before the conferees left the city. And those remaining behind felt a part of what was going to happen.

And the problem of Sunday recreation was avoided. If some congregations believed that sports should not be permitted on Sundays, while others saw no issue, spending Sunday afternoon for the trip to Forest Home, with the opening meeting Sunday evening, circumvented any possible offense without raising the question.

This sensitivity to the needs and outlooks of varying churches led Miss Mears to build conferences on the broadest possible base consistent with her loyalty to Christ. Any one church's peculiarity that might needlessly offend other participating groups was not allowed, and with none was she more insistent of this than with her own people. When her students were attending Mount Hermon conferences, Miss Mears constantly lectured them, "Here you are not the First Presbyterian Church of Hollywood; you are the Mount Hermon Young People's Conference." And at Forest Home, in spite of the fact that groups from her church frequently outnumbered all other churches combined, Miss Mears integrated leaders from the other churches into the center of the programing and tried not to let her people have advantages at their expense.

The camps thereby energized each church that took part in them. And since most of the Forest Home camp weeks, especially the larger ones, were interchurch, and with that, interdenominational, the Christian community in Southern California was solidified more than would otherwise have been possible. Many had friends in other churches whom they first met at Forest Home. This interchurch fellowship led to joint evangelistic efforts in the area, but it did not lead to proselyting. If a person came to Forest Home a Methodist, he left a Methodist. Those who knew Miss Mears' thinking never believed that Forest Home was the exclusive property of the First Presbyterian Church of Hollywood. It was her vision that it belonged in spirit to all churches who wanted to use it for the glory of Christ. Forest Home thus had no denominational preferences.

One of the prominent Baptist ministers in Southern California said one year, "I have twenty-two of my young people studying in Baptist schools for the ministry. They all made their decision at Forest Home."

Because the camps were interchurch and interdenominational, they were also interracial. All college groups were invited to the College Briefing Conferences, for example, including students from Negro, Japanese, Chinese, Mexican and other churches.

At one of the early College Briefing Conferences, soon after the Second World War, there were present a young man who had flown in Hitler's *Luftwaffe* another who had flown with the Japanese, and a third who had been in the American Air Force and had bombed Germany. None of these knew of the others' presence at the camp, and none was a Christian. At the final meeting, the traditional fagot or decision time (a fagot or stick of wood was thrown on the fire by one making a decision, symbolizing his life burning for Christ), the German stood to accept Christ. The other two were so moved that they stood by him and also received the Lord. Then the three of them, with their arms around each other and the tears streaming down their faces, sang with all those present:

> Blest be the tie that binds
> Our Hearts in Christian love.

The Forest Home conferences served as a catalyst for many a revival in local churches and on campuses, and the spirit of cooperation displayed in the conferences continued as people returned to their churches. Not the least who benefited were the pastors, Sunday School superintendents, teachers, and youth directors. Perhaps most churches experience an annual summer slump: enthusiasm sags as ministers and lay leaders go on their vacations, and programs, choirs, and Sunday School classes are recessed. For those congregations that took advantage of what Forest Home had to offer just the opposite was true. Camps played such a dominant role at the First Presbyterian Church of Hollywood that summer was the high point of the year. In fact, there was so much happening from June on that the ministers staggered their vacations through the winter months, so they could be with their people at the camps. To attend the conferences was the best way to find out what was happening in the hearts of parishioners, to follow the decisions of the youth, and to get close to those who needed counseling.

Miss Mears saw the value of the conferences also in the life of the Sunday School. She encouraged her adult classes to meet together for prayer and fellowship while at camp. At the College Briefing Conferences church groups were urged to have their own prayer and testimony time at the end of the day, and it was Teacher's custom to gather her collegians in one of the lodges for this type of fellowship. Here cabinet leaders and department members were welded together in a close bond with the Lord, which produced many ideas for future enterprises. The officers for the coming year were just entering into their new positions, and these camp prayer-planning sessions helped to map out the course these leaders would follow. Old leaders also, who had become discouraged or stale in their work, received fresh inspiration and vision.

Permeating every such meeting was one word: decision. This was the crux of Miss Mears' camp philosophy. If the Sunday School was the place where people were built up in the faith, the camp was where they made their decisions. Not only did thousands make declarations for Christ under Miss Mears' ministry at Forest Home, but innumerable Christians decided on life careers while there. No college conference ever went by without several young men resolving to enter the ministry or spend their days on the mission field. One of the elders at the Hollywood Presbyterian Church said to Miss Mears, "I don't understand it. Doesn't anyone around here ever decide anything important except at Forest Home?" The answer was simple: "If you place people in an atmosphere where they feel close to God and then challenge them with his Word, they will make decisions." An added factor was that Teacher expected people to make decisions at Forest Home. Most of what she did and said was for that purpose.

Not only were churches and Sunday School classes revitalized by her conferences, but campus Bible clubs were energized and often initiated at them. Often during a testimony time students from the same school would announce their intentions to win their campus to Christ, and by the end of the week at a high school or college conference it was not uncommon to see several new Bible study groups organized for the coming school year. It was sometimes suggested that Forest Home itself should create Bible classes for the schools in the area, but this line of thought was quickly discouraged in favor of the students in conjunction with their churches taking the initiative. Forest Home was there to serve them, not to usurp their responsibilities.

The churches were also made the unit of responsibility for counselors. Some Christian camps hire counselors for the entire summer, the thought being that if a counselor is paid and remains in a given situation for the summer, he will be better trained and more efficient. Miss Mears did not agree. She wanted both counselors and conferees to be from the same churches. After all, who better understood those with problems, and their potential, than friends and fellow church members? A volunteer from a church also had a better opportunity to follow through with his people. A professional counselor would have interest in a person as long as he remained at the camp, but a counselor from the conferee's church would be able to carry on with him back home. Miss Mears stressed that as the volunteer teacher is the heart of the Sunday School, so the volunteer counselor is the heart of the camp.

But this is not to say that these unpaid volunteers were not trained; indeed they were. Again, each participating church was expected to prepare its own. At the Hollywood Presbyterian Church Miss Mears and her assistants met weeks in advance with the counselors for a given camp and covered a thorough program of training. Miss Ellinghusen, for example, prepared the counselors for her junior camps a month before the opening date. Since Miss Ellinghusen was a professional teacher for this age, she knew exactly what lay ahead of her counselors. She also invited in volunteers from other churches, and as many as forty people would meet in her home to review the conference program, the age characteristics of juniors, program responsibilities, and subject content. Miss Ellinghusen made steady assignments and expected the counselors to bring back reports, which were then discussed by all. She had her counselors examine their own relationship to Christ to make sure that they knew why they were going to the camp. It was no wonder that hundreds of juniors came to Christ during their stay in the mountains. Not the least blessed were the counselors, many of whose lives had been changed during the weeks of training.

There were of course no counselors at the college conferences, but some of the collegians were trained to lead the Bible study groups. As Miss Mears' students had group Bible studies for their weekly Wednesday evening meetings at the church, so the entire college camp had daily Bible studies conducted in much the same way. Usually after the morning platform Bible hour the entire camp would break down into small discussion units of about fifteen students each, sometimes by cabin or by church. The leaders of these units were students who had volunteered and who had been trained. These group leaders were instructed to get the other students talking about the Scripture passage that had been presented the preceding hour. These discussion times were for many the high point of the conference. Never before had they been able to ask questions about the Bible or to give their opinions. As a result dozens of collegians accepted Christ right in their group, often during the informal closing prayer time. "I had never prayed before," was a common admission, "but it seemed so natural in our small circle of friends." When a counselor heard this, he knew that he had done his job well.

It may appear an extravagant expenditure of time and personnel to train a different set of counselors for every week of a busy summer camp program. There is no doubt that to hire one group for the whole season is simpler. But at Forest Home the dividends paid off as scores of these volunteers grew into a profounder realization of their tasks as Christians.

An advantage was also found in the fact that a person who was an excellent high school counselor might be very inferior working with juniors; but with the volunteer system, counselors for each group could be chosen for maximum suitability for a given age. Thus not only was Miss Mears' Sunday School graded, but so were her camps and counselors. More work? Of course! But work was a necessary ingredient for her success.

As she put work into training counselors, so she put work into the selection of conference speakers, always managing to get the very best for her people. She flew in outstanding Christian leaders from all over the nation and the world. They came from Canada, England, Germany—it mattered not where, as long as they had a Christ-centered message. In this Miss Mears was extravagant with quality.

The first requirement of a speaker was his relationship to Christ. Teacher felt that doctrinal divergencies in speakers could be dealt with if their relationship to Christ was firm. She could have people of somewhat differing theological hues, but they had to be basically conservative. Her requisites were the deity of Christ and the infallibility of the Bible.

She did not appreciate speakers who were contentious, nor would she allow anything to sidetrack the central purpose of a conference—to win men and women to Christ and to train them for his service. She avoided conflicts and did not allow herself to be drawn into disputes. She did not believe that it was her role to hunt down liberalism, but operated on the conviction that if a person knows Christ, his doctrine will eventually head in the right direction—toward the authority of the Bible.

Starting with Christ, then, Miss Mears had a dynamic approach to conference speakers. She invited a broad spectrum of thoughts and personalities, in order to expose her young people to a variety of ideas. Being confident of her own beliefs and in God's ability to weld together divergent points of view, she did not fear differing opinions on a faculty.

And because of this conviction and her own strong will, which gave her the ability to command any situation and to make up her mind as she went along, she did not have to take refuge in previously thought-out patterns. She never viewed a set pattern as sacred. This attitude could leave conference speakers gasping for breath, for the usual task of a speaker is to find out weeks in advance what he will be talking about and how many hours he will be allotted. He can then plan out in systematic order exactly what he is going to do. But Miss Mears always demanded flexibility from her speakers, not infrequently asking them to change what they had prepared.

It was not uncommon for her to come out with this sort of analysis at an afternoon faculty meeting:

"Here it is Wednesday! The conference is half over, and what have we accomplished? Oh, the messages have been good, but we aren't getting down to business! We must have a presentation of salvation tonight." (At this point you could feel the fellow next to you slump in his chair. He had his sermon already planned for that evening!) "As I walk around these grounds and talk to the young people, I find that many of them do not know anything about Christ. Now let's pray that the Lord will

213

reveal to us who should speak this evening. This is the turning point in the conference!"

So they would pray, someone would have the unexpected responsibility of this evening's message, and dozens of young people would find Christ. Each conference was a creative experience!

This dynamic approach was most evident at the college conferences, which were Miss Mears' special interest. (The younger camps were much more programed, as were the older ones.) Henrietta Mears at a college conference was a wonderful mixture of the careful program-planner and the spontaneous improviser. She could shatter the most well-thought-through plans without warning, but always with a reason. She frequently threw aside her own ideas for the sake of something better. Often she would say that she did not want something that had already been planned. When asked what should be substituted, she might say, "Well, I don't know right now, but let's think it through and see what the Lord would have us do."

One world-famous evangelist said, "When I am invited to speak at Forest Home, I immediately exclude from my mind any message that I have already given somewhere else, and I ask the Lord to reveal to me what he wants for this particular occasion." This undoubtedly is an oversimplification, but it does illustrate a facet of the many-sided diamond of Miss Mears' leadership technique. She could say to a potential speaker: "I want you to bring the most outstanding message you have" or: "I want you to present that series on prayer I heard you give three years ago." But the planned program was never the master of Henrietta Mears; the goal was. If the target was not being reached, throw the bow and arrow away and use something else!

Every conference had to have three emphases: (1) the

acceptance of Christ as Saviour and Lord, (2) the growth of the Christian, and (3) a world vision. The first was the milk for babes; the second was meat for the mature; and the third was the task ahead, the energy for which was supplied by the first two. Whatever theme had been selected for a camp week, these were the foundation. The same was true for every age level. Christian camping was first of all Christian. A conference for children was not just a week of baby-sitting in the mountains; it was a golden opportunity to teach them the wonders of God's plan for their lives. (These fundamentals were of course applied differently for every age.)

The Bible hour, whether for children or for adults, was the pillar around which the rest of the edifice was built. This hour was usually given priority in the morning when minds were fresh. Sometimes not only were group discussions co-ordinated with it, but so were printed materials, notebooks, suggested readings, question times, and the like. For the high school camps on down the children met by cabins and discussed what had just been brought out by the conference Bible teacher. Although the platform hours could be shifted to satisfy immediate needs, the Bible hour was rarely changed. It was the anchor which held the other hours at home port.

Miss Mears saw the individual at the heart of the group, and as a result each camp was person-centered. At times the college conference would have over a thousand present, but the individual was never lost sight of. The small discussion groups, with the individual church prayer meetings, helped. For such large camps the faculty was deliberately expanded so that there would be enough faculty counselors to meet the needs. This might mean that a given faculty member would have only one opportunity to speak, although usually he had more; but every speaker was instructed that his first responsibility was to counsel and his second to preach.

Another technique to individualize the conference was to hold special seminars. If there were three meeting periods in the morning, the camp would be broken down into seminars during the second one. If only two hours were set aside for meetings in the morning—a more relaxed pace—then the seminars met in the afternoon. These seminars covered a wide range of subjects: "How to Do Personal Work," "The Ministry of the Holy Spirit," "How to Lead a Bible Study," "The Doctrine of the Scriptures," "The Art of Prayer," "The Book of Hebrews," "Your Missionary Calling," and the like. (Missionaries were on hand to discuss their fields with any interested students.) Sometimes these seminars ran for a three-day course and then began again in mid-week with a different audience. At times there were not only morning seminars but also duplicate afternoon ones, repeating the morning discussion for a new class. Thus during a week one conferee could take in a complete course in four different topics. It was not uncommon for the most outstanding leaders to come to conferences merely to conduct these seminars and then to spend the rest of their time counseling, without ever appearing before the conference as a whole. All this created a sense of intimacy. It was a marvelous sight when nearly a thousand collegians gathered in the main hall and overflowed it to sing the songs of Zion and hear the Word of God, but it was even more significant to watch them gather in small clusters with the leaders, or by themselves, to pray and to talk person to person. The main meetings were the backdrop; but the drama was played on center stage by individuals who worked with other individuals.

Miss Mears also appreciated the fact that people came

to a conference to have fun. No matter what age group, they had to be given plenty of time to enjoy the outdoors and to work off their energies. This was not a mere expedient, but a part of the spiritual program of the camp. Recreational chairmen were carefully selected, and the play periods were guarded from being infringed upon by some extra meeting. Usually the entire afternoon was available for recreation, competitions were encouraged at the younger camps, and trophies were presented to winning basketball, football or baseball teams. Teacher often took an enthusiastic part in planning and watching such events. And knowing that people love to be with their friends, she made sure that social times were built into the schedule.

The evening platform hour was after dinner, the other platform hour being right before lunch. Since the evening meeting was usually the most important time for a public challenge for decisions, many of the conferees would afterwards go to the prayer chapel or to some other place for quiet thought. Sometimes the churches would gather together in prayer groups as explained above. But most of the campers would filter down to the Club House for a soda or a hamburger, and there "spontaneous" sings would break out. And right in the middle would be Henrietta Mears, downing a banana split with gusto and singing at the top of her voice.

These Club House sings seemed to the uninitiated to be spur-of-the-moment. But those close to Teacher knew that they were calculated. She made sure that several good song leaders and at least one pianist "just happened" to be there to get things started. A couple of soloists or someone with a guitar was added. With her eagle eye, Teacher would point out to her leaders those students wandering around the campus who were not coming to

the sing, and she would hustle the leaders off to corral
them into the Club House, especially if they had not made
a decision for the Lord. In the informality of these sings,
Teacher would call upon somebody she knew in this
fashion: "Sam, I know what has happened in your life in
these last twenty-four hours, and I wonder if you wouldn't
like to share it with the others." Sam had probably been
at Teacher's cabin for counseling; now he began to tell
how he had accepted Christ. A few more testimonies
around the sodas, a prayer song or two, and Teacher
would give an invitation. It is wonderful how the smell
of onions and root beer and the fellowship of one's friends
help make the gospel more palatable!

Afterwards a string of students might follow Teacher
to her cabin for a prayer meeting. Not infrequently one
of the speakers or counselors, feeling the need for a
fresher, more vital walk with the Lord, would ask her to
pray with him.

This sort of intensive but informal planning helped
break down the resistance of those who knew all about
church but nothing about a personal walk with Christ.

Another aspect of this emphasis on the individual—
one that very few people knew about but all benefited
from—was carried out by Miss Mears' indefatigable assistant, Ethel May Baldwin. For weeks prior to each
conference Miss Baldwin worked over the applicants'
registration cards, matching names and interests for cabin
placements. It staggers the mind to think of the amount
of work that went into this behind-the-scenes labor. Camps
averaged from four hundred to a thousand people, the
responsibility for whom was repeated several weeks
throughout a hectic summer. Miss Baldwin has an astounding IBM memory. Taking names not only from her church,
but from other groups, she could calculate interests, per-

sonalities, likes and dislikes, and match them into cabins. This ability was built up through many years of just plain being interested in people.

Sometimes her helpers would marvel at things she would say: "These girls belong to the same sorority and ought to be housed together . . . Let's see if there are more from this small college in the registration from other churches . . . Now here are two fellows that should room together; they both like surfing. This is a bad situation: everyone in this cabin is a new Christian. They could easily get off the track. Let's stick one or two older Christian fellows with them to help them along." When the conferees came through the registration line, all they knew was that they had been assigned Cabin 34 or No. 87, but they didn't have the faintest inkling why.

Miss Baldwin and her staff also took care of the enormous transportation problems of moving hundreds of people up and down the mountain. Their tasks were herculean. One bright morning one of the college fellows walked into her office (after she and her helpers had been up all night) cheerfully saying, "Isn't it a beautiful day! Just think, our college conference begins tomorrow afternoon!" He was greeted by a room full of bleary-eyed stares. One of the girls began to cry and ran out into the hall. No one said anything. They didn't have to. The tables piled high with cards, cabin sheets, transportation schedules and telephone directories spoke eloquently for these faithful and unheralded workers.

The emphasis on the individual was not by chance. Miss Mears was never impressed by crowds. "To get a crowd is the easiest thing to do," she would say. "If you want a group of boys, throw a hamburger-feed. Anyone can get an organ-grinder and a monkey and have a crowd. It's what you do with them that tells the tale.

It is the individual who counts. One man, Luther, started a Reformation in Germany. One man, Moses, led the children of Israel out of Egypt. One man, Paul, carried the gospel to the Roman Empire. God always works through the individual." Teacher always asked, "Who is going?"—and let the numbers take care of themselves.

Those who had the privilege of working with Miss Mears knew that a conglomeration of top speakers, with hundreds of conferees, did not make a successful conference. It helped to have a well-planned program, and prayer and hard work brought all into order. But there had to be at least one person aflame with a vision of God's purpose. But at Forest Home this was Henrietta Mears, even though she at times made mistakes. She was a chosen vessel of the Lord, whom he used at conferences in marvelous ways. Many a time when a conference was going along well and the rest of the faculty members were satisfied, Miss Mears set off a bomb, blowing their complacency sky high. If you had asked the average faculty member if he thought anything was lacking, he would probably have said, "No." After fifteen minutes with Teacher during one of her complacency-blasting sessions, you would come to the conclusion that something was very wrong. What was needed? There was not enough emphasis on the power of the Holy Spirit. What had been said about God's concern for the lost? The morning Bible studies weren't vital enough. The conference was drifting without a purpose. They had to pray more as a faculty. The testimony times were stale. They were rehashing worn-out ideas. The conference needed something fresh, alive. In short, Moses was on the mountain top but as yet had not seen the afterglow of God's glory.

Miss Mears was always reaching toward the limitless infinite possibilities of her God. Her Christ was the one who said, *Behold, I will do a new thing; . . . shall ye not know it?* (Isa. 43:19; I Cor. 2:9). She wanted to hear; she wanted to know what more this omnipotent God was capable of.

One afternoon a disastrous rainstorm hit Forest Home. The water was pouring down in catastrophic torrents. Danger hung in the air. Miss Mears gathered several people in her cabin to pray, not knowing exactly what for. After the storm subsided, it was discovered that a huge boulder had been washed down the mountainside directly toward the main water tank, but it had stopped a foot before making destructive contact. This was but a minor miracle in comparison to what God had planned for the ministry of Henrietta Mears at Forest Home.

11

Expendable

Expendable

"Perhaps you have come into the kingdom for such a time as this." I could not forget these words spoken to Queen Esther by her uncle. I was overcome with a sense of destiny, of crisis, of God's speaking to me. All of my ministry was now in a different light. "If I perish, I perish!" But as I returned from Europe, I knew that God had called me into the kingdom for the hour.

—HENRIETTA MEARS

The ashes of a scorched era were still falling on a frightened humanity. Half-alive, mankind had barely staggered out of the night of Auschwitz and Dachau only to be greeted by the dawning fears of atomic annihilation. One year had scarcely given the world enough time to clear away the rubble of Berlin, London and Nagasaki, and begin to reorganize its peace; but already the shadows of Armageddon were lengthening across the nations, as rumors of World War III filled the ears of a terrified globe.

Young men returning from battlefields where they had given a final salute to fallen comrades, were filled with apprehension about the future. Many did not believe the fire was really out; its smoldering glow flickered along

225

their path as they searched for a surer guarantee of peace than that which their fathers had known.

In 1946, Henrietta and Margaret Mears were in South America enjoying a year's leave from their responsibilities in Hollywood. The war years had taken their toll. With diminishing male leadership for her Sunday School and faced with the increased responsibilities of ministering to servicemen, comforting those bereft of sons, and cheering anxious parents, Miss Mears was facing exhaustion and possible loss of sight. On the calm beaches of Brazil, she sought to recoup her energies. As her strength returned and Americans began receiving visas for Europe—closed to tourists until late 1946—Miss Mears began to think about visiting the fields of war where hundreds of her college boys had served.

"Impossible!" was the first response of the American ambassador in Rio de Janeiro. "Only official persons are receiving visas to Europe."

"But I am official," Miss Mears remonstrated. "Over seven hundred young men from our church fought in Europe, and I want to see for myself what conditions prevail there, so I can better counsel them as they return home."

Her logic was not lost on the ambassador, who spent an entire afternoon making long distance calls on Miss Mears' behalf. As the days passed while Henrietta and Margaret were waiting for a decision, they went to see films of the Nuremberg trials. Finally, after wearily pursuing their visas and travel papers in all the necessary embassies, they obtained the decisive permit from the American ambassador and boarded their ship, fatigued from all of their last minute preparations but satisfied that they were on their way to Europe. Margaret lay in bed with a severe cold. Henrietta spent most of the days on the ship resting, reading her Bible, and praying, not realizing that God was preparing her for the most significant work of her life.

Her eating companion on board was a young French woman whose entire family had been killed during the war. As the Mears sisters reached France, this tragedy was so often repeated that their minds staggered with disbelief. Europe stretched before them like an endless cemetery: ruined buildings and ravaged lives were melted into a giant caldron of fear and despair. Miss Mears wept as she saw the cities she had once known as gay and majestic—Rome, Brussels, Paris, Berlin—now broken and gray, seething with crime and confusion. Children were playing in the ruins and occasionally triggering an unexploded bomb; women were lined up at relief food kitchens; their soldier-husbands were limping back to homes made of shattered bricks and fallen beams; displaced persons searched for loved ones; and the aged sat silently, their eyes glazed with hopeless terror. It seemed to Miss Mears that what had been a sparkling ice palace was now melted into a brown slush.

As she traveled from one devastated country to another, Miss Mears recorded her impressions. While in Germany, in early 1947, she wrote:

It is terrible to think of that which has come upon Europe! Nine people live in one room with clothes but rags and with no money, no shoes, no food. Two out of three have T.B. Europe is prostrate, humbled and ravaged. There are over five million homeless orphans, bewildered and afraid. Their heads are often shaven as a precaution against lice and other pests. One sees children who have not only lost a daddy and a mother, but also a leg or an arm.

There are other millions of displaced persons, many of them Christians. In helping Europe's suffering multitudes, our Christian agencies are having the opportunity to take the gospel message into many camps for the homeless. The Christians have suffered indescribably for their faith. Their convictions have brought them persecution and privation beyond those which men of lesser scruples endure. Europe is on the brink of starvation. Last spring the floods and then the drought of summer resulted in scant harvests. Wheat and rye are 200,000,000 bushels under last year, when hunger was widespread. The meager bread rations have been cut further in Britain, France, Holland, Italy and Sweden.

Germany is fallen, but her fall was not cataclysmic; it had been growing for years. Rationalism, secularism, the cult of the scientific, the worship of man, relativistic ethics—all these led to the godless society of Adolph Hitler, who placed no authority above himself. He told the women that the highest service they could render was to sleep with German soldiers. Everything sacred was violated. But since this is a moral universe and God is at the center, he would not let this continue without judgment. God has brought a punishment on the nations that no one can imagine. Peoples that divorce themselves from God experience his judgment. Out of 37 civilizations, only 7 still exist. God judges nations. When character fails, nations fall.

But the same processes that brought Germany low are working in the United States today. Sixteen out of every 17 leading educators have repudiated Christian principles, and there is a growth of this repudiation in intellectual circles. Among our G.I.'s the medics and the chaplains here tell us that 60 to 80% are immoral. What has happened to these boys—lining up outside brothels? But in America we see divorce and drunkenness increasing. What is happening to our world?—crime, ruthlessness, killing, mass starvation, mass bombing, mass exportation of slaves! And there is no penitence among the nations today!

Germany is a vacuum; Nazism has left it with nothing. But communism is reaching into the vacuum. Catholicism, too, is stepping in with a definite social program. For the most part, however, disillusionment and undefined godlessness have taken over. Hardly anyone goes to church. We are in an era of spiritual revolution. Men are hating culture and religion. They are rebelling against God. The same is true of the other countries. Fifteen per cent of the men in Britain go to church. Britain has forgotten God. In a city of 100,000, only 100 young people are in a church. Thirty million out of 45,000,000 in France profess no religion.

But like the fabled phoenix bird that was supposed to rise from its own ashes to live again, Henrietta Mears saw a renewed vision of the omnipotent God ascending from the ruins that lay about her. As she and Margaret stepped on the boat to return to America, Miss Mears felt a growing awareness of God's leading. The days on the high seas were passed in quiet meditation. She began to read the story of Queen Esther. She was impressed with the seeming hopelessness of the situation when the decree had gone out for the Jews to be annihilated. Was not this as much of a threat as the crisis now facing the postwar world? Miss Mears continued to read how Mordecai told Esther to intercede before the king on behalf of her people, and how Esther reminded her uncle that if one presented himself before the king without invitation, it might mean death. Then Miss Mears came to the words that became her guiding inspiration through the demanding months that lay ahead:

Then Mordecai commanded to answer Esther, Think not with thyself that thou shalt escape in the king's house, more than all the Jews. For if thou altogether holdest thy peace at this time, then shall there enlargement and deliverance arise to the Jews from another place; but thou and thy father's house shall be destroyed: and who knoweth whether thou art come to the kingdom for such a time as this?

Then Esther bade them return Mordecai this answer, Go, gather together all the Jews that are present in Shushan, and fast ye for me, and neither eat nor drink three days, night or day: I also and my maidens will fast likewise; and so will I go in unto the king, which is not according to the law: and if I perish, I perish (Esther 4:13-16).

Although once again involved with her many tasks in Hollywood, Miss Mears felt she was being moved forward by an unseen hand. She had known power in her life before, but this was something beyond any previous experience. Her messages were filled with urgency. She spoke of what she had witnessed in Europe and what she thought was God's solution to the chaos. Those about her saw a vitality and commitment in her that they had not known before. She was living on the tiptoe of expectancy, but what she was expecting was not yet clear.

As the summer of 1947 approached, and as the international situation became more confused and threatening, Miss Mears and those working with her began to pray with increased earnestness that God would reveal what they were to do. On Tuesday night, June 24, 1947, during the Gospel Light Teacher's Training Conference at Forest Home, the dam broke and the power was released. Miss Mears ascended the platform with a controlling sense of God's presence. As the hundreds of Sunday School workers, pastors and young seminarians listened, she spelled out all that she had seen abroad.

The seeds of destruction had been long in bringing forth their fruit. Atheism and moral expedience had been at work for centuries before Hitler's rise to power. There is no mystery as to what has happened to Germany. It can all be traced out step by step. And the same is taking place in America today. There must be a Christian answer to the growing menace of communism. Leaders are predicting that within another generation or sooner we will have entered World War III, which could bring an end to civilization. God has an answer. Jesus said that we must make disciples of all men. We are to take his gospel to the ends of the earth. We must become evangelists, even though evangelism is not recognized in our day as a valid program. And we must present the full doctrine of Christian truth. God is looking for men and women of total commitment. During the war, men of special courage were called upon for difficult assignments; often these volunteers did not return. They were called "expendables." We must be expendables for Christ.

On and on she spoke, emphasizing the need for revival, for prayer, and for renewed interest in the Word.

"If we fail God's call to us tonight, we will be held responsible."

At this Teacher's Conference were four young men who were destined to take this urgent appeal to millions of others: Rev. Richard C. Halverson, then assistant pastor at the Hollywood Presbyterian Church; Louis H. Evans, Jr., the pastor's son and the president of the college department; John L. Franck, one of Miss Mears' assistants in the Sunday School; and William R. Bright, who but a few months before had accepted Christ as Saviour. After Miss Mears' Tuesday evening message, these four young men, along with several others, asked her if they could meet for prayer in her cabin. As they knelt, they were overcome by a sense of helplessness and inadequacy. They prayed on into the late hours of the night, confessing sin, asking God for guidance, and seeking the reality and power of the Holy Spirit. There was much weeping and crying out to the Lord. At times, no one prayed as God spoke to them.

Then, the fire fell. However it can be explained, God answered their prayer with a vision. They saw before them the college campuses of the world, teeming with unsaved students, who held in their hands the power to change the world. The college campuses—they were the key to world leadership, to world revival! Within two months, according to the camp schedule, the collegians of First Presbyterian Church of Hollywood were to come to Forest Home for their annual week-end summer conference. But a week end was not long enough! And only one church's group could not fulfill the vision: All the campuses of America had to be reached! But the conference was only two months away, and no advertisement had yet been prepared. Besides, a week-long college conference had never been tried before. Who would be the speakers? How could they reach enough collegians to make it worthwhile? Everything seemed to be breaking in on Miss Mears and her collegians at once. Their thoughts were rushing together like waves whipped by the wind, crashing against the rocks. The vision had come; God had spoken; and Miss Mears and the four young men went out in the early morning transformed, commissioned, expendable. Theirs was a world to conquer for Christ.

The next morning they met again in Teacher's cabin. Again, urgency prevailed in their prayers. By this time, others in the camp had heard that something was afoot. Now, less than twenty-four hours after the initial breakthrough of power, Miss Mears and these four young men began to organize their thoughts. They prayed and talked throughout the morning and on into the afternoon. First they laid plans for the coming college conference: It was to last eight days and as many collegians as possible were to be invited. Special letters were to be written to hundreds across the country. Churches had to be visited, pastors informed, youth leaders inspired. Other conferences came into view, especially the approaching high-school camp. They, too, had to be brought into this vision. There was work to be done, and it had to be done in a hurry.

That evening, Miss Mears and these four young men returned to Hollywood to speak at the college department's Wednesday evening prayer meeting. As Miss Mears entered the room, one of those present said to another, "I have never know before what it meant in the book of Exodus where it describes Moses' face shining with the glory of God, but now I see: Look at Teacher's face!" Jack Franck, Lou Evans, Dick Halverson and Bill Bright gave their testimonies of what had happened the previous night at Forest Home, telling about their vision to have a conference for collegians from across the nation. The word "briefing" was added to the title of the conference: as, during the war when the soldiers had been briefed before their missions, so the College Briefing Conference was to prepare men and women to go out commissioned and trained to win the world to Christ. Then Miss Mears spoke, reiterating her remarks of the night before. She spoke with the authority of a person who had just stepped from the presence of God. There was nothing hysterical or histrionic in her manner, nor was there anything calculated or "put on"; she was a prophetess declaring the mind of God to men. The vision was imparted to her college department, and they responded by pledging to work around the clock that other students might know what was happening and might come to the Briefing Conference.

One cannot adequately describe the pellmell, hectic thrill of those days. It was like running at top speed through a forest in the dead of night without any light, yet knowing perfectly well just where to turn, where the rocks were, where the path led. Their course was unknown, none of them having ever traveled it before. Even Teacher, with all her wealth of spiritual experiences, was astonished at the sudden demands God was imposing on them. But an inner confidence illumined her. Men are capable of breaking old patterns and striking out into the unknown if they have faith. It does not matter if they know the way, as long as they know Him who leads. And this was the conviction that was for Miss Mears and her collegians their pillar of cloud by day and their pillar of fire by night. When men know God, anything is possible.

One of the brochures sent out at this time bore this statement:

A Call to Arms: In the nineteenth century, God chose through Dwight L. Moody sixty Oxford University students as missionaries to carry the Gospel of Jesus Christ to the whole world. In this twentieth century, He is calling for greater numbers. Youth from all walks of life, from our colleges and universities, from our businesses and industries, must go forth to carry this same Gospel to millions still in darkness.

As the days rushed toward the opening of the Briefing Conference, other churches were informed by deputation teams going out from the College Department of the Hollywood Presbyterian Church. One week after the initial prayer meeting at Forest Home, Miss Mears, along with the original four young men and one other, drove to the Mount Hermon Conference Center near Santa Cruz, California, where a high school camp was in progress. At this gathering were more young men that had been trained in Miss Mears' class: Homer Goddard, Bob Ferguson, Bob Munger, Bill Dunlap and Cyrus N. Nelson, Mount Hermon's conference director at the time. As the deputation from Hollywood told these leaders at the Mount Hermon camp what had happened at Forest Home, the Spirit of God fell again bringing confession and dedication. It was decided to have the deputation team speak to the entire conference that evening. Before an audience of nearly one thousand teenagers and older guests, the four young men gave their testimonies and Miss Mears spoke. Hundreds came forward to dedicate their lives as expendables for Christ. But there was no time to stay at Mount Hermon. The deputees left that night to return to Hollywood. As they came over the Grapevine Highway and began the descent into the Los Angeles valley, they had their devotions, one praying as another drove. The early morning rays were faintly breaking through the night mists, and a new era in Christian missions was beginning.

How gracious God is! He fashioned vessels of clay to bear floods of glory. This notice appeared in some of the literature that was printed in those days, promoting the approaching college conference:

The Answer Has Come: *And it shall come to pass in the last days, saith God, I will pour out my Spirit upon all flesh: and your sons and your daughters shall prophesy, and your young men shall see visions and your old men shall dream dreams!* We believe that this day has come. Now, if ever, is the time for God again to speak and to revive his people.

God has spoken. The revival has started. On Tuesday night, June 24, at the Forest Home Christian Conference Grounds in the beautiful San Bernardino Mountains of California, the Holy Spirit spoke to a small group as they knelt in prayer in Miss Henrietta Mears' cabin. He gave them a vision with a plan for world-wide evangelism, filling them with the power of the Spirit in a manner not unlike the experience of the disciples at Pentecost. The Holy Spirit has continued to lead. Great and mighty things have been done since that unforgettable night a few short weeks ago.

There is continued evidence that this revival is the work of the Holy Spirit and not something conjured up in the minds of men. This has been demonstrated by the fact that this experience was followed by personal confession of sins by individuals in great num-

236

bers and complete consecration of life on the part of many heretofore lukewarm Christians. Such action must necessarily precede any great religious movement, thereby providing "cleansed vessels" through which the Holy Spirit may work.

The tragedy of our times is that we live in a militantly pagan world. Social, economic, political, and spiritual chaos has overwhelmed world leaders, and the urgency of the hour has brought God's people to their knees in one last plea. God, in his tender mercy and loving kindness, has granted a revival to stave off what many of our leading statesmen have termed "the complete annihilation of civilization."

This message was carried across the nation. Hundreds of telephone calls were made to pastors and their youth. Brochures were quickly written and printed by the thousands. Miss Mears herself wrote innumerable letters to young people, encouraging them to prepare themselves at the Briefing Conference for whatever God wanted. Here is a condensed example of the type of appeal she made:

Dear Don:

I need you and God needs you! I have come back from Europe and South America with an overwhelming sense of the crisis hour in which we live. The needs of the world are appalling. I believe, Don, that you are a young man of destiny, for who knows but that "you have come into the kingdom for just such a time as this." I believe God has made no mistake and that He has a plan for you in this hour.

As never before God is calling for expendables. He is watching for men to match the mountains of opportunity; he is looking for youth who will say, "I will face this hour and find my place in it, and if I perish, I perish." We need men who will put God first.

Don, you are among those we are counting on. Gear yourself into the group, and help us achieve something for God in this hour. I would that we had young men driven along by a mighty vision of what God could do if only He possesesd them. I believe young men of today are going to do things that will stagger this generation, but all this will pass. We must have young men to deal with things not of time, but of eternity.

Don, come to the college department and help us! I say again, we need you desperately. The task before us is for the many, not the few.

I do want you to come to our College Briefing Conference and sit around the table with us and discover how we can best serve in this day. We must have plans definite and workable. The conference is solely for briefing. Don, I am counting on you.

Yours in His service,
Henrietta C. Mears

Day after day the work continued. At times there was genuine fear for Miss Mears' health. She was pushing herself as never before. From early morning to late at night, she and her staff wrote, traveled, phoned, interviewed, prayed, spoke to churches, talked with pastors, organized deputation teams, programed meetings, worked on housing for the conference, and, in addition to all this, kept up with the "normal" summer pace at the church and at Forest Home, where a new camp for several hundred people had to be planned each week.

There are many theories about revivals, and certainly God is never limited to one pattern when he decides to act; but it was obvious by this time that Henrietta Mears did not believe in passive participation. In her mind, revival meant organization, planning and work. However, through all this expenditure of energy and time, she never lost her perspective. Her own daily Bible reading and prayer time was never sacrificed. Indeed, each responsibility she had she carefully weighed before the Lord in advance of undertaking it. She knew what to do because she believed God had told her to do it. During the busiest day, when dozens of major decisions were yet unresolved in her office, Teacher and her staff would take time to pray, perhaps for an hour or more. This keen sense of balance between communion with God and activity was one of the most instructive lessons to be learned from the 1947 revival. Many Christians receive a vision of what God wants, but then they wait for God to do the work. When nothing happens they become discouraged, and soon what they thought was a vision leaves them. On the other hand, there are those who work and plan, but to no avail, because there is no vision guiding them. Miss Mears showed how to release unlimited energy and power by combining both of these fissionable elements.

All during these two hectic preparatory months, lives were being transformed by the Spirit of God. Even those who had been dedicated Christians, having actively engaged in the Lord's work for years, now felt a renewing of concern for world-wide evangelism and for a more meaningful walk with Christ.

On the morning following Miss Mears' initial talk at the Teacher's Conference—that is, less than twenty-four hours after the first "breakthrough" of the revival—as the young men with Miss Mears were in prayer, God gave them a concern that something definite should be drawn up to express on paper what they considered to be their responsibilities. The thought was not to start another organization, nor to formulate a confession, but simply to start guidelines, so that standards might be before them as they sought to implement the enthusiasm God had given them. This awakening began with the approaching college conference in view, and the primary aim was the immediate evangelization of the college campuses. With this before them, Miss Mears and the four younger leaders of this movement—Dick Halverson, Louis Evans, Jr., Jack Franck and Bill Bright—drew up a pledge which they incorporated under the title, The Fellowship of the Burning Heart.

The name, The Fellowship of the Burning Heart, was based on Calvin's seal which shows a hand offering a heart on fire, around which is the inscription: "My heart I give Thee, Lord, eagerly and sincerely." A brief statement of commitment was drafted, to which were added four disciplines. The whole text read:

> The name adopted by those who wish to be expendable in this program of world evangelism is the Fellowship of the Burning Heart. It has taken as its emblem the famous Calvin seal. It is composed of those college-age youth who have offered up their hearts as a sacrifice to the Lord Jesus Christ in behalf of a needy world.
>
> Believing that the urgency of the hour in which we live demands the highest type of Christian Discipleship, I desire to unite in the Fellowship of the Burning Heart by the following commitments:
>
> I am committed to the principle that Christian

Discipleship is sustained solely by God alone through His Spirit; that the abiding life of John 15 is His way of sustaining me. Therefore I pledge myself to a disciplined devotional life in which I promise through prayer, Bible study, and devotional reading, to give God not less than one continuous hour per day. (Psalm 1)

I am committed to the principle that Christian Discipleship begins with Christian character. Therefore I pledge myself to holy living, that by a life of self-denial and self-discipline, I may emulate those Christ-like qualities of chastity and virtue which will magnify the Lord. (Philippians 1:20,21)

I am committed to the principle that Christian Discipleship exercises itself principally in the winning of the lost to Christ. Therefore I pledge myself to seek every possible opportunity to witness and to witness at every opportunity to the end that I may be responsible for bringing at least one to Christ every 12 months. (Matthew 28:19; Acts 1:8)

I am committed to the principle that Christian Discipleship demands nothing less than absolute consecration to Christ. Therefore I present my body a living sacrifice, utterly abandoned to God. By this commitment, I will that God's perfect will shall find complete expression in my life; and I offer myself in all sobriety to be expendable for Christ. (Romans 12:1,2; Philippians 3:7-14)

The original leadership of the revival immediately signed this pledge; and as the deputation teams went out to other youth groups, they were invited to join the Fellowship. And the names of the concerned grew as the conference began.

From all over the country they came, expectant and skeptical, sincere and cynical, some waiting on God for blessing, others disbelieving his existence. Many came out of curiosity; most were convinced that God was already working in their hearts; few knew what to anticipate. From dozens of campuses the delegates arrived. No one could calculate how many collegians there would be. A week-long college conference had never been tried before. All Sunday afternoon the cars and buses continued to flow up the mountain, until near evening it became all too obvious that there would not be enough places to house the hundreds of conferees. Since the 1947 College Briefing Conference, beautiful new dormitories and cabins have sprung up across the mountainsides of Forest Home; but in those days, there were not enough sleeping places to accommodate over five hundred guests. The Briefing Conference was now over six hundred; but this did not daunt these collegians who responded to the housing problems with the adventurous spirit of pioneers. Many slept in their cars or out under the trees. As the students continued to pour in, greeters were on the road to welcome them and to bring them up to date on what was happening.

It was no secret that the leaders did not have a definite schedule for the week. Outstanding God-led Christian pastors had been invited to participate—Dr. Louis H. Evans, Sr., Dr. L. David Cowie, Dr. Robert B. Munger, and others—but the one rule was accepted by all that the hour-by-hour program was to be led by the Spirit of God and no leader was to speak who had not been singled out by the Spirit working through the entire faculty, chairmanned by Miss Mears. She with a few others met in prayer all the first afternoon and later marched around Victory Circle—the open-air meeting place where the early evening testimony times were held—claiming that the walls of stubbornness and disbelief would be felled by the Lord.

The first meeting of the conference began in Victory Circle as the testimonies of how God had started the movement were again told. Then all the students were invited to share their thoughts and aspirations. Some stated frankly that they could not accept such "emotional and illogical" beliefs. Others expressed their desire that God would reveal whatever he had for them. There was an overriding conviction of sin in the hearts of many of the students, as one after another stood to ask God's forgiveness for past errors and faithlessness. Some professed Christ as Saviour, often with tears.

The testimonies went on as night fell and only the stars and a fire illumined the scene. No one moved to stop the meeting which had no real leader other than the Holy Spirit. Miss Mears was overwhelmed with a realization that God was working and that the destinies of many lives were in the balance. As the testimonies continued, she slipped out—unnoticed except by a few—and returned to her cabin; there, with a handful of the faculty, she prayed for an hour that God would have complete sway over the situation. She returned to Victory Circle and found the collegians still talking about their spiritual ambitions and problems. Stepping before them, she spoke about sin, confession, forgiveness, cleansing and the Holy Spirit. She laid before them the need to be absolutely honest with God and to submit completely to his will. She asked the some 600 students to pray that God's purpose for their lives would be fulfilled. This first Victory Circle lasted over four hours, as did those on the subsequent evenings.

Throughout the conference confession of sin continued.

One young man, a husky football player well over six feet tall, began to weep uncontrollably. He confessed that he had been living a lie since he had returned from the war, having presented himself as a hero who had shot down many enemy planes; but in reality, as he now admitted, he had been washed out in flight school and had spent the war years on the ground repairing damaged aircraft. His large frame shook as he fell on the ground, his face in the dust, sobbing and asking God to forgive him. Two nights following, this lad dedicated his life to the ministry. Several years later, this dedication was brought to fruition before many of these same friends as he was ordained.

The Men's Council President at the University of Southern California gave his life to the Lord, as did many others who were campus officers. Several of the young men decided that God was calling them into the ministry or onto the foreign mission field. One fellow, who was singing tenor in the conference quartet, gave his life and talent to the Lord. Through the years following the first Briefing Conference, God honored his fidelity and opened up one door after the other, so that as this is being written, he is contracted with the Metropolitan Opera Company and other companies abroad; but he still returns to Forest Home to sing and give his testimony.

How many are the individual stories that could be told of collegians whose lives were changed at the 1947 Briefing Conference! Ministers and missionaries who today are scattered across the nation and around the world made their decisions during that week. A large map was placed at the front of the main hall, and Miss Mears encouraged young people who felt a leading to a certain country to write their names on the place. The map was left up for the entire week, during which, prayerfully and individually, students wrote where they thought God was calling them. A student from USC wrote his name on Japan and today he is serving Christ there. Dick Halverson signed China; several years after 1947 he went to the Orient and ministered to thousands of Chinese and since then has stepped into the leadership ranks of World Vision, one of the most effective of the Oriental missions. Another wrote his name on Russia. Many students who had no clear indication of a specific country initialed campuses, considering their schools their first missionary responsibility. T. Christy Wilson, Jr., recently graduated from seminary, put his name on Afghanistan, and subsequently took up teaching duties in that inaccessible nation, becoming even a tutor in the royal house.

Not all those who came to the first Briefing Conference were converted. One brilliant and cynical lad stood at Victory Circle to defy everything that was being presented. He scoffed at the idea that he was a sinner and openly disclaimed the existence of God. Naturally everyone began to pray for him, and many tried to convince him of his error. He laughed at what he thought to be the ambition of the leaders to "get my scalp on your belt." As he left the conference, unconverted, Miss Mears continued to pray for him, affirming that God was not limited to Forest Home. The week following the conference, during the echo service at the college department in Hollywood, he sat quietly as he listened to the testimonies of those who had found Christ the week before—among whom was his brother. Finally his skeptical heart was overcome by the reality of Christ's love, and he made a profession of faith. That night he returned home and began work on a lengthy thesis in which he attempted to explain why he was becoming a Christian. Miss Mears was hesitant when informed that he wanted to read his thesis to the college department, but she finally gave way to his request. Several collegians were converted after hearing his testimony. Both he and his brother have since entered into Christian service.

Eighty-seven colleges and universities from nearly every part of the country were represented at the first Briefing Conference. As the delegates returned to their campuses, they were filled with a sense of mission to win their schools to the faith. It was natural that a large contingent should have come from UCLA, since Miss Mears lived just across the street, and many of her young people studied there. As the school year opened after the Briefing Conference, UCLA continued to be a focal point for witnessing and for deputation teams. On various occasions Bible studies and prayer meetings composed of Bruins would meet in Miss Mears' home, and she encouraged every possible effort to win young men and women on this campus to Christ. In these early years, Bill Bright was in secular business, but during the '47 revival he felt God's hand leading him into campus work. He was a leader in the college department's deputation ministry, and as such he often directed the work toward the campuses. After completing seminary years at Princeton and Fuller, he continued his student-directed missionary efforts with Miss Mears' assistance. He and his wife for years lived with Miss Mears, using her home as a center for their emerging crusade. God blessed Mr. Bright's efforts, and Campus Crusade for Christ evolved into the international work it is today.

Many were the continuing blessings begun by the 1947 Briefing Conference. Among these, three stand out: the subsequent yearly college conferences, the Hollywood Christian Group, and the influence on Billy Graham.

The first Briefing Conference set the standards for what became an annual summer conflux of collegians seeking to find the will of their Master. The week-long conferences have been for almost two decades one of the most important gatherings for the inspiration and training of university students in our time. But others were being affected, too.

What armies of courageous missionaries have marched out from Forest Home, their banners flying, their voices hymning the glories of Zion, some to labor to old age, some to meet an early martyr's death. The following notice, written by his brother, Dwight, appeared recently in a book of testimonies about the heroic medical missionary, Paul Carlson, who was slain by African rebels:

> I can vividly remember a Sunday morning when I visited Paul at Forest Home conference grounds in Southern California. I was just ten years old at the time, and it was there that I was challenged to dedicate my life to God for whatever purpose he might desire. When the invitation was given to go forward and to seal whatever commitment we had made, I turned to Paul for support and asked if he would go with me. He readily agreed, and we went forward together. Paul was 15 at the time, and he subsequently reiterated his desire and willingness to serve Christ on several occasions, always with strong leaning toward the field of medical missions. In all the years that followed, with their many and varied pressures, Paul never forgot his commitment.*

Henrietta Mears' efforts at Forest Home had a powerful influence on the lives of many other youth workers across the land, one of whom was Jim Rayburn, the director of Young Life. Mr. Rayburn has frequently expressed his indebtedness to what he learned at Forest Home:

*There Was a Man, p. 31. Fleming H. Revell Company; Westwood, New Jersey, 1965. Compiled by Carl Philip Anderson.

As a young man just out of college, and beginning to work among young people, I heard of Henrietta Mears' ministry at Hollywood Presbyterian Church and particularly at Forest Home. What I heard, chiefly her continual exaltation of the person and work of Christ, her emphasis of a personal conversion experience, and a vital and dedicated relationship to Him in the Christian walk, these things were so impressive that I tried to incorporate into my work everything I heard about her way of doing things. For example, in my first young people's camps over twenty years ago I had "fagot services" solely because Miss Mears did. I knew it was right, if she did it. Through this influence upon my life, she has had a great deal to do with shaping the progress and ministry of the Young Life Campaign.

After the conference of 1947, the exuberant young people returned to tell their friends of what had taken place on the mountaintop. Louis Evans, Jr., shared his experiences with a young starlet he was dating, Colleen Townsend. She was a Mormon by her own choice and had completed a year and a half at Brigham Young University in Utah when discovered by Hollywood scouts, who catapulted her into the dazzling heights of stardom. Lou gave his testimony to the young actress who later said, "He talked about having been encountered by Christ. He was so alive and vital—I was impressed. I attended the next conference and there I too encountered this living Christ. I didn't fall on my knees or weep. I just walked by myself and dedicated my life to Him." Colleen had been attending the college department before her dedication to Christ, but now she gave herself to the kind of unselfish and gracious service of others that has characterized her life as a Christian.

There were other Hollywood personalities who were being influenced by the effects of the revival among whom were Roy Rogers, Dale Evans, Tim Spencer, and Connie Haines. Miss Mears had long sought how to reach the stars behind the celluloid curtain for Christ. Now the Spirit was bringing them to her. In 1949 some of these met in her cabin at Forest Home to pray for guidance as to how they could win their friends in the film industry to the Lord. True, Hollywood actors and actresses attended churches, but there were difficulties, one of which was their fame. Dennis Morgan and Virginia Mayo were members of the First Presbyterian Church of Hollywood, but even in the house of God they could not escape the lingering stares of the curious. Miss Mayo frequently came on Sunday morning with a hat covering most of her face. For an effective evangelistic movement to take hold among these people, a church-centered program was out of the question, especially if non-Christians were to be interested. The only solution was to hold meetings in private homes, without publicity, the guests being brought by invitation only. At all costs, the public had to be kept away.

Since Miss Mears had a home that could rival those of the Hollywood great, and since it was located in the middle of the estates of the stars, the decision was made to begin the weekly meetings there. Dr. J. Edwin Orr had been speaking at the Forest' Home conferences, and his logical and direct approach appealed to Miss Mears, who asked him to help her reach the film capital. She felt that his uncluttered, unaffected style gave room for the Holy Spirit to work. Miss Mears knew that no tricks or gimmicks could be used on a crowd who made the mastery of gimmicks their livelihood. The secret of reaching the stars was Christ crucified and resurrected, the source of abundant life; and Miss Mears believed that Dr. Orr represented this approach. The first meetings were immediately successful. Miss Mears' spacious living room was packed with the famous, many scores of whom found the Saviour, and some of whom rejected him.

What marvels of conversion resulted! Tim Spencer, the leader of the famous cowboy singing group, The Sons of the Pioneers, had for years been enslaved to drink. Finding Christ, he was transformed. He became the president of the movement which was now being called The Hollywood Christian Group.

A beautiful young dancer listened eagerly to the testimony of Colleen Townsend as they spoke together on a set. Georgia Lee, with her husband, Ralph Hoopes, was known to millions through television, but now a new life was opening up to her:

> Colleen invited me and my husband to one of the first meetings of the Hollywood Christian Group. The next week, Ralph and I were there and listened to Dick Halverson tell of his conversion, how he had sinned and then saw that not only he but everyone needed a Saviour. There was a discussion after the message in which Dr. Orr and Miss Mears explained Jesus Christ the Saviour to us, so that Christ became a reality in my life instead of just a fact in my mind.
>
> That night, I knelt to pray as usual, but in a different way I prayed that the Lord Jesus would come into my life, forgive my sins and use me to His glory. Since that night, Ralph and I studied Scripture almost every day.

Georgia Lee and Ralph Hoopes gave themselves to the

Lord with that total abandon which often characterizes the newly-converted, but their enthrallment with Christ did not lessen as they sought to serve him with increasing zeal. Ralph eventually entered the ministry, assisted by his vivacious wife—who also accepted roles in many Christian films notably some produced by Billy Graham.

The Hollywood Christian Group grew as hundreds of Hollywoodians were converted. From 1949 to 1951 Dr. Orr chaplained the group, after which it lacked the full-time leadership of one individual. Miss Mears did what she could as adviser and confidante, but her increasing illnesses in the 1950's prohibited her from sponsoring it. As the fellowship increased in size it opened its doors to others besides just the top stars—such as cameramen and technicians—and instead of meeting in exclusive homes, it moved to the banquet hall of the Knickerbocker Hotel. In this way, what had started as an exclusive movement for a few took on a broader appeal for the many. Other groups split off the central movement, so that today there are several evangelistic efforts among the movie people. Billy Graham launched his film crusades by first employing the talents of the Hollywood Christian Group. Many of the converted stars have had their testimonies published in national magazines, and some have appeared on TV and radio to tell what Christ means to them. A few have gone into the ministry.

At Forest Home, meanwhile, the schedule was increasing and the work was deepening. Miss Mears was searching for a more meaningful walk with Christ, and the influence of her quest kindled revival fires in the souls of many discouraged Christians. Billy Graham, then a little-known evangelist from the South, was invited to speak to the 1949 Briefing Conference. He agreed to come but confessed that he was so tired and apprehensive about his ministry that he would like to be merely a conferee. He was facing a crusade in the downtown section of Los Angeles, and he was plagued by doubts concerning its outcome. J. Edwin Orr was also brought to that conference. Mr. Graham told Dr. Orr and Miss Mears about the struggles through which he was going. Billy Graham spoke at the morning platform hours, and Edwin Orr in the evening, the latter stressing the ministry of the Holy Spirit. In the middle of the week, although his messages to the youth had been effective, Billy Graham came to an impasse in his conflict. In the late hours, seated by a large fish pond, he and Dr. Orr spoke and prayed together about complete surrender to God and the infilling of the Holy Spirit. The young evangelist walked off through the woods by himself, feeling as though he were in the crossfire of a raging battle. Finally, he affirmed his faith in the God of the Scriptures and prayed that he would have the strength to go on. Having reached this turning point in his concept of his work, Billy Graham launched into his first Los Angeles crusade with a surging optimism that God was going to act. And act he did. Several Hollywood notables came forward to confess Christ. The newspapers picked up the story, and overnight Billy Graham's name was flashed across the country. It would, of course, be fallacious to say that this one experience at Forest Home accounted for the success of Billy Graham, for into the life of every great man run many streams of training and conditioning. But now and then there are registered turning points, and by Billy Graham's frequent admission, this was such a turning point in his ministry. Throughout the following months and years, he frequently visited or phoned Miss Mears, seeking advice, praying with her, and informing her of new triumphs for the Cross. It is no wonder then that he was willing to make such a statement as this concerning her influence:

I have known Dr. Henrietta C. Mears for approximately fifteen years. She has had a remarkable influence, both directly and indirectly, on my life. In fact, I doubt if any other woman outside of my wife and mother has had such a marked influence. Her gracious spirit, her devotional life, her steadfastness for the simple Gospel, and her knowledge of the Bible have been a continual inspiration and amazement to me. She is certainly one of the greatest Christians I have ever known.*

At that 1949 College Briefing Conference, an afterglow of the revival fires of 1947 ignited not only Billy Graham, but scores of young men and women. The emphasis was on the Holy Spirit, and the evening messages delivered by Dr. Orr were central. There was a depth of presentation that has rarely been equaled. Dr. Orr outlined his talks with great care, explaining point by point what the Bible teaches about the ministry of the Spirit. In classroom fashion the doctrines of justification and sanctification were exhibited for even the most untutored mind to grasp. The meetings were not short, the lecture alone sometimes extending as long as two hours. But such an obstacle went generally unnoticed as the Holy Spirit convicted young people of their sins, filled them with grace, and instructed them concerning their callings. Upon the conclusion of a lecture—leaving blackboards filled with outlines and Scripture references—Dr. Orr would usually call for a period of silent reflection and quiet prayer. The presence of the Holy Spirit was so evident that no artificial thaumaturgics had to be introduced. Indeed, the

*Barbara Hudson Powers: *The Henrietta Mears Story* (Westwood, New Jersey: Fleming H. Revell Company, 1957), Introduction.

whole affair was greatly underplayed. But sophisticated collegians stood one after the other to repent of evil deeds and thoughts and to confess Christ as Lord. Dozens of young men decided for the ministry or the foreign field.

One evening Miss Mears, in the sincerest and most straightforward way possible, shared her experiences from college days when she had been searching for more significance in her Christian life. Her face was radiant as she told of finding in the Bible the simple truths of commitment, trust and fellowship with God. Many lives were changed by her testimony.

In all of what happened, certain lessons were learned: 1) Time was given for the Spirit of God to work. The evening hours were not filled with music before the message nor with other meetings afterwards. 2) Along with freedom of schedule went an expectation that God was going to do something. Most everyone believed this, although people didn't know exactly what it would be. 3) The faculty meetings were devoted primarily to prayer. Levity was out of place, as the seriousness of the mission was allowed to settle on the faculty members' hearts. There was much weeping over the lost and crying out to the Lord for blessing. 4) Miss Mears kept the purpose of the conference ever before the faculty, and conference techniques were bent or thrown out if they failed to comply with that purpose. 5) The faculty moved, thought and prayed as a unit. No matter who was speaking, the faculty was there en masse to support him. There were no prima donnas. God himself was the soloist, and no one dared to upstage him. 6) The revival began in the hearts of the faculty before it spread to the conferees. At some of the meetings, it was various faculty members who spontaneously rose to confess inadequacies. During one altar call a young minister, prominent in the group, asked Dr.

Orr to pray for him. Dr. Orr brought him to the stage and had other members of the faculty lay their hands on him, as they asked God to take over his ministry and to glorify Himself in his life. (Since then, God has honored that prayer mightily.) It was an unforgettable sight to see several college men, previously aimless dawdlers, rise to admit their frustrated existence and to surrender to the Spirit. Many such have since gone into the ministry.

In faculty meetings and in the open conference, Miss Mears lay bare her soul. She led by being led by God. She gave herself to those about her in such a way that they felt close to her innermost struggles. A comparison can be found in the writings of Paul, where often his most effective points are made as he reveals his most private thoughts, using himself as an illustration. This mood was picked up by the other faculty members with the result that there was little "preaching down" to the collegians. They were one family seeking together the heights and depths of the grace of God.

The years 1947 and 1949 were high-water marks of revival. In the ensuing years, Teacher tended to look back on them as examples of what God could do if men and women were willing to pay the price. At times it seemed as though she had fixed them in her mind as standards by which everything else had to be evaluated. But in the mid-1950's her attitude changed, and lingering triumphs of the past gave way to the exciting realities of the present. If not in service—although that was still to be considerable—then in character, she was yet to climb higher.

12

On to Glory

On to Glory

If you ever happen to see in the obituary column that Henrietta Mears has died, don't you believe it! This old body may die, but I'll be glad of that. I wouldn't want to have to go through eternity with this deteriorating one. I'll have a new body. And what will I do when I get to heaven? Well, I am going to ask the Lord to show me around. I'll want to get in a rocket ship to inspect all the galaxies he has made. And maybe he will give me a planet of my own, so that I can start building something. Oh, it's going to be so wonderful!

—HENRIETTA MEARS

It will ever be said of Teacher that she was a living example of the truth that one does not grow old; one becomes old by not growing. Teacher fed daily upon the Word, and grew according to the dictates of God. As the Lord made it clear that she was to remain at her post year after year, for over thirty years, she used to pray, "Lord, as long as you see fit to keep me in that college department, you must make me attractive to those young people, and you must give me the message for this day and age that you want them to have."

Her sister Margaret was always close at hand to remove the humdrum of daily living, giving Henrietta the opportunity to accomplish the full life the Lord had placed before her. Margaret organized the household, bought the clothes for both wardrobes, promoted Forest Home, assisted with teas and accompanied her sister to meetings. Margaret's service was all the more endearing for its artlessness and spontaneity. At the age of 72 she was still able to delight Henrietta's collegians with her views on politics, how the Korean war should be fought, the latest trends in women's styles, the UCLA football team, and liberalism—flying from one of these subjects to another in such a way that kept the young folk bursting with laughter. She had a deep reverence for things sacred, and her labor was unto God. But she had a delightful way of erupting with cold common sense when her sister's religious fervor became—in Margaret's eyes—impractical. Especially did she enjoy poking fun at the collegians when in their youthful but immature ambitions they failed to see the larger view of life. She kept their feet on the ground, as much as her sister kept their hearts in the sky. Since Miss Margaret did not drive a car, she was dependent on others to take her about. But she was usually too proud to ask one of the students for a lift. Once in a while one would see this lady, her beplumed head held as though she ruled five kingdoms, sitting at a bus stop on Hollywood Boulevard. If you offered her a ride, she would at first refuse, affirming that she enjoyed taking the bus; but in another few seconds she would be sitting beside you, probably talking about last Sunday's sermon and emphasizing what she did and did not like. This generous, quick-witted, individualistic lady was greatly loved by the collegians. They grieved, then, when five days before Christmas, 1951, while decorating the home and getting everything ready for the season, she was felled by a stroke and less than two days later slipped quietly away.

How much our faith means when we are suddenly met with the realities of life and death! How thankful we are for the knowledge of the resurrection and eternity, knowing that we shall again see our loved ones! Tragedies occurring during holidays seem the more devastating because of the seeming mockery they make of happiness. We grieve, but not as the world grieves. Faith activates confidence.

The following Wednesday at the college prayer meeting, before two hundred collegians who knew her so well, Miss Mears bore witness to her faith; and perhaps this was her finest moment.

I had thought that I would not come tonight. Then I realized what an opportunity I would be passing up if I did not come. I have been teaching you collegians for the last twenty-five years that God is able, and that he does sustain us in any situation. I am here tonight to tell you that my God is able, that he is my sufficiency at this very moment. As life passes you by, you will be going through experiences that you think you absolutely cannot endure. But God is faithful. He will not permit you to suffer a temptation which you will be incapable of bearing. And this I know, that if we will commit our way to him, and will trust in him, he will bring all these things to pass.

The history of her life for the next years was a demonstration of the rightness of this faith.

After her sister's home-going, the matter of what Teacher should do about continuing to live in the large, six bedroom home filled her thoughts. Should she sell it and move to an apartment? It did seem foolish for one woman to remain in such a large home. Yet the thought of the cramped quarters of an apartment appalled her. And of course there was always her work, toward the fulfillment of which she could use a large home. As these thoughts flitted across her mind, a good friend, desiring to help at this time of Teacher's loss, phoned and asked her if she would like to go and see a home which she was putting on the market. She knew Miss Mears liked beautiful homes. And so they went.

In Bel Air, directly across from the UCLA campus, they drove up the driveway to a house resembling a small castle. "These lovely grounds have a dramatic sweep and look so restful. And those redwood trees, the only ones in Southern California, would make an ideal meditation garden when it wasn't being used for a barbeque." Unconscious that such thoughts were passing through her mind, Miss Mears went inside. As she wandered from place to place, the thought kept coming back, "I have plenty of furniture to fill these rooms. I wouldn't have to buy a thing unless I wanted to. And that dining room—big as a football field—well, almost—my collegians would love it!" Some of these thoughts were escaping her mind and coming out of her lips until finally her friend, greatly amazed, said, "Why, Miss Mears, I didn't bring you here to sell you this house! I just thought you would enjoy seeing this beautiful place."

Not wanting to encumber herself with any "white elephant," Miss Mears set about to discover whether or not the Lord approved. No one could ever hurry her by offering the thought that someone might buy something out from under her. If that happened, then the Lord didn't want her to have it. And that was the very thing that did happen! When she learned that her "dream house" was sold, it didn't faze her. There were some speaking engagements coming up, and the conferences would occupy her full time at Forest Home, so apparently the Lord didn't want her to have the house. It was settled!

But was it settled? One day a short time later, Bill Bright casually remarked, "Miss Mears, you know that property on Sunset that you were looking at—well, there's another 'For Sale' sign on it." Then the Lord revealed that this was his plan for her life, and everything began to unfold in rapid succession. If the Lord were not in it, what would she ever do with a house that was even larger than the one she now possessed? The unfolding of the plan had begun. One of her "sons" wanted to buy the old home, in which he and all his friends, along with Miss Margaret, had enjoyed many, many happy times. Bill Bright expressed a willingness that he and his wife, Vonette, move into the new home with Miss Mears and help with the expenses, and pointed out that he could carry on his campus work from there. That settled that! And eleven years of happy association followed. Vonette was the perfect hostess and took over where Miss Margaret had left off. And thus God set his seal upon the entire venture—beyond the shadow of a doubt.

The Venetian goblets, acquired when she and Margaret had been in Europe, were a delight and pleasure to all who gazed at their beauty as they were brought to life in the lighted display cabinet; handcarved ivory from Hong Kong, India and Africa lay side by side with a pearl covered Bible and a carving of the Last Supper, in the beautiful curio cabinet, along with other objects too numerous to mention; handpainted figures of Napoleon and the Battle of Waterloo ringed a table lamp which reflected the scene in a mirror on an exquisite marble and gold table. Soon every piece of furniture and other *objets d'art* had found their place.

As some of her collegians were being shown the new home and wended their way through the delightful rooms, they arrived at Miss Mears' suite. The most intriguing, simple object to "her sons" was the black marble bathtub sunken in the middle of the floor. David Cowie burst out with, "Well, fellows, this proves it! We have matured! If not, I'd be sitting in the tub, casting for that big, shiny fish, and you'd be turning on the water!"

Then came the night when God's blessing was invoked upon this home and household, and it was dedicated to the Lord for all the plans he had for its future service. After this, Miss Mears, with the Brights, settled down to the usual task of just living, day by day doing the things before them, ministering to those who rang the doorbell, lifting voices in song and laughter with the groups that filled the rooms, knowing God was in their midst. And so, for more than a decade, this home served as a holy shrine where hundreds met the Saviour, going on their way with lighter and happier steps as they went down the stairs and out to bring their witness of the greatness and goodness of God.

Things happened in that home which read like a story-book. At first there was genuine concern that Napoleon would get knocked off the table by some awkward football player. This was more the concern of others than of Miss Mears. Her philosophy that "one would act like a lady, or a gentleman, if so attired," held true. Teacher always used every gift and anything she possessed, not carelessly or cautiously, but carefully. She felt the difference in people was their power of appreciation, no matter whether it was a breathtaking sunset, a handsome set of Limoges china, Napoleonic lamps, a hungry child or a person's need of Christ. Her *objets d'art* became the cultural training ground for those big, awkward football players. But the *objets d'art* remained in their places. And surprisingly, most remained in one piece! Her collegians had valued and appreciated the beautiful!

When the Bright's son, Zachary, arrived in this very adult household and among these *objets d'art*, the rule still held—nothing was put away. That most intriguing room, filled with all those nice things to investigate, became the "no-no" room. The times did come, of course, when he escaped notice and went to sit on the top step, gazing into that most interesting looking room. To Teacher's great delight, she might come upon him unexpectedly to hear him muttering to himself, "No-no."

Teacher dearly loved children. She could have spent her entire day with this precious little boy who had invaded her life and won her heart. She observed his reactions to life, and would talk to him by the hour to draw out his responses. They were great pals. More to discipline herself to remain at her work in her den and not play with Zachary, than for any other reason, she installed a modern fold door in the open archway. One day as Miss Mears and Miss Baldwin sat working on the davenport, they noticed the plastic drape being slowly pulled away at the floor level. "We sat quietly," recounts Miss Baldwin, "smiling and nudging one another, until two little eyes peered up at us. We could contain ourselves no longer and burst into hearty laughter. A delightful, gleeful squeal arose from the other side of the drape at having found Aunt 'Aret.' We jumped to our feet, pulled back the drape, and there ensued many happy hugs!"

But one time there was a possibility of tragedy taking place among those *objets d'art*. For several mornings the potted plants in the den were found turned over. Every inch of the house was searched, but nothing else seemed to have been touched. What could be going on in the dark of the night to cause such a thing as this to happen? Then in the dead of one night, Teacher awoke to a noise in her room. She listened and listened to find out where it could be coming from. Should she put on a light? Should she get out of bed and investigate? Was the noise coming from her large, walk-in closet? Yes, that was it. Something was in there! With a bound and a dozen steps, she had the closet door closed. Then she grabbed the telephone and woke up the Brights over in the other wing of the "Castle." Excitedly she related that suspicious noises were coming from her closet and that she had shut something in there. Bill Bright routed out Dale Bruner, another member of the household at that time, alerted other sleepy members, grabbed a broom and a box, and all dashed up to Teacher's room and gazed at the suspect door. What to do? Finally, Bill opened the French doors to the roof, and marshalled everyone across the roof and behind the French doors on the other side. Then armed with the broom and box, he cautiously opened the closet door. Muffled shouts of warning kept coming from the excited participants whose view of the scene had been shut out. As the closet door opened, out darted a much frightened skunk, and before Bill could make use of the broom and box, it bounded out the doors and away over the roof. The faces peering out the French doors on the far side only caught a glimpse of a shadow and knew whatever it was had gone.

But this was not the end of the skunk! Miss Baldwin tells what happened: "He returned nightly for many nights as no clue could be found to where he got in. As the 'skunk stories' materialized, Teacher saw her silver gleaming in the lining of their nests, as one story went. And as things grew more tense, she was steeling herself to the grim fact that everything would have to be burned if he attacked. The greatest concern though, was that he might knock over some of the *objets d'art*. Then we learned that moth ball granules stopped a skunk from moving into an area. We finally located a carload—well, almost—and generously sprinkled them around. I think we were trying to asphyxiate the skunk. But his nocturnal wanderings finally came to an end before he could do any damage. We discovered a possible place where he might be coming in, and the next morning the trap revealed a baby skunk. For such a little feller, he certainly had had the household in an uproar for many a day and night!"

Miss Baldwin relates another episode:

"Then fire came, but not nigh Miss Mears' home at 110 Stone Canyon Road. It was touch and go for a time. The Bel Air Hotel just up the street had been evacuated. If the wind decided to blow down canyon, the fire would certainly reach Sunset Boulevard and 110. But the wind continued to blow up canyon, and those gorgeous homes burned like matchsticks. Folks were standing on the roofs of the buildings on the UCLA campus, watching flames and black smoke belching skyward. Miss Mears and a group of us were standing on her roof filled with horror at what our eyes could see, our ears could hear, and our imaginations were conjuring up. The horrible black smoke rolled up, and up, and up. The airplanes added their confusion to the roar of the fire that was eating, eating, eating—where? The moments were tense and filled with dependence upon God. One felt completely helpless. Our hearts ached for those who were already going through this living hell, as their homes were caught up in the pathway of the roaring flames. We prayed that God would rescue individuals and permit no life to be lost. As we stood on that roof, we could not know that shortly the report would read that over 400 homes had been devoured, lifetime keepsakes melted and disintegrated in the heat, everything lost except the clothes on one's back. This made one stop and ask, 'How much do things really mean to me?' It was heart-rending to view nothing but the chimney of the fireplace left standing to represent homes costing $100,000, or $150,000 or more, for home after home in this elegant Bel Air Estates. One could not help but ask, 'Why them and not me?' And the only possible answer one could find was to live close to the Lord, and if he allowed the fires to come that he alone would sustain no matter what might happen."

Many momentous happenings were destined to take place in Miss Mears' new home. The work of Campus Crusade for Christ was growing rapidly. With Bill and Vonette Bright and other members of the Crusade staff living with her, Miss Mears was always in close touch with the student movement.

A broad-shouldered football star at UCLA named Donn Moomaw was converted through Bill Bright's influence. It was a common spectacle on Saturday afternoons to hear some fifty thousand fans chanting: Moo-maw, Moo-maw, Mooooo-maw!" and the opposite side roaring back: "Moo-maw, he-haw!" Donn's new faith quickly caught fire, and seeing the change in him, many came to know his Christ. Miss Mears loved this explosive, open-hearted fellow, and many were the hours they talked and prayed together.

When Donn finished his university studies and was headed toward seminary, he needed finances, and thus he was very happy when an American professional football team offered him a contract. There was only one hitch —he would have to play on Sundays. He asked Teacher if she would come to see him play on Sunday. "Donn," she said, "you already know my answer to that." Donn searched the Bible, committed his future to the Lord, and rejected the contract. A short time later, a Canadian team gave him a bid—with no Sunday games. Not only did it meet his financial needs for seminary, but it introduced his name to British sports fans, a fact that enhanced his witness when two years later he joined Billy Graham in London during the Harringay Arena Crusade.

There were many other conversions and spiritual transformations in her home, as well as meetings of rejoicing for what God was doing.

An idea had been taking shape in Teacher's mind: She had been recalling the Christian organizations which had been brought into existence since she had answered the Lord's call to come out to the Hollywood Presbyterian Church. "Why, some of my own young people have been instrumental before God in founding some of these organizations," she mused. "They have much in common. Wouldn't it be wonderful if somehow we could all get together and share what the Lord has been doing, and pray together?" As the thought took root and grew, over fifty closely-knit organizations appeared on the list she was making. "We leaped to action when she told us her idea," recalls Miss Baldwin, "helping to get out invitations, preparing the day's speaking and prayer schedule, and getting in supplies to feed the group. The day finally arrived. The doors of her home swung open wide, and she stood welcoming her guests and friends. One does not expect to have an experience like this, this side of heaven! In they poured, eagerly shaking Miss Mears' hand or giving her an embrace. They came with such joy and exuberance that one felt they had been waiting a long time for just such an opportunity to share and pray together, as Teacher had made available to them. She reveled in the successes of the Lord, and wept, and smiled, and prayed, for one whole day, and on into the evening hours, as she listened to one after another tell what the Lord had accomplished through him and his organization. Truly our hearts did burn within us, as the mighty workings of God, our Father, were brought to our attention.

During the 1950's Miss Mears' influence was felt around the world. But especially in America did she have the opportunity to share her insights and successes with others engaged in Sunday School work. Time and again she traveled to cities across the nation to speak at Sunday School conventions, inspiring pastors, teachers, superintendents and directors of Christian education. One match can ignite a forest. After her tours, fires were burning in thousands of hearts in hundreds of churches, as pastors and educators went back to their tasks with renewed vision.

In recognition of her leadership in Christian education, Bob Jones University granted her an honorary Doctor of Humanities degree.

And the influence of Gospel Light Publications (Press was dropped in 1956 since they had no presses and did no printing) grew beyond expectations. Cyrus N. Nelson, one of Miss Mears' collegians who was associated with Gospel Light in the 1930's, left his post as Director of Mount Hermon Conference Center to assume the responsibilities as President of Gospel Light.

William T. Greig, Sr., Miss Mears' cousin by marriage, had for many years been a partner and executive in a large Minneapolis printing firm. He gave valuable counsel during the 1940's in the technical phases of Gospel Light's publishing program, and spent most of his time in 1949 and 1950 in California working with Dr. Nelson. Having sold his interest in the Minneapolis printing business he was free to move to California in 1951 to devote his full time to the growing concern. In 1950, as Gospel Light was entering the period of its greatest growth, Bill Greig, Jr. became involved and launched the Minnesota offices at Mound, near Minneapolis.

With these men taking the reins of Gospel Light, Miss Mears assumed the role of Editor-in-Chief. Freed of major management and administrative responsibilities, she was now able to devote herself more fully to her many other involvements such as Forest Home, and especially her first love and responsibility, the Hollywood Presbyterian Church. All of this reflected Miss Mears' conviction that her work must pass on into the hands of capable men who could not only carry on after her death, but who even during her lifetime would expand her original vision beyond what she herself had seen.

By 1958 the Gospel Light staff had multiplied five times what it had been but a decade before. TEACH magazine, a new publication for Sunday School workers, was soon to become the leader in its field passing on information and inspiration to tens of thousands of Christian educators around the world.

The original curriculum had been enlarged and was undergoing constant improvement to keep pace with the times. Gospel Light soon was publishing over 700 individual items and circulation was running in the millions.

Demands from around the world saw overseas circulation boom in the 1960's with major distribution outlets in Toronto, London, Johannesburg, Sydney, Auckland, and Tokyo. Every month shipments were going to over 80 countries of the world and reports flowed in of transformed Sunday Schools and people being reached with the Gospel.

The wisdom of this decision gradually to commit her ministries to others was made manifest in the 1950's by a series of illnesses she suffered. In 1951, shortly after returning from a trip around the world, Miss Mears collapsed while addressing the women of the church. The doctors could find no cause, so the diagnosis came back that everything was fine. But those close to her felt that they knew the cause: people had been telephoning for counseling appointments with her, and when they learned that she would be back in less than two months, they decided no one else could help them. They would say, "Oh, I'll just wait until *she* gets back." This happened time and time again. Thus the cares of the world literally submerged her, and the physical body just could not take it. While she was in the hospital, Miss Mears and Miss Baldwin often smiled about it, as Miss Baldwin would say to her, "This is the Lord's way of letting you get away from everyone's problems."

When her strength returned, she and Miss Esther Ellinghusen decided to take a trip around the world. Their excitement ran high as they visited schools, mission stations and hospitals. One evening, some missionaries drove them through the red-light district of Hong Kong, and the two Americans were invited to help pass out tracts to the unfortunate streetwalkers. Miss Mears and Miss Ellinghusen were filled with enthusiasm, as in the semi-darkness they handed hundreds of brochures and slips of paper to eager hands.

On university campuses in Japan they saw well-printed Communist literature being read by hundreds of students while Christian materials were very scarce. Oriental pastors bemoaned the absence of adequate Sunday School manuals, and wherever Miss Mears and Miss Ellinghusen went, church workers asked them for help in supplying their children and young people with literature. This cry began to stir in the ladies' hearts a desire to see something done.

On Formosa they visited the compounds, schools and hospitals of Lillian Dickson, the indefatigable "angel" to thousands of homeless orphans and lepers of that island. While visiting one of the homes for lepers and seeing the helpless folk living—and dying—on bare boards, the two visitors learned from Mrs. Dickson that they were in desperate need of mats to serve as mattresses. Miss Mears and Miss Ellinghusen immediately wrote out a check to pay for one hundred mats.

Upon returning to the States, they began to encourage others to become interested in the work of Lillian Dickson, and in the next few years they introduced her work to many churches and groups which provided assistance for her. Miss Mears and her friends, notably Miss Eleanor Doan (on the staff of Gospel Light), did much to encourage the subsequent formation of "The Mustard Seed, Inc." the organizational title by which Mrs. Dickson's work became known to hundreds of thousands of American friends.

The growing demand for Gospel Light materials in foreign languages continued to burden Miss Mears and Miss Ellinghusen. "When I see children in Hong Kong sitting on a curb poring over Red comic books, students in Tokyo University districts with their arms loaded with Communist literature, and similar scenes throughout the world, by God's grace, I must do something," Miss Mears told friends. The same burden was beginning to haunt Dr. Nelson and Mr. Greig as they received letters and reports from various parts of the world asking for Sunday School literature in national tongues. Finally in 1961 steps were taken to organize GLINT—Gospel Literature in National Tongues—and money began to come in for translation programs in India, Africa, South and Central America, and Europe. The vision immediately caught fire as missionaries pledged their support and time, and money was raised. Within a short period, over one hundred thousand children were reading Gospel Light Sunday School books in Greece, and translations of the same books were being introduced into major linguistic areas of India under the direction of Miss Anna Nixon.

The stories associated with this new venture bore the seal of God's approval: A converted Hindu, now a leper, was skilled in languages, but he could not write for lack of fingers. He found a friend who could act as his scribe, and the two worked together, the leper dictating his translations to the scribe until several books were available for printing. And neither would take any pay for their work, saying, "It is our gift to Jesus who gave himself for us."

Often at a GLINT board meeting Miss Mears would say, "Let's send $100 or $200 just to encourage their hearts that someone cares about their literature translation program." And often a report would come back that the GLINT check had arrived at the very moment a bill had to be paid.

Reports abounded of churches in far-off countries doubling and tripling in a few months time as the Sunday School manuals were introduced. As had happened in Hollywood, now in India, Africa, and in more than a dozen other places, young people were being converted and trained for Christ's service. Dr. Nelson was appointed president of GLINT as the new ministry rapidly grew to take its place in the front ranks of twentieth-century missionary advances.

But other miracles were to take place in the closing years of Miss Mears' life:

In 1957, while sailing with friends across the Pacific, Miss Mears realized her eyesight was once again deteriorating. Even more ominous, pains in her eyes were rapidly increasing. The sight in her good eye became impaired. Upon arrival in Australia, the new trouble was diagnosed as a rupture, and Miss Mears was told to return to America and her doctor, and not to prolong the trip past the projected cruise. In California her ophthalmologist, Dr. Paul Reed—a nationally honored specialist and esteemed Christian leader, said to her, "There is nothing I as a doctor can do for you. But as a Christian, I suggest you pray and ask others to pray with you."

Miss Mears knew that her sight lay in the hands of God who had created it, and that God alone could intervene and stop the deterioration taking place in her vision. As prayer ascended on her behalf, God did hear and did answer.

The next time Dr. Reed examined her eyes, he found no further deterioration in her good eye. God had stretched forth his healing hand once again on her behalf. Friends were amazed to find her reading again.

A new dimension began to open in her mind. She had long studied the doctrine of the Holy Spirit, and all her life the ministry of the third person of the Trinity had been a reality in her experience. But now Miss Mears began with growing eagerness to seek out a fuller understanding of his potential in her life. What an unexpected thrill it was for those who were close to her! Here was this beloved friend, this old warrior now approaching the end of her course—having accomplished as a woman enough to satisfy most ambitious men—searching, seeking, stretching for yet untapped reservoirs of divine power

that her life and ministry might attain to even more sub-
lime heights of holy accomplishment. "I have enjoyed
spiritual gifts," she would say. "I have had the Spirit's
presence. But now I want everything that he has for me.
I want all the gifts." And with a surprisingly youthful
earnestness, she set out again to know God better. The
observable outcome of this pilgrimage was seen not so
much in her teaching or organizational ministry—for these
realms were more and more being committed to her suc-
cessors—but in that most important sphere of all: a holy,
peaceful life. Henrietta Mears mellowed after this experience, becoming even more sympathetic, gracious, kind
and secure. Her eyes were seeing with deeper penetration
the opening doors of eternity.

Early in 1963, Miss Mears was attending a garden party
sponsored by some of the women of the church. Recognizing a musical friend in the crowd, Miss Mears asked her
to play something for them, and began to lead the lady
to the piano. But the soloist apologized: "Oh, Miss Mears,
I am not really in practice. I'll play for you next year."
Miss Mears registered a kindly disappointment, but only
a friend standing next to her heard her whisper, "I'll
not be here next year."

During her latter years, Miss Mears had pondered the
question of her retirement and how she could possibly
go about it. But each time she took any steps in this
direction some new challenge would arise, and it soon
became evident that because of her own willingness to
serve and remain active, retirement was out of the question. When she finally realized that God did not want her
to retire, she accepted the decision with renewed energy,
comparing herself to Caleb of old, whose strength was not
abated in old age. This decision now gave her determina-

tion to rise above any handicaps, and to give herself to the service to others.

As always her home was open to guests seeking her spiritual guidance. She continued to attend the teachers and officers meetings for the Sunday School and she was present at most of the functions of the college department, staying late counseling students. The executives of the class continued to meet with her on Saturday mornings, and the group more than ever expressed its love to their beloved friend, who, regardless of personal health, was giving herself to her beloved collegians whom she always considered her family. It seemed that Miss Mears actually relished the opportunity to test God's promise, *As thy days, so shall thy strength be* (Deut. 33:25), accepting her infirmities as obstacles to be overcome by the determination of her courageous spirit.

During the day of Monday, March 18, 1963, Miss Baldwin drove Miss Mears past new construction sites in the San Fernando Valley. Both of them talked excitedly of how rapidly Southern California was expanding, of the influx of people to the area, and of the opportunities this presented to reach them with the gospel. They returned to Miss Mears' Bel Air home still animated over what the future held for their work. Tuesday evening, Miss Mears talked at length on the telephone with Jack Franck about the coming prospects of Forest Home—so many new ideas were in the offing that thrilled her. When she finally turned her light out, her heart was singing with the adventures of what still lay before her.

The next morning, her housekeeper, Mrs. Shearer, found that Miss Mears had finally slipped through the veil between the present and the hereafter, which she had described over the years as being so very, very thin. Someone remarked, "It was nothing new to her to meet her Lord alone, for she had often done so. This time she just went with him." On her desk were found the preparations of several Bible messages which she was to give in the near future, among them the lesson she planned for her collegians at their Easter breakfast.

Nearly two thousand people filed silently into the sanctuary of the First Presbyterian Church of Hollywood to witness the most triumphant memorial service that most of them would ever see. Scattered throughout the audience were hundreds Miss Mears had personally led to Christ, some of them ordained ministers. Many were the young people in the crowd, who at this moment were maturely aware of God's presence. The opening words were: *I am the resurrection, and the life: he that believeth in me, though he were dead, yet shall he live: and whosoever liveth and believeth in me shall never die* (John 11:25,26). And the soloist, one of Teacher's boys, sang with profound feeling: "How Great Thou Art!" The choir, under Dr. Hirt's majestic leadership, resounded forth with Luther's call-to-arms, "A Mighty Fortress Is Our God," as prayers of thanks and rejoicing rose from hearts overwhelmed with the glory of God.

Many tributes were uttered, including one sent by telegram from Billy Graham: "I am certain that Henrietta Mears had a great reception in Heaven. She made a tremendous impact upon my life and ministry." Dr. Raymond Lindquist spoke of her energy, enthusiasm, and her ability to bring a person to his own fulfillment. Dr. David Cowie mentioned her talent for showing a person his unlimited capacity to be filled with God's ability. Dr. Richard Halverson recalled her many wise counsels, especially concerning her advice to stay in one place in order to establish a lasting work, and not to move about from church to church. Her work at Hollywood was possible, he emphasized, because she stayed there for thirty-five years, turning down many invitations to minister elsewhere. The Reverend Louis Evans, Jr., unfolded in his prayer a scene all were thinking about: "O Lord! We look upon Heaven now, and can see nothing but rejoicing, for she is meeting all those whom she has known on this earth who have gone before, and all those whom she has not known on this earth who have waited for her all these years. Indeed, O Lord, Heaven throbs with rejoicing on this day for thy saint, who walked in simple victory, because she walked in simple trust."

Dr. Cyrus Nelson summarized her accomplishments:

Because of Dr. Mears' deep love of her Saviour and her church, she had a great love for the world. She believed that for the needs of all people in all places Christ was the answer. Consequently, when she envisaged the work of the local church, she saw the church universal. "People must be called by God," she said, and she prayed the Lord of the Harvest to send forth his laborers. It is a remarkable fact that over 400 young people went into Christian service under her influence. In 1962, there were more than 40,000 delegates at Forest Home, coming from 40 different denominations and hundreds of churches and groups. Billy Graham, in 1949, found a renewed dedication at Forest Home, which enabled him to begin his now-famous Los Angeles Crusade. Writing in *Christianity Today,* he says: "I remember walking down a trail, trampling alone in the world, almost wrestling with God. I dueled with my doubts, and my soul seemed to be centered in the cross-fire. Finally, in desperation, I surrendered my will to the living God as revealed in Scripture. Within six weeks we started our Los Angeles Crusade, and the rest is now history." Dr. Mears also played an important part in the world-wide ministry of Campus Crusade for Christ. Bill Bright, the founder, listened to her one evening with intensity and conviction, and after her challenge, he knelt before God. This was his spiritual pivot from self to the Saviour. Then she opened up the doors of her home, and for almost ten years, thousands of students crossed Sunset Boulevard from UCLA to hear the gospel there. The Hollywood Christian Group was born in her home. She was a founder of the National Sunday School Association, and a member of many boards of international Christian significance.

Her global vision also saw the potential of the printing press and in 1933 she founded Gospel Light Publications, together with Miss Esther A. Ellinghusen, Miss Ethel May Baldwin, and D. Stanley Engle. Today this ministry touches more than 20,000 churches and mission stations across our country and the seven seas.

Her last, and perhaps destined to be her greatest world-wide ministry is GLINT, a missionary foundation formed to translate and distribute Christian materials around the world. And so GLINT was born in 1961. You will notice that facts stirred Dr. Mears to action.

The open casket banked with the numerous floral tributes seemed to be but another platform from which she was speaking. And many young hearts asked themselves, "I wonder upon whom her mantle will fall?" But her mantle already lay on the shoulders of thousands upon thousands who had been directed to Christ by her life.

The choir began to peal out the heroic themes of Handel's "Hallelujah Chorus," and while the audience stood to honor the King, minds turned from the passing of a friend to the glory of the Risen Lord. As the last chords reached into the silence, a man whispered to his neighbor, "Dear Teacher! Even in her death she pointed us to Christ."

Officials at the Forest Lawn Memorial Park said that it was the largest crowd at a graveside service in twenty years—an astounding fact considering that many of Hollywood's greats are buried there.

> To God be the glory—
> Great things he has done!

Four Talks
by Henrietta C. Mears

I. THE ROMANCE OF THE SUNDAY SCHOOL

(This message was delivered at the Baptist General Conference in Portland, Oregon, in 1957.)

Nothing in this world thrills me so much as to talk about the Sunday School to Sunday School workers. I say this because I want you to realize how serious is this occasion. There is no conference that is being held around the world today over glass-top tables, considering millions or even billions of dollars, that is as important as the meeting you and I are holding tonight. Those conferences deal just with time, but the kind of business you and I are talking about touches eternity.

We are living in a very strange world: We are neither in inflation nor depression; we are neither in war nor peace. Every government is in a static pause, wondering what to do. But as we look at the faces of our youth, we see that they are exploding. I have discovered with my college men and women that they do not have the seriousness that they once had, and how can I blame them? A young man came into my office the other day and said, "Miss Mears, I am going off now to the Marines, and I will be gone for two or three years." I told him that I thought he was going into medicine. "No, I don't think I will," he answered. "It will probably be three years before I get back to school, and the course is so long and strenuous that I think I will do something else—what, I don't know yet. I'll have to decide later." Here was a young man who had the noblest ambitions and the highest desires to do the right thing in his life, and now he is marching off to war not having any idea what he is going to do afterwards. I have found the same thing with hundreds of young people, as I have talked with them across the country. Nobody knows what to do nor what kind of day tomorrow will be. They have to live and be prepared for today.

And so I want to talk to you about the Sunday School, because I believe that you and I have a solution to the dilemma facing our youth.

We would be very proud to say that we are a professor at Oxford or Columbia University; that would be an honor. But the men and women I am addressing are professors in Christ's college. Is there any calling higher than ours? You and I are teaching in the best college in the world, for it was founded by the Lord Jesus Christ. The Textbook was written by the Holy Spirit, and the students are boys and girls, men and women whom God made in His image. This is the most important business in the world.

We have the most significant Textbook to teach, but it is probably the most poorly taught book of our times. I say that to a Christian audience, because you will understand me. We often blame the school for turning our boys and girls away from their faith in Christ and having them lose that which we think is supreme. But I tell you that as teachers of the Word of God some of us have made our boys and girls despise the Bible. We have taught it so disgracefully, without any significance or any relationship to their lives, that they have said in their hearts, "When I don't have to go to Sunday School anymore, I won't."

The reason I started writing Sunday School material was that when I first went to Hollywood, a young man dangling a Phi Beta Kappa key on his chain, who was studying to become a doctor, said to me, "Miss Mears, what's wrong? I have gone to Sunday School all my life, and yet if I had to pass an examination on the Bible, I would flunk." That rang in my ears. Then a junior told me, "I don't want to go to Sunday School any longer; it just gets dumber and dumber." So I determined that something ought to be done about poor teaching. When I went to Hollywood in 1928, I decided that if I were going to establish a school, the kind of curriculum I would be using was of utmost importance. What books would we have? How was the material going to be presented? What were going to be the requirements of my teachers?

First, I looked at the Bible. So many churches were complaining that "it just isn't getting across to the children." And so they were introducing everything but the Bible into their curriculum. But I knew that there was nothing wrong with the Textbook, it was the way we were teaching it. Do you think that a professor at Oxford must know his subject before he stands before his pupils? Of course he must. And yet you and I are teachers, but we don't know our Textbook. It was my joy, two years ago in London, to have lunch with C. S. Lewis, who is such a stimulating and knowledgable conversationalist and author. Afterwards, I said to Dr. Goodwin-Hudson, who was my escort, "Isn't it a shame that we as Christian teachers do not know our subject as well as Dr. Lewis does? If we did, boys and girls would be challenged and their lives would be changed!"

My heart is thrilled when I see what the Word of God can do. Come some Wednesday evening when you are in Hollywood and visit our college prayer meeting. You will see some two hundred young people meeting around the room in groups of ten to fifteen, studying the Bible. The other night was beautiful: the ocean was appealing, the mountains all around called to them, and yet those collegians were there at church to study God's Word. I have discovered that if the Bible is taught the way it should be that it will be like a powerful magnet drawing youth unto the Lord Jesus Christ. What a supremely superb Textbook we have!

Then the Sunday School is the greatest work in the world because of its consistency: boys and girls, young people, men and women, for whom Christ died. Is there anything else like it? We know that twenty-five per cent of American families move every year, many of them seeking better schools or a healthier climate for their children. We do everything for our children. How important they are! When I stand outside my college department on Sunday morning and watch those magnificent young people pouring into my class, I pray: "Lord, I don't know why you keep me here so many years; I don't know why you have me the teacher; but as long as you do, I demand of you that you will give me an attractiveness for these students, that you will help me say a word for them about their most important decisions in life." I am overwhelmed with the possibility that here may be a Martin Luther, or a John Knox, or a Calvin, or a Carey. Every Sunday morning I realize that I am facing the most important people in the world. Those who are stepping into my Sunday School class today may be stepping out tomorrow to become leaders of nations.

I know what my purpose is when I teach those students. If we were playing basketball but not making any points, we would say that we were not achieving our purpose. Our goal is to win students to Christ and to train for leadership. It is not enough merely to introduce them to the Saviour, although that is the first step. We must show them what their lives can be if they are completely given over to Christ and trained for his service. I look at an all-American like Donn Moomaw and say to myself, "I am so glad that Donn has come to Christ, but now I want him to realize what he can do if Christ possesses him completely." And I see other young people in our class like Colleen Townsend, and I pray that God will take over their lives one hundred per cent for his glory. I want them to have the experience Saul of Tarsus had when he saw Christ and said, *Lord, what wilt thou have me to do?* (Acts 9:6).

The purpose of our evangelism is not simply to introduce men and women to a Saviour, but to a Lord. Your ministry as a Sunday School teacher will be productive if you will let boys and girls know that God has a purpose for them, that God wants them to be commissioned soldiers in his army. I love to think of Elisha as he went into the room where the dead child lay and put himself over that body with his eyes to his eyes and his nostrils to his nostrils and literally breathed into him life. As teachers we must learn to do that very thing—lay ourselves over against young people that they may understand what we are talking about, and that we may learn more of what they are thinking.

Many of you here are bored with teaching in the church.

Saturday night rolls around, and you say, "Horrors! I haven't prepared my lesson yet." And you are ready to quit. But you will discover that if boys and girls are coming to Christ and finding the purpose God has for them, you will never want to stop teaching. Teaching God's Word will become the most exciting adventure of your life.

I have had the thrill of going around this world many times, and practically every place my plane lands—whether it is in India, or Hong Kong, or the islands of the sea, or Africa—I find a young man or woman who has come up through my college department and is there preaching the gospel of the Lord Jesus Christ. How I thank God! I was in the Congo last year when one night, at a little meeting, I saw a young woman beaming from ear to ear. She was the wife of a doctor. She came up and said to me, "Oh, Miss Mears, you know I was in the college department, too, and at Forest Home I made my decision to come over here." And there were five others in that room who had made their decisions under my ministry in Hollywood. Three years ago I was in Beirut, and one of the missionaries invited some of the professors from the American University, along with a few nurses, to a reception for me. Then our host said, "Several years ago Miss Mears came to our church in Berkeley and challenged some of us about our service for God, and about two hundred of us came forward to say that we wanted to do whatever the Lord willed. My wife counted up tonight and discovered that fifty-six of those who came forward are now on the foreign field."

Now these are the results I have seen. It isn't because I am anything, but if we are vehicles of the Spirit of God, he will perform miracles. In myself I can do absolutely nothing, but in him all things are possible. The

Lord Jesus says to you as a teacher, *If any man thirst, let him come unto me and drink; and out of his innermost parts shall flow rivers of living water.* Men and women, I expect that! I expect it from God because he wants me to have all of his blessings in my life. God wants results. How powerful we can be in Christ!

I know another thing about a Sunday School: It can be built. I have discovered that most of you want to build bigger Sunday Schools, but I advise you to think about building better Sunday Schools. I can honestly say before God that from the first moment my feet entered the First Presbyterian Church of Hollywood, I never tried to build a bigger Sunday School. My only concern was quality. Size came as a result. A Sunday School can be started anywhere, and it can grow. But you will say that we have had success because ours was in Hollywood. Listen, any problem that you have, I have had in Hollywood three times worse! Hollywood is the most terrible place on the face of the earth to organize anything solid, because it is the most transient city imaginable. It is a city of make-believe, of falsity, of broken homes, of sophistication. But God has seen fit in his mercy to erect a far-famed Sunday School there. I believe as I look at that city objectively, that the Lord has said, "I am going to establish a Sunday School there so people can see that if it can be done in Hollywood, it can be done anywhere." What competition we have with the great white way of sin! Young people are sold on the auction block to the highest bidder. You know the enormous salaries they offer young people in the entertainment world. There is temptation all around us. But it is a delight to see on Wednesday night a hundred junior highers and one hundred and fifty high school students praying that God will use their lives for his glory. We are but three blocks from Hollywood and Vine, yet day after day God blesses our church as people are converted and commissioned to go out with the gospel.

When my sister and I first came to Hollywood, we were driving out in the suburbs one afternoon looking for a place to eat. As we rode along, we saw among the groves a tiny shack with dozens of cars around it. We knew it must be good because of all the people, so we stopped and went in. Why, the fried chicken was absolutely delicious, and the boysenberry pie was delectable. It was Knott's Berry Farm, which today covers acres and acres of land. In those days it was the most inaccessible place you could imagine, but because everything was so excellent, people came from miles around. That was a lesson to me: I knew that it did not matter where our church was located; if we had something good, people would come across the country to get it. A few years ago my plane landed in South Dakota. You know how flat that state is. I felt that someone had hit me on the head and flattened me out! There was not a tree, or a mountain, or hardly a person in sight. The superintendent of a Sunday School came to the airport to meet me, and as we were riding over the plains, he pointed to a speck on the horizon—we were literally out in the middle of nowhere—and he said, "You see those buildings over there, Miss Mears? That is where we have our Sunday School bursting with children every week." I was amazed. Since then I have never worried about location. If the product is good, the people will come.

Don't try to build a bigger Sunday School. Don't have a visitation campaign to get more people. Build a better Sunday School. Have a place for every person, every age. If you don't have rooms for junior highs, you cannot invite them. If you don't have a place for young marrieds, you won't have them. If you don't have a place for the babies, they will not be there.

Now, I have a pet peeve: I detest paper cradle rolls! Little booties hung up on the wall with little pink ribbons —I despise the horrible things! I want real, live, honest-to-goodness babies! We have just finished an educational building for our babies including children up through the primary department. We spent half a million dollars on babies. One of the elders raised his eyebrows and asked if such a building was necessary for "just the babies." I told him that such a building was the most necessary structure in the world; for if the parents have a place to put the babies, they will come with their children and in turn go to the young marrieds' class. Thus we have a Sunday School atmosphere from the very beginning. Besides that, our psychologists and educators tell us that we have no idea what impressions are made on little children: beautiful music, lovely colors, stories. We have learned to condition them to love the house of the Lord.

Do you have a place for every age in your Sunday School? And do you have a program for every age? Think through the age characteristics of each group and gear your program to them.

And is your program as good as it could be? When I went out to Hollywood, there was a restaurant in Santa Monica where we used to take our out-of-town guests. It was the most luscious place to eat: If anything was supposed to be cold, it was crisp and delicious. It was all delightful. One Sunday sixteen years ago I entertained some friends there and we were served day-old pumpkin pie. I have never been back since. I don't even know if that place still exists, and I don't care. You will say that

I am being too hard on a restaurant. Oh, no I am not. I don't intend getting stung twice. So I find in my Sunday School that if we have one bad Sunday, we lose people. We are in the kind of business where everything has to be perfect.

How poorly we sometimes conduct our services! Have you ever been in a department when things go something like this: It is 9:30 and we are supposed to begin, but the superintendent comes rushing in about twenty-four minutes of the hour and says, "Hello, everybody. Oh! aren't the books out yet? Well, go down and get them, please. Those junior highs are making so much noise this morning! . . . Will somebody go down and get the hymn books? Now who will play this morning? Mr. Jones . . . He isn't here? Well, Mrs. Smith, you play. Come on, Mrs. Smith, we'll choose a song in the key of C, if that's all you can read . . . Oh, good, here are the books. Please pass them out . . . George, don't throw them, just hand them . . . That's better. Now let's sing hymn 262. Oh, it's got four flats; that won't do. What song has just the key of C? All right, now everybody sing with all your power: Glory to God! Now what about the announcements? Who has the announcements? Well, I understand the Boy Scouts are meeting next Friday . . . It isn't next Friday? Well, come next Sunday and you'll find out when the Scouts are meeting. And the teachers are going to have a picnic. Is there anybody who can tell us about the picnic? Are the children invited? Do you know, Mrs. Smith? You don't . . . Well, anyway, there will be a picnic . . ." Now, doesn't that just thrill you down to your toes! You can hardly wait to get back next Sunday. It's so challenging! So exciting! And you love to invite all your friends, too, because it is so wonderful. Rubbish! We should weep over our programs. They drive people away from the church.

If a man wants to build a place for a large industry, he doesn't phone up the cement factory and have bags of cement piled on his lot, or phone up the lumber company and have stacks of lumber piled up somewhere. He doesn't start to order the material until he has a plan. Have you a plan for your Sunday School? Have you drawn up the blueprints of what you want it to be? When we were thinking about a new building for our junior highs and high schoolers, the elders told me to write down everything I wanted in it. Well, that was a big order, but I did. And, you know, everything I wrote down we have, and much more. If you don't draw up a plan, you will never have anything accomplished. Be ambitious in your plans. I have discovered that if we present definite plans to people, they will get interested and pay for them. When they saw what we wanted for our high school young people, they offered to pay for the chairs, to lay the carpet, to give for the stained-glass window. When we dedicated that building, we did not have one cent of debt. Now, men and women, be ambitious for God.

If you are going to build a magnificent Sunday School, you have to have magnificent plans. When I go to New York and look at those gigantic skyscrapers, I think of the meticulous calculations that were made over every square inch. When we sailed through the Panama Canal, I thought back how every foot was carved out with sweat and blood. And we build chicken coops for God! You think you can always add on to a chicken coop, so you set up a little building, and in fifty years you add another little building. We want skyscrapers for God! I challenge you to go home and ask God what he wants your Sunday School to be. You may not be the superintendent or the minister, but you may be a layman. I believe this is the generation when laymen are to lead the churches. Definitely! What do you want to see in your church? Idealize! Dream dreams!

When we started to build our Sunday School in Hollywood, I realized we needed lesson material. So we sat down and started to write. We mimeographed them every week for the children. Then we called in our educators and discussed how to improve them. We went through the entire Sunday School grade by grade, week by week, until we had our curriculum. And I tell you the truth that in two and a half years we grew from 420 to 4200. Parents brought their children from everywhere. A family of five came from Balboa—fifty miles round trip. They drove from all the neighboring communities, because parents wanted children to be instructed in the Word of God. Distance was no problem. That is the way to build. Put something into it, and you'll get something back.

But let me tell you that Sunday School is work. I have 567 officers and teachers in my Sunday School. That's quite an army, isn't it? Many of them hold down very responsible positions in the secular world. Some of my superintendents spend as much as thirty-five hours a week working on their department. I don't know how they do it. Some of them are teachers in the public schools; others are housewives. But they have learned to organize their time. Their departments scintillate. Boys and girls are finding Christ. Of course they are! Their teachers are putting themselves into their work.

There is nothing easy about Sunday School; it demands everything we have. It is a labor of prayer. It is labor of intelligence. It is labor of muscle. I have marks on my neck for which I thank God. When I first came to Hollywood and tried to build a conference, I would sit at the phone, and my secretary would give me the numbers I needed, and I would phone and phone, urging this boy or that one to come to camp. "Well, I'll go if Jim is going," so I would have to phone Jim. "Well, I'll go if Ed goes," so I would have to phone Ed. Then I would phone the other two back and tell them that Ed was going. And so it went, hour after hour, until boils literally broke out on my neck. I am glad for those scars.

Let your teachers know exactly what is required of them: be definite in your assignments. I never give my teachers long lists of names to call. It discourages them. I give a teacher three names. Then he is ashamed if he cannot report on just three people. When a teacher calls me up and says that he is going to have to resign because he can't call on all his pupils, I ask him if he has time to call on one boy a night. Certainly he can do that. Well, in ten days he has called his entire class. When teachers see this possibility, they do not feel overwhelmed with impossible assignments. I have one man who does just that: he phones one boy a night. And he has been doing it for fourteen years. How God has blessed him!

Recruit the most qualified people you can find to be your Sunday School teachers. Don't lower your standards one inch. There was a man in our church who was the president of thirty-two banks, a rather busy person. He was the type of man I wanted to teach a class of our high school boys. Mr. Porter was a Christian gentleman, who loved God and was successful in the world. "What a challenging influence he could be on these young fellows," I thought. So I took a card and wrote his name at the top of it; then I wrote the names of the twelve boys under his and handed him the card.

"What's this?" he exclaimed.

"It's your class."

"Oh, Miss Mears, there must be some mistake. I haven't said I was going to teach," he emphatically replied.

"I know that," I answered. "But I want you to look these names over. They are a wonderful class, aren't they?"

"Yes, they certainly are, and I hope you can find someone to take them."

"Well, Mr. Porter, I think I have found someone—you are the person I want to teach those boys."

After we talked about it a few more minutes, he said, "Yes, Miss Mears, I would like to tackle those youngsters, but I will have to reorganize my business, for right now I am too busy. Give me six months to put things in shape, and I'll do it." Eventually he did take that class, and, oh my, how he has influenced those fellows! What an investment of time he has put into them! He knew it would take work, but this man knew how to work. He wasn't afraid of it.

I have had so many people say to me, "Oh, Miss Mears, I wish I could do all the things you do. Why, I would give anything if I could have the results you have in your Sunday School!" Well, let me tell you right now that I don't believe you! You watch the organist play so beautifully at your church, and you say, "I would give anything to be able to play as she does!" But your mother and father spent hundreds of dollars on your music lessons when you were a child, and you were too busy to practice. Instead, you went out to play with your friends. So it is with your Sunday School class: You don't have results, because you don't take the time or make the effort to do anything about your teaching or to learn more about your students. I tell you truthfully that I have never seen a teacher who was willing to invest time and effort into his class who was not successful—that is, if he were teaching the right age class.

Maybe some of you need to think about changing the age level of your teaching. Some people are amazingly adroit with juniors, but they have no ability whatsoever with high school pupils. When I see a teacher foundering, I call him in and ask if he is happy with his class. "Now that you ask, Miss Mears, I am not. I have been meaning to talk to you about this for some time. You know . . . I just don't think I'm cut out for this group." And he begins to tell me all about his difficulties. As he talks, I try to evaluate the situation, and I suggest another age for him to take.

Not everyone can teach a class of junior high boys. It takes nerve and skill. Have you ever seen a junior high teacher trying frantically to get order maybe like this: "Now listen, fellows, we're all going to pay attention today . . . Bill, take those spitballs out of your mouth. I see them. Put them out. Here, give them to me . . . John, don't you laugh at Bill. He is not funny at all, and I don't care if your father is the minister, you are going to leave this class if you are not respectful . . . I see you, Tom. Now put your feet on the floor. Bill, don't laugh. I mean it! Tom, take your feet off the table, and now! Bill, give me those spitballs . . . Now we're all going to be respectful in God's house. *In the beginning was the* . . . Tom, stop kicking John. *In the beginning was* . . . I said we are not going to start until everybody is quiet!" Wouldn't you think that here was a teacher in perfect command? Know at what age level a teacher is his best, and analyze the reasons for unruly classes.

No doubt you listened several months ago, as did I, to the life of Helen Keller. I learned from that story one of my greatest lessons of pedagogy. Here was a child who couldn't see, hear, or speak. She couldn't be put in with the other children. What was to be done? Then

Miss Sullivan—what a gifted teacher!—took Helen's hand and put it under water, then she placed the hand on her lips as she carefully pronounced the word "water." And slowly the outside world began to walk into that brilliant child's mind. Isn't that what faces us every day in our Sunday Schools? We don't realize that sometimes there come to us children who have absolutely no conception of spiritual realities. They can neither see nor hear the marvels of heaven. They don't understand what we are talking about. We must be ingenious if we are going to penetrate into their minds. Have you had the privilege of taking a boy or girl that has been brought up in a non-Christian home, where there are no sensitivities to the words of Christ, and then introducing that child to the Lord? Oh, how we have to take them by the hand and lead them one step at a time! We must, as it were, place their hands on our lips, so that they understand every heavenly sound.

Teaching is work. We all wonder how Miss Sullivan stood the physical strain while working with Helen Keller. But it will be the same with us. If you really mean business with God, there will be many sleepless nights, many days without rest. I have learned to judge my own spiritual condition by the people who are pounding at my door and ringing my phone. If I am not getting calls at one o'clock at night from my college students or at six o'clock in the morning from people who are distraught, wondering what to do with their lives, then I know something is wrong with me. We must be spiritually available. If you are not willing to pay this price, you are in the wrong business. My family constantly tells me that I am going to suffer an early death, because I push myself too hard. Well, I have never felt better in my life, and I am older than most of you in this audience.

Work won't kill you; but being frustrated about what you are supposed to do next will. How wonderful to know that you are in the place where God wants you! Why, you can keep going and going, because you have a confidence that orders your life. I praise the Lord tonight for such a confidence. It can only come from Christ.

Yes, we must be willing to work, but we must not work alone. A Sunday School cannot be built by one person. Don't ever say, "I just can't get anyone to help me," because that admission gives you away. One of the most important secrets you and I as leaders have to learn is to inspire others to lead with us. We must learn to designate tasks. I have found that people will do anything if I do not load them down with too much, and if I am specific. If you will not suffocate a man with responsibility, but give him just enough, you will have him coming back to you for more later on. This is one of the ways by which we are able to inspire people's confidence in us and in themselves. Be prepared when one of your teachers comes into your office. Think ahead of his responsibilities, so that he will realize that you see his problems. When you call all of your teachers together, have a definite plan. Don't say, "Well, I wonder what we should talk about tonight." That will inspire no one. Men and women today are looking for places where they can invest their time and energies; they want something to do. Don't let them down by not having a clear-cut plan of action.

On the evenings when we have our teachers' and officers' meetings, two hours before the rest of them come, we gather all of our superintendents, presidents, and staff together for a cabinet conference. It begins at 5:15, the first Tuesday of every month, and I expect everyone to be there on time. We can't run a Sunday School otherwise. I spend practically the whole day in definite, meticulous preparation of what the procedure is going to be, so that each cabinet member will know exactly what we are talking about and what he is required to do. My job is not to run that Sunday School of several thousand students all by myself. I wouldn't last one hour if I wanted to. I must inspire my cabinet, and they in turn go out to inspire and inform their teachers. If the Sunday School is big business, let's run it like a business.

But although the Sunday School cannot be run by one person, it can be destroyed by one person—the minister. If a minister is not interested in the Sunday School, it will die, positively! If a minister vetoes projects because they cost too much, or if he cannot see the possibilities of expansion, that's the end of it. One of the greatest problems in Sunday School work is the minister. And often this is so because he doesn't know what to do. He's afraid of the Sunday School because he doesn't understand it. How many ministers are at their wit's end over their youth; they don't know how to organize them. My own minister says to me often: "I don't know what I would do without you, Miss Mears; I just couldn't take care of the young people without this Sunday School." We must be sensitive to a minister's headaches. He has his assignment of keeping the church organized and making it function properly. There are so many committees, meetings, talks, funerals, weddings, calls, and so forth. It's a miracle that more of our ministers don't crack under the strain. But if you are a minister, may I say this to you: You may not have all the time you would like for your youth, but be appreciative of the plans that are brought before you regarding your Sunday School. Learn as much about it as you can. Be sure to drop in at the teachers' meeting once a month to say an approving word. If our minister didn't encourage my teachers ever so often, I don't know what I would do. They would feel so left out. Why are many of our most successful Sunday Schools disunited from the church? Is it not because the Sunday School is ignored by the minister? He never makes an effort to let his teachers know how important they are in the life of his congregation. The church school should be an integral part of the church; if it isn't, neither school nor church is functioning properly. We must not have little churches within churches. The minister is the key.

Often churches have men's classes that become so powerful that they are divorced from the over-all program of the church. They have their mission projects, socials, and Bible studies, while the rest of the church straggles behind. I know definitely that for a Sunday School to grow and flourish, it must work as a part of the church. We take particular care to keep our Sunday School classes informed about church-wide missionary projects, special days, building programs, and the like. We want everyone working for the same end. Go back to your Sunday School and look at it. Is every department feeding into your church to make it strong in missions, in preaching, in music, in giving? Does your Sunday School encourage your minister? We must have united churches where Sunday School and minister are working together to win the youth to the Lord Jesus Christ.

What are we doing about all these things? Years ago, I went to a conference and I heard a splendid challenge on what a Sunday School teacher should do. I was so moved! But when I went back to my hotel, I got into bed and began to fall asleep. Suddenly I realized that I would forget everything I had heard that night—the summons to be a better teacher, to set high objectives for my Sunday School, to understand the various ages and what their needs are for curriculum—unless I did something right then and there. So I turned the lights on, took a piece of paper, and wrote down ten steps I wanted to take in my class. The first was a decision to win every girl to Christ as personal Saviour. Then I determined that my girls were going to know the Word of God in a life-transforming way, that they were going to find in it the call of God to be witnesses. Ten goals for my class—they nearly killed me, but through the months I saw each one fulfilled. What a tremendous assignment that was! But my ministry was revolutionized.

Now, what I have told you tonight is the truth. I don't care where your church is located or what your problems are, you can make something marvelous out of your Sunday School.

Many years ago, in the little town of Beardsley, Minnesota (with a population of only 850), I took my first public school teaching position. I went one night to a prayer meeting, but no one else showed up except the dear, faithful, old minister. So the two of us talked about prayer meetings, and he said that he believed in them because his mother had always gone to them. I said to him, "Well now, *One* [can] *chase a thousand, and two put ten thousand to flight* (Deut. 32:30), so let's go out and invite people to come to prayer meeting." Then I asked him about classes. He said that he had a young people's class of about eight boys, but they were very much of a disappointment to him. His wife had invited them to dinner, but they had thrown the rolls around the room, smeared butter on the walls, and made a mess of her beautiful table. He was most discouraged about these fellows, so I asked him if I could have them. I was just out of college, and he looked at me as if I had lost my mind.

I called on the boys and got them out. We opened the Bible and began to talk about God. Soon the class began to grow. Then two of them said, "Miss Mears, we don't know anything about the Bible, and we were wondering if we couldn't have an extra class during the week." I invited them over to the place where I was staying. My landlady had a little parlor with a tiny table around which these two boys and I sat. Soon the parlor was filled as these two began to bring their friends. Our hostess then let us use her dining room, and when that filled up, we moved into the even larger kitchen. We put boards on the stove so we could have a table. In the summer, we opened the windows so that those who couldn't get in could at least stand outside to hear the Word of God. And finally our little class grew to over a hundred boys. Can you imagine a Sunday School class of a hundred boys in a town with only 850 people in all? I don't know where they came from. But they were hungry for the love of God.

Will you stop looking at your problems and wringing your hands in despair? If you will present God's Word so that it meets the needs of young and old alike, you will have a successful Sunday School. How I want the youth of our land to know Christ! They are so frustrated and out of focus. If we don't take the gospel to them, no one knows what will happen to our country tomorrow. Realize this, men and women, that you have the privilege of taking the good news of Christ's love to these young people.

I wonder if you will pray with me the prayer that Paul uttered when the Lord met him on the road to Damascus: *Lord, what wilt thou have me to do?* (Acts 9:6). I don't care what your situation is, God has something for everyone of us to do in this perilous age. We have come to the kingdom for just such a time as this. Will you salute your General and say, "Lord, whatever you tell me to do I will do"? If we salute the General, it is to take his orders. *Lord, what wilt thou have me to do?* Not my church, not my minister, not my friends—but me! *Lord what wilt thou have me to do—today?"*

II. WHO ARE THE YOUNG PEOPLE YOU TEACH?

Youth today find it increasingly difficult to understand themselves; their parents are even more perplexed about them. Perhaps there has never been another time when young people have been so motivated to go to extremes, to act with such intensity, to revolt, to take up new causes, to sacrifice themselves for ultimates of good and evil.

We of the older generation have the temptation to impose upon the young our preconceived ideas, to force them to accept our ways of doing things, our patterns of thought. But they do not want these premeditated, predigested patterns; they want, rather, to work out their own conclusions. Our duty is to help them do this, to aid them to understand themselves. And to accomplish this, we must know what our youth are striving for. We must know what our students want to know.

They are, first of all, in the process of getting an education. This includes more than attending a university; it embraces all that the twentieth century offers. There is the quest for reality, for changeless standards in a changing world, the desire to comprehend the drives and customs of peoples in other lands, to understand how people fit together in a world that has erected so many barriers. Education today must be practical, meaningful, satisfying. It cannot deal with mere facts; it must teach students how to think for themselves, how to discover the meaning of life, how to live a purposeful life in a world seemingly without purpose.

So many of our teenagers are prematurely leaving school to become self-supporting. They are cutting their education short and thus limiting their potential for future development. Part of this problem is economic: many families are unable to support a young person in college, or, even more urgent, the income a teenager can earn is needed to help the family budget. But more than that, young people want to be identified with their world, to break away from family responsibilities, and to be independent. Our life today is geared to the immediate: Wars, riots and revolutions speak of the hour in which we live; as a result, the long-range view is lost. The challenge to youth is "What are you doing this moment?" not "What is your life going to be twenty-five years from now?" Consequently, many of them fail to see the importance of a prolonged education.

Along with the question of education goes the problem of choosing a vocation. More and more vocational guidance is being offered in our schools. In the church it is becoming increasingly important to relate this vocational guidance to the young person's faith. He must be helped to see how his life can have meaning and fulfillment in the context of his Christianity. Would it not be a marvelous advancement if we in the church would be more concerned with the guiding of our youth in their choice of careers that will do honor to their religious convictions?

Our young people, furthermore, want to know how to select a life partner. Many of them are afraid of marriage. How can we blame them when so great a number see broken vows in their parents' homes? Our age does not stress marital fidelity. And yet one of the strongest yearnings of youth is to have a happy marriage. A great joy of my life has been to see hundreds of young people come to my college department and there find their future husband or wife. I make it a point to encourage my students to seek their future partners in our group, for I know that there is no better place to start building a home than in the fellowship of God's saints. But we must be much more concerned with this aspect of our work. I am all in favor of marriage counseling in the church. We do everything possible to help our students in this respect. Just recently we concluded a series on dating and marriage for our high school and college students. We invited in various experts to answer their questions, and we showed sex-education films, which we borrowed from the public school film library, because I want our teenagers to learn about these things in the context of the church and not to be ashamed to ask their ministers anything that is on their minds.

The teenager also is trying to decide where to invest his life in this modern world. Where are his energies, his education, his family responsibilities and his faith going to find their maximum accomplishment? This is a generation of doers; action is the key. But there is a growing concern that there be a purpose behind action. Our young people want to believe that their lives are counting for something. And this restless striving for meaning is perhaps affording to us our grandest opportunity to direct the minds of our youth to God.

But we must be careful to counsel rather than to advise. Kindly counsel is more prized than expert advice. The young person's deepest problem is how to feel his own significance. And if he is made to think that he is incapable of solving his perplexities by himself, he will never be confident of his maturity. Parents should realize that their example is more important than their commands, that it is better to help a teenager come to his own solutions than to force upon him parental prejudices.

One of the mothers of our church had a very unruly teenage son who was constantly getting into trouble. Finally, the distraught woman took the boy to a psychologist. After the youth took the tests, the psychologist said to the mother, "I find your son quite normal, Mrs. L—, but I think you should make an appointment with me as soon as possible." The problem was not in the son but in the mother, who was trying to force the boy into her own pattern of life and was not allowing him to find out for himself who he was and what he wanted to be.

Since students offer to us the challenge to conserve their lives for Christ and his church, we must realize this thrilling fact: Christianity has always been a youth movement. As we look over the pages of church history, we find, more often than not, that brave thrusts into the unknown have been led by the young. Can we not expect the same from the generation that is now upon us? Can we not see in them the most powerful potential the church has? We must consider the child or young person as an end in himself, a dynamic personality, capable, under God, of realizing his best self. We must lead these souls to the point where they are set aflame with the adventure of serving Christ. And to do this we must enlist their basic desires.

There are five basic tendencies in the heart of every young person:

1. *The urge for security:* This is the most basic drive of our existence. Life is called upon to preserve life. The animal seeks to protect its young by foraging for food and providing warmth and shelter. Man, too, strives for economic security, physical safety and social protection. This is why many of our young people seek at such an early age economic independence, for they have learned not to lean on their parents for security.

We all have an urge for spiritual security. Augustine reminded us that there is a Divine-shaped vacuum in the heart of every man, and it is not filled until it is filled by God. People are amazed that in Hollywood we have been able to interest so many hundreds of young people in Christ; but I have not had to interest them in him; such an interest is already in their hearts. All I have done has been to direct that interest. Hollywood is saturated with insecure people. There is nothing one can depend on there. But we have presented the Lord Jesus Christ as the one who can satisfy that emptiness. I have seen many of our young people go out to the most insecure areas of this world—to jungles and mountain highlands—leaving all the comforts of civilization to preach the gospel. The only explanation I can give of such a daring leap into the unknown is that these people have possessed an inward security that equips them to face external uncertainty.

2. *The urge for recognition, status or promotion:* This drive is especially a part of our American society. Youth likes to receive credit. Even the disciples asked Jesus who among them was the greatest. And Peter was concerned with his reward when he reminded the Master

that he had left all to follow him. Ambition and position, courtesies and fashions, advancement and prestige—all are a major part of our life. Young people demand recognition, attention. How important it is to commend them when they do well. As the new officers take over their responsibilities in our college department, I am very careful to have a special meeting so that the class knows who they are and can hear their objectives. I ask our minister to preside at this installation in order that as much dignity as possible might surround these young leaders. I want them to feel the importance of their responsibilities. In so many Sunday Schools I visit, the teachers and officers have never been made to realize their value; as a result they put little into their work. In our church, our ministers have had the marvelous ability to commend the workers. Hardly a Sunday goes by that mention is not made of the beautiful way the choir robes are ironed, or of the lovely flowers, or of the fine job the ushers are doing. This sort of recognition makes people feel appreciated. We all love praise. Most certainly our youth need it. I am so disgusted with the way our newspapers play up juvenile delinquency and yet have so little to say about the commendable actions of our youth. How can we expect our young people to do good when all our emphasis is on their crimes? In the church we should take every opportunity to recognize the virtues of our teenagers.

3. *The urge for new experiences and adventures*: In our generation more has been learned about the universe than in all the previous history of mankind. This is the age of discovery. Those who think that there are no more frontiers to conquer are out of contact with their times.

Young people today are willing to try anything—jazz,

sex, riots, dope, and religion. They love to take risks—
it's part of the game of life. Now Christianity must be
presented to them as an adventure! One of the most basic
mistakes we make in our churches and camps is that
we take the thrill out of religion; we fail to show them
the adventure in the gospel. So much of our preaching is
without enthusiasm. No wonder people fall asleep in
church! Teenagers want excitement. It is my prayer
every Sunday morning as I step before my collegians that
they may see in my message the challenge of doing big
things for Christ. I know that they are ready to do anything, and I want this spirit of adventure to be Christ-
directed.

For several years now we have been sending from our
church summer deputation teams—a dozen or more young
people going across our land and to various foreign lands
to work with missionaries and in church camps for the
summer. In this way their minds meet the world; they see
how other people live, what they think, what the needs
are in Harlem, down South, or abroad. As they come back,
they share their experiences with the rest of the class.
This program has done wonders for our college department. Missions are becoming relevant; the cry of the
world is becoming a part of our planning, our decisions.
Some of these deputees are now returning abroad to
study, while others have already decided to give their
lives to foreign missionary work. We have begun a program at Forest Home that is affording the opportunity
for twenty or more young people to travel abroad for
the summer, under the auspices of the College Briefing
Study Cruise, to learn of missions, and converse with
those around this globe who have their finger on the pulse
of what is happening. This too is bringing a world vision
into our college conferences and is making an overseas

career a serious consideration for hundreds of college students. Our young people are learning that following Christ is an unparalleled adventure.

4. *The urge for social response:* The Lord Jesus Christ chose twelve men, as the Scripture says, to be with him. What a social fellowship that group of men must have enjoyed! How they must have encouraged one another! As teenagers today are governed more and more by social pressures, we in the church are beginning to understand how to take advantage of this fact. I watch the activities of my college department with an eagle eye to make sure the students are getting plenty of wholesome outlets for their social urge. In fact all that we do—whether it be prayer meetings, deputation teams, Bible studies or fun-times—has a social significance. Young people will not work alone, but they will do practically anything in a group. I am not afraid to invite non-Christian students into the different areas of our class, because every activity is dominated by the Christians. And when the newcomers see what a good time everyone is having, they are attracted to Christ. This is a part of our evangelistic group-dynamics—using the influence of the group to win individuals to the Lord.

The group is the lever to move the individual. Here comes a shy student all wound up in his difficulties and feelings of inferiority. As he enters the group, he realizes that he is accepted just for what he is. He also learns that many of the others feel the same way he does but that they have learned to overcome their shyness. Soon he forgets himself and begins to realize his strength. As he is given a responsibility, he begins to understand his own importance in the class. If he momentarily fails, the others are there to encourage him, so he quickly bounces back with renewed confidence. Before long he is willing to tackle nearly anything for Christ. He has learned in the group to be a leader.

5. *The urge to help, aid and cooperate:* This drive is in the heart of everyone, but in some it is more developed than in others. It is our job in the church to cultivate and direct it. People love to help others, because there is nothing that gives such a deep sense of self-importance and usefulness. *It is more blessed to give than to receive* (Acts 20:35). Sharing creates a sense of personal interest in a mutual understanding.

Not many years ago, our college young people were quite concerned about a mission in one of the poor sections of Los Angeles. A man and his wife had worked for years with impoverished Mexican families, and for several months our students were going to the mission, visiting, taking baskets of food, sewing, organizing baseball games, and the like. One of our young men, a business major, put on a campaign for the mission, setting three goals before the department: 1000 prayers, 1000 dollars, and 1000 pounds of clothing. This drive caught on like wildfire, and in a short time we were over the top in every area. How exciting it was to see our young people respond to this need! And they had so much fun in doing it.

Hitler rose to power, in part, because he convinced the youth of Germany he needed them. Youth will respond to this type of challenge. Let your young people know where they can serve in the church. Emphasize the service of singing in the choir, leading a club, working in the camps, teaching a class. Let them know that they are needed.

Along this line, I cannot stress too strongly the importance of allowing teenagers to express themselves. Let them talk. As much as possible let them do what they want to do. Our job is to channel their bursting energy into creative service, not to dam them up. When I was teaching high school in Minnesota, I saw a gang of fellows who always stood outside the center of activities. They were critical of everything and everyone. So I organized a "wranglers" club and asked these fellows to join. The one rule of the group was that you had to say whatever you were thinking. These lads began to air their dissatisfactions—most of which concerned their own personalities—and once all these negative things were brought out, they began to express themselves more positively. It was not long before they were sharing their life ambitions. Out of that group went some of the finest students I have ever seen, and it was my pleasure to recommend many of them to Yale and Harvard. Our "wranglers" club was perhaps the most important phase of their education. There is no impression like expression.

Put a flower in the sun and it unfolds. Put a young person in a group and he will blossom. Allow him to express himself. Release his dynamic powers. I am very cautious not to put words into the mouths of my young people, because it is not important at all for them to memorize ideas that I have created; rather I strive to get them to state their own beliefs. If a person is going to be a witness for Christ, he cannot be a robot, repeating phrases he has heard from another. He must develop his own conception of Christ, studying the Bible for himself, and allowing the power of Christ's life to flow through him directly.

One of the most effective methods of witnessing, we have learned from the communists: the cell—a small group of committed individuals working for the conversion of one other person. We have in our department a system of triangles: Two Christian students write their names on two sides of a triangle. On the third side they write in the name of a non-Christian friend, for whom they pray. As they witness to that friend and he accepts Christ, they bring him into the triangle and build him up in the faith. When he is mature, the three of them pray for another non-Christian friend. Upon his conversion, the original triangle is split into two, and the whole process starts over again. I have seen dozens of these triangles at work in our group.

These, then, are some of the characteristics of our young people and some suggestions how we can take advantage of them for Christ. If there are three words that summarize youth today, they are: adventure, achievement and enjoyment. The striving of their nature speaks to them in these terms. But the world in which they live diverts them from the Christian influences which could give these proper direction. But how rewarding it is when they do find Christ as their personal Saviour and begin to fulfill their ambitions in him. One tall, good-looking collegian told me just a few weeks ago, "Since I have accepted Christ, I have had more joy than in all my Christmases, birthdays and holidays combined." Although this fellow had every advantage socially, in our Christian group he found the meaning of life. All I did was to create an atmosphere in which God could speak to him.

But there are many blind alleys that can trap even our Christian youth, and we must warn them to keep their eyes open. We should know what they are and avoid them.

1. Our society teaches that *money is the real measure of success*. We are not content to have enough for a comfortable life; we want to have more than enough, an abundance of wealth. This, again, is a reflection of our twentieth-century insecurity. Now, I want my Christian collegians to have a proper attitude toward money, and the first thing I teach them in this respect is that they have a financial obligation to God.

Every year, in early December, we have a church-wide campaign when we encourage everyone to make a pledge. For our youth budget we have special pledge cards which we present in our Sunday School. Since I believe very strongly in the scriptural admonition of tithing, I present to my collegians God's promises and commands about the first tenth of their income belonging to God. Because of this emphasis, our college department has always been capable of supporting many missionary programs and paying for its own projects.

The financial structure of our college group is somewhat different from what is the rule in other churches. We take two offerings a week. The Sunday morning offering, including the money received in the youth-pledge envelopes, goes toward the fulfillment of the church budget. We believe that our department owes its first loyalty there. But on Sunday nights we take up another offering, all of which goes to the department's treasury. Thus our college department is a financial unity in itself, with a treasurer, its own bank account and books, budget and total financial program. This has been authorized by the Session, and an annual report of moneys handled is submitted. There are many advantages to this independence: First of all, it teaches our collegians financial responsibility—the responsibility to give and the responsibility to administer wisely. Secondly, the students are more willing to give when they know where their money is going. We have learned that if we ask them to give toward the church's benevolence budget, they have no idea what their money is going to be used for—we have many missionaries from our church, and it is hard for collegians to become acquainted with such a large group of them. Our Session, therefore, has allowed us to take over the support of several missionaries who have gone out from our department. Our young people know them, they correspond with them, and feel a part of their work. As a result, more money is raised. Interest breeds generosity. Thirdly, giving is a spiritual exercise, a form of worship. So, instead of agonizing through a yearly financial push, just waiting until we can get to something more "spiritual," we make giving a part of our dedication to Christ. And the thrill that some of our young people have had when they see how God has honored their faithfulness! God will never be any man's debtor. I have seen young men and women try to outgive God and then stand back in amazement as God gives back to them many times over their original gift.

The results of all this are quite amazing. In many churches, the college department is fortunate if it is allotted one or two hundred dollars from the general budget for its own activities. As a result, there is always a tension between the young people and the church. The collegians say, "The church doesn't appreciate us"; and the Session replies, "We don't have any more money to give to the college group." Both suffer. But when the collegians are responsible for raising their own money (of course, their bookkeeping is supervised by the Session), they outstrip all expectations. Would you believe that our college department budget last year was $20,000? That included the youth pledge, support of missionaries and all of our department functions. Compare that to the two or three hundred dollars the average church can give to its college group, and you will begin to see the possibilities of letting the collegians work independently. They love the challenge.

I am overjoyed when I see one of our young men going into business. I encourage him to do the best he can, but also to remember that his first financial responsibility is to God. In this way God is at the center of his life—including his business life—and not money.

2. Another blind alley says, *Get what you want at the least cost to yourself*. Hollywood is a place of quick success. Consequently, our young people think that success is something that you either have or don't have, and there isn't much you can do to bring it on. But another, subtler temptation among Christians is to think that there is nothing we can do to gain success, for, after all, everything is a gift from God. All you need do is pray and God will make you prosperous. But that is not how God works. I find that I must emphasize over and over again the need for preparation. Moses was eighty years in preparation for what God wanted him to do. And young people must come to terms with their obligation to equip themselves for a career that will bring honor to the gospel. Preparation—there is absolutely no substitute! We live in an age of immediates where the long-range view of life is lost. Men and women, to be successful in a world of fast-paced competition, must learn to sacrifice, to prepare, to sweat, if their lives are to have any meaning at all. I like what Bob Pierce says: "For any worthy project, many people may work, but one person has to bleed." That's what it takes! We must be willing to bleed if we want to accomplish something of value. And would to

God that our young people would bleed for the sake of the gospel!

3. *Personal desires are the proper criterion for conduct.* This blind alley sets up self as the ultimate norm and goal. Now there is nothing wrong with feelings and desires as long as they are controlled by the Spirit of God; but today desires have run amuck. We must watch the emotional life of our young men and women. Savonarola appealed to feelings and transformed Florence into a model of righteousness. But Robespierre appealed to feelings and turned Paris into a pandemonium of immorality. Feelings cannot be made moral ultimates.

4. *It doesn't pay to be good.* Teenagers don't feel "in" unless they are willing to be bad. We read the other day of a junior high girl who refused to smoke with her companions. One afternoon they caught her and told her to take a cigarette. When she rejected it, they burned her body all over with cigarettes. It costs to be good!

But our teenagers must also see the reward. A young man taking up politics for a career is faced with a dilemma: to compromise his beliefs in order to win votes, or to stand firm and thereby alienate supporters. This is especially difficult for a Christian, who wants so strongly to serve, but who has deep convictions, which, he feels, cannot be sacrificed. I try to encourage such a fellow to remain true to his faith, knowing that God will honor the man who honors him. It has been a pleasure to watch such a young man grow up in our church. When Newt finished UCLA, he immediately set his face toward a political future. I have known very few men like him. He absolutely refuses to engage in anything that would cast a shadow on his witness for Christ, but God has given him favor with men. What an inspiration to see young men, strong in mind and body and dedicated to God, step forward to become statesmen! In my college department I have been training for statesmen. A statesman is one who sets his own interests aside and works for the interests of others, being governed by noble ideals and being willing to expend himself for their fulfillment. The world today needs Christian statesmen.

5. *Freedom is to be gained by ignoring law.* The distinctive of this age is lawlessness, rebellion against established authority. Nearly every day there is a new riot, another revolution, one more government overthrown somewhere in the world. And the trend is toward more and more lawlessness. Especially do our youth feel that to be free they must break the law, disobey their parents, seek out forbidden pleasures. I do not think that many of our rebelling young people actually want to hurt their parents. But the parent, they feel, is a symbol of domination that must be overcome if freedom is to be won. But our youth must be made to see that freedom from discipline and self-control is no freedom at all, but the most terrible kind of slavery. A train is not free that refuses to run on the tracks. Oh, for the first few seconds it may think it has found independence, but in the next moment it will crash. It always seems so shortsighted of the Communists, working in our country for the overthrow of our liberties, that they do not realize, if our way of life goes, they will be the first to suffer slavery. We in the church must re-establish a respect for law and authority. But to do this is no easy task, for the church has lost its once widespread respect in society. It is so important, therefore, that we have excellence reign in

our church work, in order that our young people learn to admire the house of God.

In all that I am saying the important thing is this: We must understand the youth we are attempting to win to Christ. We must learn what are their immediate and ultimate goals. If you do not as yet apprehend your young people, start now to make a first-hand study. Begin with interviews. Christ did this: nearly every personal conversation he had was an interview. He, of course, knew what was in the heart of man and used questions to make people think; but we can follow his example to learn more about those we work with.

Another good method to find out what young people are thinking is the forum. Have them write out their questions for a panel of experts. We have used this method many times for our Sunday evening college hours. It causes people to think and to express their problems. At Forest Home, too, we usually have a panel program, when the conference faculty spends an hour or two answering the conferees' questions. Listening to those questions tells me what I should be emphasizing in my Sunday morning lessons. Also at Forest Home, at the beginning of a conference, we ask the conferees why they have come. Why are you willing to take out seven days to attend this camp? What are you seeking? Right then and there we know where the rest of the week is headed.

A doctor puts his patient under observation. Let's find out what makes our young people "tick." Keep your eyes and ears open. Know what the interests are of each youth, boy or girl, you teach. Keep a record of those interests and talk them over with your students. Be willing to learn from them.

Our aim is the development of a Christ-like personality.

Youth want to know where they are going. "What am I living for?" "Why am I here?" All of their existence must be integrated around their answers to these problems. Why does John want to be a doctor, or Mary a teacher? What is the purpose behind that choice? These questions must be answered for life to be meaningful. We want our young people to find a life work, not a work for life, or a work to live. Of course they want a good life, but God has to be in the good or else nothing will be left. But that is not all:

As I lead my college men and women, there are certain objectives governing my methods:

1. *Help young people to see themselves in a moral mirror.* James calls the law of God a mirror in which we see our true image. In this age of moral relativity—when every man does what is right in his own eyes—men need to know what is right and wrong. And I find that my young people watch my life for a standard. We must be so careful what we are and how we act, for if there is no consistency in us Sunday School teachers, our pupils will never be inspired to learn for themselves. We must help them to see how they stand in comparison to Christ.

2. *Help young people to see themselves as they really are and to overcome cynicism.* Always approach problems positively. The world's thinking today is fragmented; the whole is lost from sight. People therefore don't know what life is all about. This lack of wholeness leads to distrust, pessimism, cynicism. To be negative is more socially acceptable than to stand for something. Difficulties are

more easily seen than solutions. We must restore a confidence in young hearts which encourages them to seek answers and which says that answers can be found. If we show our youth that they are sons and daughters of God and that he has a purpose for their lives, this confidence will be well on its way. The Christian view of man is the realistic view, and it alone can lead to a constructive, positive attitude toward life.

3. *Encourage them to find the highest motivations for their lives.* You can lead a child to facts but not to truth. You can show him work but not service. You can teach him ideas but not ideals. You can introduce him to Jesus but not salvation. There comes a point in the teaching process where the student must decide what he is going to do with the facts he has learned, what meaning he is going to give them, how they are going to affect his life. These higher principles of truth are learned not so much by the mind as by the attitude. There is a difference between learning to obey the law, and obedience. A child can be taught when and where not to obey certain rules. But the higher objective is to teach him the principle of obedience and to encourage him to apply this principle whenever it is needed. He thereby learns to think through every circumstance for himself. The Pharisees had no problem in knowing when and where not to obey their many laws; but they failed to choose correctly when they were faced with the ultimates of moral decision in Jesus Christ. They had learned to follow laws; they had not learned to make moral choices. It is the same with our young people. If they obey laws merely because there are policemen forcing them to do so, they will never be mature beings. The policeman must be on the inside; the

oughtness of any situation should be self-evident to their moral consciousness. The sensitivity cannot be inculcated by rote learning. It has to be allowed to grow on its own initiative. All we can do is to supply the water and the sunshine of God's Word.

4. *Encourage them to make their own decisions.* The age-long conventional procedure with youth has been for their elders to decide their major questions for them. From pulpit, school and breakfast table young people are told what choices to make, what associates to have, what amusements to engage in, what character to form, what personality to develop, what sweethearts to reject, and until recently, what vocation to choose. One freshman at Harvard wrote back to his dad, "All I have done in coming here is change drivers;" by which he meant that as his father had made all of his decisions for him before, now his professors were taking over the control of his mind Is there any wonder so many of our college freshmen lose their faith? They have never been allowed at home to think problems through for themselves. We must help our youngsters to turn the light on for themselves. What they want is information, methods, principles, not dictation or decisions. Youth tires of continual lectures and sermons, of overmuch counsel and advice. They want, rather, sympathetic help to do their own thinking. I have made it a practice never to do something for a young person he can do for himself. He may not realize that he can do it, and thus he may ask for my help. But I know in the long run that if I help him recognize his own ability, he will be happier, for he will have learned how to take responsibility on his own shoulders.

Many Christian parents feel it is their obligation to keep their children from worldliness. And certainly this is true. But the Christian parent must realize that his control must diminish as the child grows toward maturity until finally the young person is totally answerable for his own life. When should this stage be reached? It varies. But certainly as the student enters college, and, say, by his second year, he should be expected to stand on his own two feet without parental pushing. There is a clear distinction between parental encouragement and suggestion, on the one hand, and dictation and nagging, on the other. My niece, in the presence of her mother, once said to a friend, "Oh, I can't do that. Mother won't let me." But her mother corrected her by saying, "Darling, you may do what you wish. But I prefer that you don't do that." I know that that is a daring attitude, but it is the only way that our collegians are going to learn moral responsibility. Dare I say that it takes the issue beyond legalistic obedience into the higher realm of a loving loyalty?

There is an increasing spirit of independence that makes youth come to clashes when you would thwart them. We as educators must recognize this "spirit of the times" and learn how to skirt around it. If we don't, we will lose our children completely for Christ. Is it any wonder that Solomon prayed for wisdom to govern his nation? We need the wisdom of Solomon in dealing with our youth. There are no easy solutions, and sometimes we shall have to say to the oncoming generation, "We of the older generation don't have all the answers. You young, brave hearts will have to make your own decisions." But one thing we can work for is certainty: that our young people love the house of the Lord, that they feel comfortable and accepted there, that they trust us as teachers and ministers, and that they learn to transfer this trust to God.

5. *Assist them to see that God has a blueprint for their lives.* The most important thing for a Christian youth to discover is the plan of God for his life. What is more exciting than to search for the divine plan for one's career? What can give deeper satisfaction than the sense of building according to that scheme? There must be life objectives. Paradoxically, the starting point for life is at the end. One must determine where he wants to go and then devise ways and means to get there. An engineer decides what he wants to build, and then he proceeds with the plans how to build it.

Whom shall I serve? What service shall I render? Who should help me in this service? When shall I serve? These are the controlling decisions of life. Every life must be centered immovably around answers to these questions, or it will be swamped and swept by winds of adversity and emotions.

Although our psychologists speak of the integrated life, much of modern education builds youth around self, encouraging him to live a self-centered life, where the chief aim is the advancement of self. But Christ taught that a man finds his true self only when he is willing to lose himself in God's plan.

This is our supreme task as Christian educators: to gear youth into Christian service—regardless of what the specific occupation may be—and to encourage the utmost skill in the fulfillment of this service. It is comparatively easy to enlist young people for any idealistic cause. The real test comes in continuance. And expert service is quite another thing. Americans are nibblers—they rarely engulf something to perfection. But the church today needs experts in doing the will of God. This is the pre-eminent challenge we have to give youth today.

III. TRAIN UP A CHILD

Should a teacher stress the development of the pupil or the mastery of the subject matter? This is the question that is being asked everywhere in the field of Christian education.

I am convinced that learning is more than the ability to repeat the sayings and ideas of another; rather, it is a dynamic development of the conduct and character of the pupil. The woman at the well is a good example of a person who was transformed by Jesus' teaching. She did not learn mere facts that were to be repeated for an examination; facts alone could never have produced the radical transformation that came about in her attitude. A life that had been self-centered became Christ-centered. The twelve disciples were far different men at the end of their training school with the Master Teacher from what they were at the beginning. The duty of an educator is to build personality. This change in character should include a modification in the pupil's ideas and ideals, in

331

his aspirations and appreciations. Everything that is included in his activity and thought should be touched. We must watch the behavior of his mind and heart as well as of his hands and lips.

A teacher has not taught a lesson until his pupil has learned it. Learning in Christian education is not the mere acquisition of ideas; it is the integration of ideas into the personality. Real teaching should help the student to demonstrate an increased ability to meet the problems of life and to act on his own initiative. As he comes in contact with the experiences of others, his own experiences are enriched. This is learning one's lesson.

Jesus was called a teacher rather than a preacher; and as a teacher, he constantly tested his disciples to see what they had learned. He would send them out to see how much they had comprehended, and they would return, realizing all too well their need for further instruction. Christ, the Teacher, expected results in his teaching. Do we? Note what Jesus did with Peter. Were Peter's ideas modified? Was his behavior changed? What kind of preacher did he turn out to be? Peter was a problem pupil—vacillating, impetuous, and at times fearful—but Jesus recognized in him the leader of the crowd and the bold preacher at Pentecost. Who is the problem in your class? Are you teaching him anything? I am not asking if he is acquiring a fund of information, but rather if he is evidencing a new life, with new aspirations and accomplishments. An honest answer to this question may revolutionize your whole teaching ministry.

Our task with boys and girls is training. God says, *Train up a child in the way he should go: and when he is old, he will not depart from it* (Prov. 22:6). This law is infallible. Why, then, are we often prone to think that it does not work? Because we do not train our students. We tell them what they ought to do. We preach to them truths. We tell them stories. But we do not train them. Learning is not only knowing but doing. A coach does not line up his team on the bench and tell them how to play football; he sends them out on the field; and as they practice and make their mistakes, he corrects them and shows them how to improve. This is training.

Education is not only the acquisition, but also the use of knowledge. It involves growth and action. Christ not only taught men, but he lived with them and guided them in every action. We find our summer camps of great value, because in living with young people, we can effect a change in their whole conception of what Christ expects of those who bear his name. The Lord saw to it that his pupils applied his teaching. He did not think that he had fulfilled his obligation as a teacher by merely meeting with them once a week and telling them wonderful truths. He entered into their very lives and plans, and they developed under his training. Too often we seek to hand to the learner an accumulated stock of information. We wrap up our knowledge and deliver it in a package at the pupil's door. An untrained teacher is often only a good delivery boy.

Here are questions the successful Sunday School teacher should ask himself:

1. Do I study the lesson thoroughly myself so that I understand it?

2. Am I doing all I can to help my pupils understand the lesson and to retain it in their memories?

3. Do I have them try to deduce their own applications from what they have heard?

333

4. Does my teaching really influence their lives, or does it seem dull and removed from their immediate interests?

Don't be occupied only with passing on a store of information and beliefs to the next generation; rather be interested in the growth of personalities. Give those before you a new outlook on life. Start where the pupil is. Deal with his problems as they really are, not as you think they ought to be. Work for the growth of his entire personality, not just his mind. Teach your students to think. Help them to make choices. Religious training must necessarily involve a child's mind and will; if it does not, it is weak. To be able to think and to make wise decisions as a Christian is of the utmost importance. This is your duty as a teacher. We want to have our youngsters stand firm in the face of temptation and meet their problems without fear of failure.

Do not ask, "How many facts in the life of Christ do my pupils remember?" But, "How much do my pupils know of Christ? How has their love for him increased? Can they say: *For to me to live is Christ* (Phil. 1:21)?" We want them to have values and judgments born of God's will.

Jesus said, *Come unto me . . . and learn of me* (Matt. 11:28,29). Are our pupils learning of Christ? Our chief business as Christian educators is to help our students know God and his Son Jesus Christ to the point where their lives are transformed.

IV. DIMENSIONS OF LEADERSHIP

Are you a carbon copy of someone else? Most people are. Even in the church the majority of men and women fall into common categories of sameness, without individuality.

When I was a teenager, I heard my mother say of a rather nondescript fellow, "When he walks into the room, you are not aware that anyone has come in. You think, rather, that the wind has blown the door open." That trenchant criticism cut into my mind and made me think of the type of person I was, and I resolved that I was going to be different, that people would not think that just the wind blew the door open when I walked into the room. And so I began to ask myself, "What makes an interesting personality? How can I develop my personality so I will be able to attract men and women to Christ?" The Lord's promise seemed to summarize everything that I was thinking: *I am come that they might have life, and that they might have it more abundantly* (John 10:10).

Here was where I would begin—with Christ's abundant life.

I think of Jesus as vital, alert, enthusiastic—full of zest and zeal. So much emphasis is placed on the suffering and dying Christ—and certainly that is essential—but rarely do we see paintings or hear sermons that reflect the vitality of Christ's personality and the life he wants us to have. Christ is the ideal leader—men leave their professions, their homes, their companions to follow him. He inspired them to do their best, to be their highest self. Jesus must have been a physically vibrant person, radiating energy and confidence, mental alertness and interest in everything about him. Think of him being able to speak to a crowd of many thousands of people—without a microphone! See him walking through cities, his head high, his shoulders thrown back, bursting with good will, kindness, courage and faith! No wonder the multitudes followed him! He was enthusiastic about the kingdom of God, and his enthusiasm ignited the hearts of others. There is nothing so contagious as that kind of fervor. Jesus went about his work wholeheartedly, and his eagerness inflamed the adventurous spirit in the men who became his disciples.

We all stood in amazement at Churchill's ability to rally the disheartened spirits of the British to heights of courage and sacrifice during the frightful years of the war. Was it not because Churchill himself had an explosive faith and determination that inspired his countrymen? Men will always respond to such courage. Livingstone marching through Africa brought England to her feet in admiration. Luther defying Europe's tyrannies changed the course of history. There was nothing halfhearted about these men.

They radiated their vision, setting nations on fire for truth and liberty.

I have learned that I can teach mere facts to any boy or girl—that's not hard at all. But the only way I can lead a child to Christ is to show Christ living in me. I must be enthusiastic about my Saviour, allowing his life to burst beyond the narrow walls of my personality, to overflow my mind and to push out the limitations of my soul.

Is it not our aim to attract men to Jesus? How is it, then, that we spend so little time making ourselves attractive? Many dear Christians believe that all they have to do is be willing and God will do the rest; but they are so wrong. "There is gold in those hills!" Yes!—but the gold must be mined. Surely God is there to live through us, but we must mine not only his personality but our own. We must refine the gold; then mold it into a beautiful image. Am I attractive for Christ? Is my life gold-brilliant or brass-dull? The rich young ruler, the woman at the well, Nicodemus, and thousands like them were drawn to Christ. Of course he was divine: what he said and did was exceptional. But Scripture encourages us to follow his example. Am I the kind of person people seek out?

Now, when we speak of being attractive, we usually think of the external appearance, and this, indeed, should be a concern if we want to be effective witnesses for Christ. What do my clothes look like? Am I neat? Do I dress with taste? Clothes advertise the man. What kind of image of Christ do people get when they look at the way I dress? The Bible states that *man looketh on the outward appearance, but the Lord looketh on the heart* (I Sam. 16:7), and that is true; but let us not forget that man does look on the outward appearance; and as long as this is so, we should take advantage of it. My appearance makes a first and lasting impression on people as to what I am inside. Clothing can speak worlds about a person's soul. I have four standards for my dress: it must be neat, becoming, in style, and economical. A person doesn't have to be physically handsome or beautiful to have an attractive appearance. What he does with what he has reflects what he is.

But of greater importance is emotional balance. Jesus asked Peter, *Lovest thou me?* (John 21:15). That was Peter's most basic lesson in emotional stability—where was the object of his love? Emotional balance speaks not only of maturity of feelings but of a proper relation between feelings and the intellect. A person who is all brainpower with no feeling is as unbalanced as one with no intellectual control over his emotions. But more than that, I want to have healthy attitudes toward people. So much can be accomplished by an optimistic, positive, happy spirit. Such disposition is contagious. Why should I be a glum, sour Christian? I don't see how it is possible to be a glum Christian if we really understand the meaning of "Christian." Some of God's people have never learned to have fun, to laugh, to see the humorous in life. Is it any wonder that they are ineffective witnesses for Christ —who is life?

But if a leader should be able to laugh, he should also be able to weep. Knox was heard to cry out in the night, "Give me Scotland or I die!" His love of God and country swept like fire across the highlands, through the towns and into the hearts of his people. God cannot work through lifeless, loveless, listless Christians. Before he can use us to kindle the hearts of others, we have to be burning with a passion for his cause. Very few men today are ardently devoted to a cause, be it spiritual or secular. When a reporter asked Mussolini how he was able to become ruler of Italy, the dictator replied, "Looking around Europe, I saw many vacant throne rooms. All I did was to step into one of them." How pathetic when the leadership vacancies have to be filled with selfish, destructive tyrants! Oh, that Christians might step into some of the vacant throne rooms so numerous today! But it will never be until we weep over the world's condition, until we are consumed with a compassion to proclaim Christ. No man is great if he has never wept over sin. So much of our Christian work is characterized by a smooth professionalism. Why is it that, although our church programs run like clockwork, so few people are profoundly reached for Christ? Do we leaders not lack depth? Haven't we forgotten how to weep over the lost?

How much do I love other people? My father advised me when I was very young, "Henrietta, be sweet with your lips." I want to try harder to live up to that. Shall I use my mouth to destroy people, or build them up?—to tell of their faults, or to encourage their faith? How powerful is the mouth! Empires can be built or ruined by it. Souls can be damned or saved by what we say. How much people want to hear loving words! One day I told my mother that I was lonely. I shall always remember her kind reply: "My dear, the world is dying for a little bit of love. Go find someone who is as lonely as you are and love that person." That is the essence of our Sunday School work—loving people for Christ.

A leader is also mentally alert. A person that is a powerhouse of new ideas guarantees the success of a Sunday School. James A. Garfield, when teaching in Hiram College, was asked how he managed to hold the close attention of his students so constantly. His instant reply was,

"I never give them cold victuals." A leader must be able to think ahead, see solutions, create plans and understand people. He should be courageous to face facts and to accept new ideas.

And he certainly must be able to perceive possibilities in situations and people. George Washington Carver saw health, industries, synthetics, soap, oil, butter and much more—all in a little peanut. John Calvin came to Geneva, the "playground of Europe," known for its licentiousness, and saw possibilities. Calvin transformed Geneva, so that, for a hundred years after his death, it was known around the world as the "schoolroom of the Reformation." People often are amazed that I will spend time on this fellow or that one. "Why, Miss Mears, he is about the most worthless scoundrel there is! Why do you waste your time?" But I have resolved never to consider anyone worthless. Think of what God did with Mel Trotter—his life was ruined, enslaved to drink, hopeless! But God saw the possibilities. A leader brings out the best in people. It does no good to criticize, to harp on weaknesses. Emphasize the strong qualities. Expect great things. Have confidence in others. Let young people know you trust them. Be encouraging, positive. And you will be astonished at the results.

A leader, moreover, has an inward strength, which sustains him through every conflict. The Christian's spiritual power comes from him who said, *Be thou strong and very courageous . . . I will not fail thee, nor forsake thee* (Joshua 1:7,5). To know God is to have a reservoir of sustaining force that never fails. This fortitude pervades every nerve of the Christian as Christ lives within him and fulfills God's perfect will. It is not something we pump up. We can't work for it. We accept it as a gift. When my mother died, and I felt that God was calling me into

340

his service, I was broken with the thought of my weaknesses, and I prayed, "God," if you want me to serve you, you will have to give me the strength." After studying my Bible for many weeks, I came to the realization that God wanted to give me the power of his Holy Spirit, and that all I had to do was receive it. I cannot describe to you what happened in my life. From head to toe I was a different person. In my mind reigned a peace I had never known before, convincing me that God was in me working out his plan.

Many years later, as I was analyzing how we know the will of God, Paul's words set my heart on fire: *Wherefore, my beloved, as ye have always obeyed, not as in my presence only, but now much more in my absence, work out your own salvation with fear and trembling. For it is God which worketh in you both to will and to do of his good pleasure* (Phil. 2:12,13). If I had God living in mo his life controlling my life, his desires my desires, his mind my mind—then as I worked out my will, I was actually working out the will of God! Again I was overcome with joy. The secret of power and of being in the will of God was not something that I had to sweat and strain for; it was, rather, what I had to recognize as already present in my life. God's will is God himself, and that is my power: I was transformed with the thought. This was the most daring idea I think I have ever had regarding leadership. It has given me strength to sustain any defeat or to face any challenge. Think of it: our frail, dying bodies—the temple of God's Holy Spirit! Now I want to take that idea and let God use it to bring every thought into the mastery of Christ. I am a Christian leader insofar as Christ leads me. Therefore, my mind must be led by him. Thus Christ leads me as I lead others.

My mind is crucial in my leadership. I must, first of

all, be loyal to truth—I must love it. Do I fill my mind with noble thoughts, inspiring ideas? It has always been very difficult for me to read, but I still do as much as I can, or have others read to me, or I travel, or listen to lectures. I want ideas in my head. I want to be challenged by great thoughts. To the very day I die, I want something new to think about. But I also want the type of mind that can sift facts and retain what is valid. I court criticism, because everything I am doing can be improved. I fear lest at any time I shall be unable to face the facts of my existence, of my work. A leader must be a realist; he cannot hide from his failures. When we were writing the Gospel Light materials, we had a committee composed of the teachers involved in our Sunday School While they were still fresh in our minds, we tore the lessons apart, venting our dissatisfactions, rewriting, improving, upgrading. We wanted the very best, but we knew we couldn't achieve the best without criticism— constructive, positive, creative criticism. Our minds had to be open to reality, to change, to any valid idea, for the Christian education of boys and girls depended on us.

In all of this, I have learned to be bold. So often, one of my collegians, when asked to take a job in the department, will say to me, "Oh, Miss Mears, I don't think I could do that. You know, I haven't had much experience along that line, and I am afraid I might let you down." "Now, John," I reply, "it isn't a matter of can you do it; rather, will you do it?" Then I explain that very little in this world would have been accomplished if men refused to do things until they thought they could do them. We never know until we try. And working with collegians, I have discovered that they are always capable of more than they think they are. And aren't we all? The psychologists tell us that we don't use but a fraction of our mind's potential. Is this not why the Lord tells us to be bold? *Be strong in the Lord, and in the power of his might* (Eph. 6:10)! Over and over Paul tells us to be strong, courageous, bold, daring, fearless, confident in Christ. I love the book of Acts—every time the early Christians prayed, something happened: fire fell, the house was shaken, they were filled with boldness! Now it is not a vain, boastful, senseless recklessness that is encouraged in these passages. Rather it is a confidence inspired by the mind of God. It is his strength, working power.

We are as Joshua of old. Moses is dead. Now here is the land of Canaan stretched out before us, and there is a mighty people we are to lead into that land. Their future lies with us. Let us therefore as twentieth-century Joshuas hear God's command:

This book of the law shall not depart out of thy mouth; but thou shalt meditate therein day and night, that thou mayest observe to do according to all that is written therein: for then thou shalt make thy way prosperous, and then thou shalt have good success. Have not I commanded thee? Be strong and of a good courage; be not afraid, neither be thou dismayed: for the Lord thy God is with thee whithersoever thou goest (Joshua 1:8,9).